# Contemporary Challenges

## CONVERSATIONS WITH
## CANADIAN
## NATIVE AUTHORS

# Contemporary Challenges

## CONVERSATIONS WITH CANADIAN NATIVE AUTHORS

**HARTMUT LUTZ**

**Fifth House Publishers**
Saskatoon Saskatchewan

**Canadian Cataloguing in Publication Data**

Main entry under title:

Contemporary challenges: conversations with
 Canadian Native authors

 Includes bibliographical references.
 ISBN 0–920079–75–X

1. Authors, Canadian – 20th century – Interviews.
2. Authors, Indian – Canada – Interviews.
3. Indians of North America – Biography.   I. Lutz, Hartmut.

PS8089.5.I52C6 1991     C810.897     C91–097147–1
PR9188.2.I5C6 1991

This book has been published with the assistance of The Canada Council
and The Saskatchewan Arts Board.

Fifth House Publishers
620 Duchess Street
Saskatoon, SK   S7K 0R1

Printed in Canada

*For Ruth*
*who hosts our friends*
*who spends weeks and hours alone*
*and who supports us all*

# ACKNOWLEDGEMENTS

▼

There are so many individuals who have supported my work on this project, and nearly each of them to such a degree, that a book could be filled just telling about the help I received in the form of hospitality, time, interviews, books and articles sent, transcriptions made, typing done, or meals and rides provided. Instead of writing about each of them individually, I can only mention their names here: Marge Adams (Vancouver), Lori Alexson (Regina), Andrea Bellegarde (Regina), Barbara Blyth (Saskatoon), Marlene Brant-Castellano (Peterborough), Eleanor Brass (Regina), Paul Chartrand (Winnipeg), Sue Deranger (Regina), Glen Douglas (Penticton), Parker Duchemin (Ottawa), Willie Dunn (Ottawa), Renate Eigenbrod (Thunder Bay), Irenka Farmilo (Ottawa), Rita Flint (Icker), Barb Frazer (Penticton), Ethel Gardner (Vancouver), Albertine Gosselin (Regina), Konrad Gross (Kiel), Janette Heath (Regina), Jennifer Hillard (Winnipeg), Helen Hoy (Lethbridge), Peter Kelly/Kinew (Winnipeg), George Kenny (Thunder Bay), Wolfgang Klooss (Trier), Sheila and David Latham (Lethbridge), Kendra Lerat (Regina), Ralf Lischewski (Osnabrück), Stan Manoakeesick (Winnipeg), Dennis Maracle (Vancouver), Virginia Maracle (Winnipeg), Horst Martin (Victoria), Mechthild Massarrat (Osnabrück), Robin McGrath (London, Ont.), Gloria Mehlmann (Regina), Anne Ostermeier (Osnabrück), Wilfred Pelletier (Ottawa), Bernie Selinger (Regina), Barbara Smith (Victoria), Rosalee Tizya (Vancouver).

To all of you: Thank You! I hope we'll all meet again!

Support from the following organizations is gratefully acknowledged:
External Affairs Canada, for a Faculty Research Grant in 1989; Fachbereich Sprach-und Literaturwissenschaft (Department of Linguistics and Literature Studies), University of Osnabrück, for funding to help transcribe some of the tapes; German Academic Exchange Service, for sponsoring my year as a guest professor at the Saskatchewan Indian Federated College in Regina, Saskatchewan 1990/91; the Saskatchewan Indian Federated College, especially Bernie Selinger, for office space, computer, and funding to let Albertine Gosselin and others help me with the tapes.

Thank you all for making this possible!

# TABLE OF CONTENTS

# PREFACE

▼

The spoken words of Indian and Métis authors contained in this collection were recorded over a period of a little more than a year (September 1989–December 1990). But what a year it was! It was the most productive time in Native literature in Canada yet, and at the same time it was a very crucial period in Native/non-Native relations.

When I visited Canada for five weeks in the fall of 1989, the appropriation of Native voices by non-Native authors was discussed widely, and most of the authors I met addressed the issue with great passion. Then, in the summer of 1990, after the arrival of my family and myself in Regina, the Oka standoff put the issue of Native national sovereignty on top of the agenda. At the same time, Native literature in Canada went through an unprecedented boom. While the proliferation of texts by Native authors and the increasing attention their works receive from non-Native academia and critics may indicate that Native literature is on its way to becoming established in the mainstream, the appropriation issue and the Oka confrontation clearly demonstrate that there are fundamental rifts between First Nations people and non-Native people in Canada. These rifts are manifest in the inequality of economic, social, and cultural power between the two groups. An ongoing internal colonialism affects all layers of Native/non-Native relations in Canada, including the arts. Openly or subtly Native literature reflects both the Indigenous traditions and the colonial situation. Approaches to Native literature not acknowledging the colonial legacy or the specific cultural background of the authors are hampered by intellectual denial and will remain peripheral to the issues Native authors are concerned with. In that way, Native literature represents a challenge to contemporary literary criticism and the reading public at large.

## Native Literatures in Canada

Native literature in Canada is "new" only in its literate book form. The lonely example of Emily Pauline Johnson's (Tekahionwake) publications in the early 20th century stresses the general absence of printed texts by

1

Native authors. While Native people continued their oral tradition throughout the century that lies between treaty-making and the present, there are next to no books by Native authors until the 1960s, when Canadian Natives were made citizens of Canada and received the right to vote. Even then, texts stemming from the oral tradition were usually collected, translated, and often heavily edited by non-Native missionaries, anthropologists, and hobbyists. Moreover, they tended to represent Native "tales" from the igloo, the smokehouse, or the campfire as "quaint" or "exotic," fit for ethnological inquiry perhaps, but not for serious literary studying.

In the 1970s Native authors began writing down their own (hi)stories and expressing their views on Canadian society. But even seminal books like Harold Cardinal's *The Unjust Society* (1969), Maria Campbell's *Halfbreed* (1973), or Howard Adams's *Prison of Grass* (1975) were until recently dismissed as "protest literature" (*Oxford Companion to Canadian Literature*), not really considered part of Canadian "literature" as defined by English departments and literary scholars in the mainstream. However, this attitude is beginning to change dramatically due to the proliferation of Native texts on the market, and due to the struggle of First Nations authors addressing non-Native colleagues on the issue of "Native voice." Since 1985, *Whetstone Magazine*, published by the University of Lethbridge English Department, has had three issues on Native writing; in 1987 Thomas King guest-edited a special "Native" volume for *Canadian Fiction Magazine* and together with Helen Hoy and Cheryl Calver edited an anthology *The Native in Literature: Canadian and Comparative Perspectives*; and in 1990 the University of British Columbia celebrated its 75th anniversary with a double issue of *Canadian Literature* dedicated to Native authors in Canada. In the same year, Oxford University Press published the first book-length survey, *Native Literature in Canada*, by Penny Petrone.

Such critical attention reflects the momentum developed by Native authors and their writings. In the performing arts, Canada has for years been represented internationally by Native actors and playwrights. The two Oscar nominations Canadian actors have received in the last 20 years both went to Native actors: Chief Dan George (1971) and Graham Greene (1991). Micmac-Métis singer Willie Dunn's record *Willie Dunn* came out in the early 1970s and was rereleased in Germany several years later; singers/actresses Buffy Sainte-Marie and Alanis Obomsawin enjoy a stable international reputation; and three Native dramas have represented Canadian culture abroad: George Kenny's *October Stranger* (Monaco 1978), Tomson Highway's *The Rez Sisters* (Edinburgh 1988), and Evan Adams's *Dreams of Sheep* (Sydney, Australia 1990). It is, above all, in the field of drama that Native writers have found national recognition, starting with Tomson Highway's *Rez Sisters* tour of Canada in the fall of 1987 and followed by an abundance of new plays by other playwrights, including Daniel David Moses and Drew Hayden Taylor (both 1990).

In the 1980s Native women in Canada began writing themselves into Canadian letters. Beatrice Culleton's *In Search of April Raintree* (1983), Jeannette Armstrong's *Slash* (1985), Ruby Slipperjack's *Honour the Sun* (1987), and Joan Crate's *Breathing Water* (1989) are first novels by a new generation of authors addressing the lives of Métis and Indian people in Canada today. Lee Maracle's *I Am Woman* (1988) went beyond the format of the novel, combining west coast Big House oratory with poetry, memoir, and political essay in a book on oppression and liberation which presents "theory coming through story" (Maracle). Two years later, her as-told-to autobiography, *Bobbi Lee: Indian Rebel*, originally published in 1975, came out in a new edition by Women's Press, prefaced by a powerful essay reflecting the colonial structure which the then-current Oka standoff exposed. Her latest book, *Sojourner's Truth* (1990), a collection of short prose pieces, combines "oratory and European story." Lenore Keeshig-Tobias, co-founder of the Toronto-based Committee to Re-Establish the Trickster, began editing her magazine *Trickster* in 1988; in it she publishes works by new and established Native writers. Anthologies such as *Telling It: Women and Language Across Cultures* (1990), *Writing the Circle* (1990), and *Living the Changes* (1990) bear witness to the involvement of authors like Jeannette Armstrong, Lee Maracle, and Emma LaRocque in literary/political alliances with Eurocanadian writers/editors. Often, such cooperation across the boundaries of class and race is very painful, evoking feelings of guilt and shame on the non-Native side, as Maria Campbell's and Linda Griffith's *Book of Jessica* (1989) demonstrates with moving clarity and in painstaking detail. In at least one such project Native women writers seriously scrutinized and finally fought the non-Native editing of First Nations literature: Marie Annharte Baker and Sue Deranger campaigned against Jeanne Perrault and Sylvia Vance's anthology *Writing the Circle*. In another case the experience led to the resolution "I'll never do it again!"(Campbell). The concern about appropriation looms large in all Native writing, because after centuries of colonial dispossession and oppression, Native people have learned to be suspicious of outside "help" or interest. In this context, anthologies collected, edited, and published entirely by Native people themselves are vitally important, and Native presses work hard to address this need. Theytus Books and the first International School of Native Writing at the Okanagan nation's En'owkin Centre in Penticton, British Columbia, directed by Jeannette Armstrong, have produced two such anthologies, *Seventh Generation* (1989), a collection of poetry edited by Heather Hodgson, and a year later *Gatherings*, the first issue of the school's *Journal of First North American Peoples*, containing writings

3

by both students and more established Native authors, whereas Pemmican Press's anthology *Our Bit of Truth* (1990), edited by Agnes Grant, still falls short of the all-Native ideal.

Thomas King stands out as the most successful Native promoter/ writer of First Nations literature in Canada to date. His anthology of Native short stories, *All My Relations* (1990), is based in part on the texts first collected in *Canadian Fiction Magazine* (1987). His first novel, *Medicine River*, came out in hardback in the spring of 1990, and went into a Penguin paperback edition the same year. He is currently working on another anthology and a second novel.

Other authors also had breakthroughs in very recent years. Jordan Wheeler's first monograph, the three novellas in *Brothers in Arms*, established his name among Native authors in Canada in 1989. Several poets, female and male, came out with their own books in the same period: Bruce Chester (*Paper Radio*, 1986), Beth Cuthand (*Horsedance to Emerald Mountain*, 1987, and *Voices in the Waterfall*, 1989), Joan Crate (*Pale as Real Ladies*, 1989), Annharte (*Being on the Moon*, 1990), Wayne Keon (*Sweetgrass II*, 1990), and Daniel David Moses (*The White Line*, 1990).

As new writers emerged in this intense period of Native literature production, more established writers also continued to write and be published. Pauline Johnson's *Moccasin Maker* was reedited by A. LaVonne Brown Ruoff in 1987, Basil Johnston moved from rendering the oral tradition to writing a personal and collective memoir of his generation in *Indian Schooldays* (1988), Rita Joe's *Song of Eskasoni* came out in 1988, followed by the (private) republication of her first book of poetry in 1990, and Howard Adams's classic *Prison of Grass* came out in a revised and updated edition in 1989.

### Appropriation

At first glance, the appropriation discussion in Canada closely resembles the "white shamanism" discussion in the United States more than 10 years ago. Again, Native authors are speaking out against the misuses of their cultural heritage by non-Natives who claim varying degrees of authority and initiation, and who produce books for a growing market that is increasingly hungry for specific aspects of Native cultures. In the process, the appropriators gain money, fame, and prestige, while at the same time obliterating those in whose voices they speak or claim to speak. In the US Gary Snyder's "shamanist" poetry, Ruth Beebe Hill's novel/film *Hanta Yo!/Mystic Warrior*, and even Hyemeyohsts Storm's beautiful new-age and hippie cult-novel *Seven Arrows* came under heavy attack from Native Americans, precisely because these authors appropriated and then sold aspects of Native spirituality in their works. Regardless of whether they

4

distorted them or presented them with degrees of authenticity, regardless even of whether the authors could claim some Indian ancestry, many Native people were outraged by the fact that, after centuries of material dispossession, relocation, and genocide, the colonizers were finally reaching for Native spirituality, the essence of their identity.

In Canada today, authors who produce books about Natives, and especially those whose narrators or personae assume Native voices, are asked to "move over" or to "stop stealing Native stories." Unlike most of their colleagues in the US 10 years ago, non-Native authors in Canada have reacted widely and publicly to such demands, and their reactions have ranged from compliance (Anne Cameron stopped writing in the Native voice), to defiance (Lynn Andrews continues her writing), to outraged cries against "censorship" (George Bowering, Betty Jane Wylie, and many others). To me, this last reaction against "Native censorship of non-Native voices" seems the most compelling/telling and ideologically intriguing one.

In political and economic terms the outcry against "Native censorship" is clearly a gross overreaction. In no way are Native authors able to enforce anything like censorship upon mainstream authors today. Colonial disempowerment does not allow that. Native authors know this situation only too well, and significantly, not one of those who came out on the issue did actually and seriously advocate a state of censorship. Rather, there have been appeals for equity. Mainstream authors have been asked to use self-restraint, to step aside and give Native authors their chance, to be quiet for a while, to learn from and listen to First Nations people before writing about them, and to at least seek their permission before telling their stories. According to storyteller/writer Alexander Wolfe, the oral tradition practised a "copyright system based on trust." In the storytelling tradition he comes from, the teller would make sure to give credit to whoever owned and told the story before. Anything else would be considered dishonest, just as in Western academic discourse not giving credit where credit is due is despised as "plagiarism" and punished severely.

The outcry against "censorship" uses a very honourable, democratic, and emancipatory argument, because in the course of history censorship has been imposed by dictators, enemies to our humanity. The issue calls to mind the horrors of censorship and book-burning under fascism and Stalinism. It arouses strong emotions of indignation against a group said to be bent upon tearing down the achievements of the humanist struggle for civil rights and intellectual liberty. And yet, to cry out against "Native censorship" in the light of the very real economic and social disempowerment of Native people, is as misleading as the cry against a so-called "Indian menace" in pioneer days, which according to historian Francis Jennings was in reality "the boomerang effect of the European menace to the Indians" (*The Invasion of America*, 1975, 37). By leaving out the central issue in Native/non-Native relations, the inequality of power between both groups, "Indian censorship" becomes a scapegoat, serving in turn to silence/censor Native appeals for equal opportunity and fair representation in the literary world. Nor is it in keeping with the ethics of multiculturalism to discard as negligible concerns stemming from a "copyright system based on trust." Censorship and trust are mutually exclusive.

Within literate cultures words are reproducible, stories can be stored for ages, lost myths may often be restored by piecing together literary shards from various sources. In the oral tradition the mechanisms of documenting, retrieving, or authenticating texts are limited to living individuals mastering language, and oral texts are only "one generation removed from extinction" (B. Johnston). The spoken word, the verbatim rendering of traditional stories, deserves the utmost attention and veneration. Many of today's Native authors in Canada define themselves and their work as part of the ongoing tradition of storytelling. Non-Native authors who maintain that anybody should be able to tell anybody's story and write about anybody else's culture may be unaware of the particular significance the word has in the oral tradition. Appeals not to tell Native stories are also appeals not to destroy what has carefully been preserved over many generations and what often holds the power necessary for survival in the future. It would be difficult if not impossible to codify this "power" aspect of the oral tradition in written laws designed preeminently to protect private material property. What is called for is a rethinking with open minds and hearts, a struggle for an ethics of respect that has nothing to do with censorship.

The appropriation discussion in Canada has challenged non-Native authors to enter a dialogue with Native writers and readers unparalleled elsewhere. On both sides, some of the voices are shrill, others are muted. Some non-Native authors have begun to fundamentally rethink, refeel, and redirect their writing (*Books in Canada*, XX.1, 1991, 11–17). Perhaps some of the conversations in this book can serve as encouragements to continue the process of listening and learning.

### Listening

After this remarkable "outburst" in Native literary creativity, mainstream literary scholars in Canada are discovering Native writing as a new field of exploration on which to test their critical theories, and as a literary scholar, perhaps I ought to make haste and join the race to stake my claim in this new territory. But listening to almost 30 Native storytellers, oral historians, and writers has given me a lot to think about before joining the race.

"The oral tradition," I wrote in 1987, "transcends European notions of *genre*" (Lutz 1989, 90). This statement has since "haunted" me. I have read it in somebody else's book on Native literature in Canada, as well as on the back of a recent anthology of writings by Native women. I have even "carelessly" repeated this observation in an article on "Native Literature in Canada Today," in which I subdivided texts by contemporary Native authors into—what?—genres, of course!

After having talked to many Native authors, I have begun to realize that the truth of my sweeping generalization of four years ago needs to be brought to bear upon Native writing in Canada in general, since many authors follow their oral storytelling traditions very consciously. And here I am, with newly raised questions of methodology. How does a critic/scholar begin to "structure" the vast amount of texts? How is it possible to categorize without over-generalizing or without getting lost in "petty" individual detail? One way would be a strictly chronological approach, another one an approach by author; both may lead to the meticulous boredom of encyclopedias.

In the US the situation seems quite different. There, the established novelists themselves are usually university professors of English, who draw at least as much on their academic training and literary skills as on the traditions of their Native ancestors, whose language many of them do not speak due to centuries of cultural ethnocide. In Canada at least three Native languages, Cree, Inuktitut, and Ojibway, are going strong, and many others are likewise spoken on a daily basis. The ties of modern Native literature to the oral tradition seem far stronger here, and the languages, in turn, are tied to the land (as Maria Campbell, Ruby Slipperjack, Tomson Highway, and others stress in their interviews). How can Western literary criticism accommodate this relationship? How will critical theory deal with a statement like Maria Campbell's, that non-Native writers in Canada have "lost the Mother"?

Unless such a comment is brushed aside as "non-academic" in a gesture of colonial arrogance and/or academic provincialism, it posits a serious challenge to contemporary academia. It would require an amount of cross-cultural learning on the side of non-Natives which could seriously question (and thereby "impede") the progress of literary-theory-development in mainstream academia. And yet, it behoves non-Natives to stop to listen because Native ways of perceiving and dealing with life "derive from an ecosystemic, nonanthropocentric perspective on the world" (Krupat 1989) which our planet is in dire need of.

Literature provides an avenue into the perceptions of reality by other people across cultures and generations. Native authors show their readers views of a reality far more complex than that which the European linear, causal mode of perception can accommodate. Native authors in Canada have access to cultural traditions that have enabled their ancestors to survive under extreme conditions and in ways that have enhanced the lives of all members of their respective societies, as well as endowing them with a deep respect for all their relations, be they rocks, plants, four-legged, winged, finned, or scaled. This collection of conversations with Native writers in Canada, it is hoped, will provide us all with challenging thoughts to help us in our struggle for a world in which even our great-great-great-great-grandchildren, seven generations from now, will be able to live to the full potential of their humanity.

## Collecting and Editing

What the reader finds on these pages is only the visibly worded part of an extended process of meetings and conversations with many Native people in Canada. For reasons of space, theme, or other "technicalities," only about two-thirds of all conversations are actually included in this collection. They are given here in chronological order, reflecting the process I went through.

In the fall of 1987, while pursuing research on contemporary women writers in Canada, I also met with Native individuals whom I was directed to: in Alberta, Martin Heavyhead gave me some personal oral history, and Leroy Littlebear took me along on a tour of otherwise inaccessible Blackfoot pictographs near Writing-on-Stone; in Saskatchewan, Medric McDougall and Walter Fiddler met with Wolfgang Klooss and myself and gave us some oral history while showing us around St. Louis, Duck Lake, Wakaw, and Batoche; in Winnipeg, Peter Kelly/Kinew told me about a film project he was involved in, and I also met with Paul Chartrand at the Native Studies Department; in London, Ontario, Robin McGrath introduced me to Alan Chrisjohn, director of the School of Native Journalism at Western University, who told me about their program and his former involvement with *Akwesasne Notes*; at Trent University, Marlene Brant-Castellano talked to me about system theory and Native American perception; in Ottawa, Parker Duchemin brought me together with Greg Young-Ing and Wilfred Pelletier.

Two years later, I returned to Canada to do research on Native literature. Howard Adams, comrade and friend, directed me to Rosalee Tizya of United Native Nations in Vancouver, who told me about oral history. The next day Ethel Gardner of the First Nations House of Learning, UBC, spoke to me about the importance of the Sto:lo oral tradition and told me how to find "Bobbi Lee" (Maracle). In Victoria, I spent several very enjoyable and memorable hours with Barbara Smith at her house, a visit which told me much about her writing, but left me puzzled about the intersection of Native identity, feminist spiritualism, appropriation, and oral traditions in her sources. A meeting with Lee Maracle, whose *Bobbi Lee* (in German translation) was the first Canadian Native text I ever read, made me more aware of the dangers of appropriation and the unreliability of sound-recording equipment.

A day after our meeting we were both on the same plane to Penticton, British Columbia, where Jeannette Armstrong just happened to be opening the En'owkin School of International Native Writing, and I was privileged to visit with them for several days. While on the second day students and instructors went on a physical orientation excursion to traditional Okanagan sites not accessible to me, Elder Glen Douglas told me stories for hours, ranging from Okanagan traditions to his personal experiences with residential schools, missionaries, and the military. I will be forever grateful for his patience, generosity, and trust. On the final day of my stay, Jeannette Armstrong took the time off her incredibly busy schedule for an interview, and I now understand that that was the beginning of this book. That interview is the first one included in this collection, reflecting verbatim her impressive oratorical skill.

After having met teachers and students at En'owkin, things went along by themselves, and my five-week trip from Vancouver to Ottawa gained considerably in momentum. While visiting with Fifth House Publishers in Saskatoon, Maria Campbell happened to phone and an interview was arranged, 10 minutes later Tomson Highway happened to phone, and I changed my itinerary to be able to meet him in Toronto. While reading a paper in Regina at the Saskatchewan Indian Federated College I met with Beth Cuthand and Sue Deranger, and Bernie Selinger, head of the English department, offered me a guest professorship. In Winnipeg, on the day I interviewed Jordan Wheeler, the Manitoba Native Writers Association just happened to be having its first meeting. In Thunder Bay Renate Eigenbrod introduced me to George Kenny and Ruby Slipperjack, and I had conversations with both of them. Finally, on one very intensive night in Toronto before flying back to Europe, I met with Lenore Keeshig-Tobias in the early evening, who told me during the interview that Maria Campbell and Linda Griffith were launching their book at the Theatre Passe Mureille that night, so I ran, and Pauline directed me to the underground station,—"miraculously" I made it there in time. The next morning I met with Tomson Highway at Native Earth Performing Arts, and then spent two hours at Beatrice Culleton's home for a long conversation, before jumping into a taxi to snail my way to the airport during rush hour. All the while, I was not thinking of a book.

The book idea came in the fall of 1990, during my stay at the Saskatchewan Indian Federated College. Instead of writing a book about Native literature, which was my original intention, I felt it was more "appropriate" to prepare the recorded conversations for a separate publication, since there are so few texts available in which Native authors and critics express their views about their own writing. Fortunately, Martha Gould and Fraser Seely of Fifth House lent their support to the idea. The remaining interviews were recorded in a somewhat more planned fashion.

Deliberately, the collection includes conversations with both well-known authors and little-known or even hardly published ones, because they all are embarked on the same project. In my questions, I followed a few recurrent topics, but I also included ad hoc issues spontaneously. The influence of the oral tradition forms one theme through most of the conversations; the question of what makes each writer write is another one. A recurrent strand is also the relationship between Native writers and (non-Native) critics, and the topic of appropriation commanded much of our time. A question about a message to non-Natives/Europeans/my students in many cases led to global aspects and our relatedness to our Mother, the Earth, but also addressed the equally vital issue of overcoming perceptional barriers that need to be removed for the sake of future generations.

Other questions involved the specific works of individual authors, the "Nativeness" of Indian or Métis literature, and the "borderlands" position of people of mixed ancestry between two or more cultures. Some conversations may turn out to be interesting only to those readers who have read specific texts by the individual Native authors themselves. Finally, a number of topics are bound to my own person, my German, historically charged background, the north German region I come from, and the people I am involved with.

While this book "grew" on me as I went along, and many "happenings" and the "moccasin telegraph" supported me on many occasions, the issue of appropriation always loomed large in the back of my mind. Editing Native manuscripts as a non-Native may result in renewed forms of appropriation. In the hope of minimizing this risk, the copyright remains jointly with each interviewed author and myself.

In terms of the actual process of editing, each author received a word-by-word transcript of the whole conversation before signing her/his consent to publication. The transcripts were then edited by the authors, myself, and a copy-editor, to smooth the transition from conversation to written texts.

To me, it seems very fitting that this first collection of Native opinions on Native literature is based on spoken words. It is in keeping with the oral tradition. At this point in time, and in the light of the many unresolved questions and conflicts of which the Oka-issue afforded the public only a small glimpse, it may have been less challenging that these conversations were conducted between Native authors and a non-Canadian, but I am confident that many more exchanges will (have to) follow. Throughout the process, there was much learning for me, and I thank you all for giving me your time and attention.

Hartmut Lutz
March 1991
Regina

# JEANNETTE ARMSTRONG

▼

*Jeannette Armstrong, grand-niece of Hum-Ishu-Ma (1888–1936), the first Native American woman novelist, grew up on the Okanagan Reserve near Penticton, British Columbia. She received a sound traditional education and went through mainstream schooling at the same time. She earned a diploma in Fine Arts from Okanagan College, and a B.F.A. from the University of Victoria. Since 1978 she has been working in various cultural and political capacities for the Penticton Band, and in 1989 she became the director of En'owkin School of International Writing, the first centre in the world where Aboriginal people learn and teach how to write and publish their literatures.*

*Jeannette Armstrong has published two books for children,* Enwhisteetkwa: Walk on Water *(1982) and* Neekna and Chemai *(1984). Her internationally acclaimed novel,* Slash *(1985), follows the development of a young Okanagan man, Thomas Kelasket, who grows increasingly involved in the Native struggle for human rights and self-determination.*

*The interview was recorded on 13 September 1989, at En'owkin Centre, two days after the official opening of the school* (copyright: Jeannette Armstrong/Hartmut Lutz).

---

**HL:** *Slash* is the first novel by an Indian woman in Canada. The first novel by an Indian woman south of the border was also by an Okanagan woman.[1] Were you aware that you, as an Okanagan woman, were setting a precedent?

**JA:** Well, when I wrote *Slash*, I wasn't aware that it was the first novel by a Native woman in Canada. I knew that there were Native women writing, and, I guess, I never really differentiated, I never thought about it in those terms between "biography, autobiography," and other things that Native people, and women in particular, were writing.

I was aware of Maria Campbell and of Lee Maracle's book. Also, I never set out to do that. I'd like that understood: I never set out to set a precedent or to be the first Native woman novelist!

My real quest was to present a picture of that time for a specific purpose. We were talking about that historical period, trying to determine how best to get that information to Native people, young people in particular. We wanted a tool to use in education, to give not just the historical documentation of that time but, beyond that, the feeling of what happened just prior to the American Indian Movement, and what happened during that militancy period—and that's, frankly, what came out of it, the spirit of the people, and the rise, and the groundswelling, and *how* that occurred, what the people were feeling, what they dreamed, and what their pain and joy were during that time. And it was the only way in which, without a lot of money, I could see developing something that might be worthwhile.

Another reason attached to it, in terms of working with the Curriculum Project, was developing materials for the schooling system. The opportunity was there. The thing that needed to be said was answered.

My intention was to accomplish two things. It was to be able to talk about that period and some personal experiences but also, because I wasn't really deeply involved in the movement, to talk about the experiences of others, whose pain and pleasure I did experience, and which as a result influenced me, and other people as well.

I was aware of Hum-Ishu-Ma's writing, Mourning Dove. She is my grand-aunt, and a direct relation to me. But I was more aware of her collection of Okanagan Stories. I knew of the existence of those, and then read them. After that I read *Kukidjuwea* (non-Native people call it *Cogewea* or whatever!), the novel. It was hard to find because it was out of print, but it has since then been reprinted. I've read it, and I have a copy of it. But I knew her also as my relative from my mother's stories, although I never met her because she died before I was born. But I knew about her, and I knew a lot about her. She was my mother's aunt. I heard the things that other people said, the people who knew her. Other elders and my family talked about her. And, of course, I was intrigued because she was my relative, my blood relative. And I was intrigued by her thinking.

So, there was a definite connection there, but not directly to the novel in terms of her being the first Native woman writer of a novel in North America.

*HL:* In a way, I see your novel as a historical novel because it covers quite a span of very important history. It is also didactic in that it teaches people about what it was like. In that way, it is part of the oral tradition, which told people who they are, and where they are headed, and where they came from.

Did you design the novel to stand in that tradition, with that function?

*JA:* One point I was clear on: I wanted to give to my grandchildren what I felt, and what others felt through that time. I wanted to give it to them from our perspective, as truthfully as I could. I wanted to be able to hand it on. I wanted them to know the heart of the people during that time.

And I know that the oral tradition will carry some parts of that, pieces of that, and various experiences of our people, because we are an oral tradition people, and that continues. Anywhere you sit at our tables, you'll hear pieces and parts of that all the time. It comes up all the time. People are talking about it and relating those stories, just as I heard the stories from my aunts, and uncles, and grandparents, and elders in my community.

I have a good picture of what life was like in the early part of the century leading up to the 1950s. I have a good picture in my mind of what things looked like, and what things were like, and what things people did — not from reading history but from our oral tradition. I have a pretty good picture of that time period.

So, an oral tradition *will* be there. It is remaining and it is intact. But those oral traditions teach a certain number of people in our community, whereas a written piece like a novel can reach further than that. It is an important documentation, not only, I think, for our people, because of some of the political insights that were reached and for some of the insights that are wrapped up with philosophical world view *and* political insights together, that came about during that period, which for our purposes we're calling the "rebirth," or a "renewal." I prefer to call it a "renewal" because it was always there and was just being renewed! I think it's an important documentation for those people who colonized this country and who continue to make mistakes in terms of the colonizing process in this country, attempting to assimilate Native people. I think it's an important piece of information for not only our children and their grandchildren and our people and the practices of where our heart is, but also for those colonizers.

**HL:** Can you say something about the characters?

In our previous discussion I said that in a lot of Native novels characters are presented in quite a unique way as part of an ongoing or larger tribal group. So, there's not much focus on the individual in the Western bourgeois individualist sense. And, also, since they are part of a larger web, other characters move around, characters come in from the outside. They maybe are not even introduced, they just have a name and then there's a conversation with somebody else. This, for an outsider, is very different from what we as Western European readers are used to reading. And I found that in other Native American literature as well.

**JA:** It's difficult for me to make a comment about it which could make comparisons. But what I could comment about, is the process of writing. That's what I know best about.

I've been criticized by non-Native critics in terms of character development in the novel. I know that. I see the weaknesses in the novel as anyone does, in terms of writing a first novel and going back and reading it and saying, "Geez, I could have done that differently! I should have! Why didn't I?" (LAUGHS) And then that's true! It happens all the time.

But, in terms of the characters and the character development of Slash as a character in the novel, in the writing process I couldn't isolate the character and keep the character in isolation from the development of the events in the community, and the whole of the people. And I know! I took creative writing, so I know what I should have been doing, but I know what I couldn't do and make the story for my people.

The question of his connectedness to his family, to his friends, to his people, and to the outer world always entered in, all the time! All the time. More than Slash as a person! So, that was, I guess, one of the decisions I had to make in terms of writing the novel. I couldn't do both. I found that it didn't work. I couldn't. Maybe, perhaps, later on, when I'm a more mature writer, I may be able to do that. But for me it was natural, it was important to be able to work with the character as a part of other things. Simply a part of other things in terms of the community. So, when you see Slash in terms of his family you can see what his character development was. The same way with his friends, when he was out on the trail. The character development of the people around him, the pieces of character that come in and out, are all part of *his* character development, or his being, or whatever, and the relationship of his thinking to those things.

And looking at it from my point of view as a writer, it can't be any other way! With Native people it can't be any other way. That's how we are as a people, in terms of our thinking and our doing things. And if I hadn't presented it that way in the novel, it wouldn't have been readable for our people, or it wouldn't have been understandable, or real, or truthful. Because, as I was saying, it's difficult for us to look at things in a separate way. Everything is a part of something else. Everything is a part of a continuum of other things: a whole. There's a whole bigger picture there, that things are always a part of. The characters I presented are all parts of that whole.

In some cases I've had comments about Pracwa, the old man, the vividness of his character and his strength as compared, for example, to Joe, the uncle. But I'd drawn parts of the character that I present—I don't know if you have a clear picture of what Joe looks like!—you shouldn't have! The part about Joe that should be coming clear is his mind and his ability as a spiritual medicine man to work with. So, you never really know if he's tall or short or clean-cut or whatever—and that's intentional! The part of him that is important for the story is his spiritual leadership and knowledge.

16

**HL:** And it also leaves him to be part of something much larger!

**JA:** And also, in the terms of Pracwa, he's clear. You can see what he looks like. He has a moustache and he has greying hair—and his brilliant eyes and the intensity of his character, and his personality, and the intensity of the words that he uses. The character Pracwa is a person who played a part in which people related to him as an individual, and as a person, because of the strength of his leadership. What they responded to was that personality, the charisma of the person, and the physical appearance is a part of that. So that part is important to bring into the characterization.

So, I heard people say, "why bring in somebody like Pracwa and make him a vivid character? And then somebody like Joe who really had an influence on Slash—why don't we see what he looks like? I'd like to know what he looks like!" And that kind of thing. But those were the reasons why I drew on the parts of them that were needed for the development of Slash. So Slash is building. His character contains all different ones, including the women that he was involved with. So we see those women in different parts. We see those women presented as characters themselves in different ways.

Anyway that's basically what I was thinking.

**HL:** One woman character is based on a historical character—Anna Mae Aquash?

**JA:** I never intended it to be that. But I've been *asked* the question, and I guess there are two questions, really, in that: (1) Were some of the characters real people? (2) Were they based on real people?

I would say, "yes, they're based on people," but historically and in terms of content as presented in the novel, no! They definitely were not those characters!

But, do you remember that character as well, the friend of his that committed suicide, and that was in the papers and so on? That's a real character! But I never ever introduced that character as a person in the novel itself. The reason I didn't want to do anything like that was because I didn't want to write a story about those people, those individuals. They have their own stories to tell, or their people who knew them and were close to them have stories to tell about those people.

I wanted to be able to make and draw together characters who in people's minds form real characters. So, the reason for bringing in a person—that one woman figure you were talking about—there were women like that. There were *very* strong women, and they were very essential in terms of the work, and the militancy in the movement, and the thinking of the people during that time. But a lot of them were very, very unique in terms of the specific characters and personality, and I didn't want to take one of those people and present them in any way. So, I presented circumstances that were similar. So that through the similarities

17

there would be an allusion drawn to a possible personality, but not an attempt to develop that character as if it were that person.

*HL:* I think what comes across very well in that novel is that, although the central character is male, the strength of the whole movement, then and today, and I think in the future, lies in the women.

*JA:* I'm glad you say that, because that has been a question in every workshop that I do by feminists ...

*HL:* Because you chose a male character?

*JA:* Because I chose a male character!

*HL:* Yes, you did that. Maybe that's unusual, but there's also the way he learns about women.

*JA:* And the way he comes to terms with real strengths, in terms of human strength. For me *that* development is an important one for males!

*HL:* Yes, and he's going through that and realizes the stamina of women.

*JA:* And it's important from my point of view that I'd take a male and transform him into that, through female power, through "soft love" or whatever you may call it, and make it happen. I guess my choice, too, had to do with practical things in terms of choosing a male character.

But I've been asked that. That question has been thrown at me, and I say, "Well, I don't talk about it in this way!" I can talk about it in this way that it is a very feminist book, and it really works with, and talks about, female thinking and the empowerment of people through love, and compassion, and spirituality. And whether you want to call it female power, that's beside the point, but that's currently what it's being called. I think it's human at its best.

And it's not dependent on sex, men and women. But currently women, womankind, I guess, has been promoting that thinking. And so it's being called "feminist thought." And I disagree! I think it's fundamental to our thought as humans, and the real humanity in us!

I like to say that when I'm asked that question.

So I can take a character like Slash, and I can give him that quality, and he can still be male, and still be powerful, and still be believable as a male, and still be wonderful and beautiful as a human being, and have males read that and not be threatened, or not be put off by it. And I think I have accomplished that because I have had macho men out of the American Indian Movement come up to me and talk with me about that. They told me, "You said something that I missed. I'm just finding out about that." People who come out of that period, who have been involved, have said, "Those were some of the biggest mistakes that we made!" And I'm not saying that's true for all of them. There was a lot of egotism among both men and women.

I'm glad that you say that, because that part of it I was very cautious

18

about, and not sure about. And it's something I really wanted to do with that novel!

**_HL:_** There's another thing! I read a lot of contemporary Native novels before I read *Slash*, and I found out that a lot of the characters—and they're not just standing for an individual but for a whole group and maybe for all people—sort of go through a development that is a circle from, say, a healed or a whole person, with "tribal identity" as Deloria defines it,[2] and then there's a separation, and then that separation leads to alienation and at the bottom to conflict. And a lot of people then just don't make it back any more. They just drop off, they commit suicide, they get killed. Then there's a return, but the return may be just physical and it needs another level, a ceremony or some renewal, so that they can come back to that first position.

And looking at Slash and the people who go along with him, I have the feeling that it is the circle[3] that he is going through. Would you agree with me?

**_JA:_** I would, and I was very intent and careful about that! I know the writing of novels requires a certain dynamic that you set up as triangular, rather than circular. And I had decided at that point, I could have started with a person who is angry, and frustrated, and full of hate, and all the things that Slash was in the novel, and that's where other people have started.

Or it would have started at a childhood which made him that. It would have started at his childhood, for instance, he would have been beaten up and battered, in all kinds of ways abused by foster parents, and then it would just carry on from there, and would grow bigger in terms of how he reacts to life, and what makes him militant. There were those people! There's no doubt about it! A lot of people that were in the American Indian Movement were people from that background.

But my purpose was not to talk about that development of pain in people. I wanted to present a picture of a healthy family, where a healthy wholeness was there, and how that could be transformed, and changed, and corrupted; where that falling apart happens, and then where that bringing back together then happens. To bring back to wholeness.

But then there is a process of documented learning in between. A person could come in at the middle of it and say "this was, that's me!", or a person could come from the other end of it and say "yeah, that's where I started out, and what happened?"

I wanted to be able to do that as a whole, as a circle, as a continuum. And I wanted to take him from health and bring him back to health again and go through the whole process. And in a lot of cases that's what happens anyway. As children we are born healthy. We are healthy and happy until at a certain time something happens that destroys that. It can be when we are very young or older, as a teenager, or whatever.

And I think that circle is a circle that has to happen in people, many people! And if we present a picture of that happening, the process of it happening, the process of thinking, then we have a complete picture in terms of a comment, in terms of a political process, and a spiritual growth. And I wanted that! I wanted the people that were reading that, the Native people who read this, I wanted to put in their mind, with an understanding, what that process is. So—I don't know if it's in the prologue or the epilogue—when he says: "I'm closer as a man now, closer to that 17-year-old boy, closer than I was," that's the beginning of the indication that there is a circle.

*HL:* And then, structurally you have the prologue and the epilogue, and then there are four parts, four directions in the circle.

*JA:* Native people have asked me, "Is this accidental that there are four parts, and it's like the Four Directions, and there are the prologue and the epilogue being the direction above us and below us?" And I said, "No, it wasn't, actually!"

I did prepare myself in the Indian way for this novel. I asked for the guidance to write it. And I fasted for the guidance to write it. I didn't decide, "I'm gonna write this!" I didn't just decide that I know everything. I asked for help and assistance, through the same process from the Okanagan.

And I asked for it, because I knew that I don't know all these things. But through the guidance, and my right approach in terms of its use and benefit for the people, that I would be given an opportunity to present it in a way that was healthy and beneficial to the people.

*HL:* So how long did it take to write that? How were other people involved?

*JA:* The research took two years. I never started writing for two years. I did what is called a literature search. I read everything I could get my hands on. And I read everything by Native people, and I read everything by non-Native people. I read the press and everything else. I did a lot of research, written research. I had piles of stuff in the back there. I read every Indian newsletter, newspaper, anything that was written by magazines, that I could get my hands on, that I knew of, that gave a point of view about that, or by Indian people being interviewed.

*HL:* Could you name some titles or some books that you could recommend if somebody else would want to ...

*JA:* There weren't any books! Not at that period of time, cause this was, you were talking about 1980. And we were talking about a time just previous to that. So, there were no books. Now there are books coming out, but at that time there were no books available about the period just before that, the 1960s and 1970s.

So, what I had to do was go and find anything that was written. *Akwesasne Notes*, of course, was the most comprehensive Native voice there was at that time. And then there were others. They were less accurate in terms of the rising militancy and the thinking, the politicizing of the people. And then, there were magazine articles in which there were interviews with people, which were done by *Penthouse* and done by other national magazines. And I did collect them all. I have major newspapers in the back room there, which I did the research on. And then I mapped it out chronologically, historically. I actually did a chronology of events in the country.

***HL:*** One can follow that in the book! I always use the back or so and take little notes, and then I check up on that. But there's a whole chronology.

***JA:*** The chronology is 300 pages, and I've been told that it should be published, just because of the dates, and events, and people, and things like that, that were happening. I've never considered doing that, because I'm not a historian, and all of it is a point-form chronology. Like in 1976, on this day, Wounded Knee or whatever happened, so and so were there, and so and so talked to so and so — that kind of stuff! It's not an attempt to tie the events together as a historian, it's a straight chronology; but it was useful for me to produce that, so I could see the things that were transpiring, and see a pattern in what was happening. And then in the writings of the people, and things that were being said in the newsletter, in papers, there were people who write things, like the people who put together the interviews.

I did interviews. I talked to as many people who were involved in the movement, on both sides of the border, as possible. And I would sit down with people and sometimes, at some point, the people said, "No, I can't talk with you about that." But the saving factor was that they knew who I was, and they knew how I was involved. And they knew that they could trust me. And they knew what I was doing it for. I wasn't hiding that: "I'm doing a book, and the book is going to be like this. It's not going to be about you; I'm not going to do a history of anything that ... I'm talking about a time period which affected me, and which affected many people, and I want to talk about it."

People were willing to sit down and talk about it. And I talked to them not just about the historical occurrences, but their feelings about it. That was the most important part, I think, in the research. "What were the things that made you feel that? How did you feel at that particular time? What were the emotions, and what were the things that were happening, that caused these things in your life? Give me an idea about it!" Just getting them talking about it! Quite a few times it brought it all back. And sometimes, in some cases, it was extremely painful for those people who talked about it.

21

So I was really indebted to most people. And in particular to one person, who I got to know very well, who was extremely useful and truthful to me, because that person wasn't one of the leaders at the head of the movement. The person, I guess, is closest to the character of Slash, in terms of the way that person operated. He was always in the background, he was always thinking about things, he was always trying to analyze and understand things, and he was always trying to be on top of the things in terms of what would happen. And he was always misunderstood, and was always put down by some of the people who were involved.

*HL:* There was too much macho rivalry!

*JA:* Yes. And probably he could have been, if things were turned around, one of the strongest leaders. A real one! One of the real, stronger leaders. Because, things that went wrong, he would say beforehand to them.

*HL:* That's so obvious close to the end, when the sovereignty issue and the land claim issue comes up, that he sees much further than ...

*JA:* There were several people like that! One person in particular, who said, "I gave up, I gave up! I can see all these things. I understand them. But why? Why? I can't do anything about them! All I can do is try to live my life and pass on things I know." He was so frustrated at the time when I was talking to him. But I thought, "That particular character trait I want to pull out of there!" Because so many of the other character things were obviously blatant and there, for everybody.

I won't name any names, but some of these guys were pretty prominent. And I didn't want to draw on them or use them in any way.

*HL:* I think that's one of the strengths of Slash, that he remains outside of that. So he is also a critical observer of what's happening, and nobody can now turn around and say: "Well, it's a history of AIM from the AIM perspective." It's not!

*JA:* It's not, and it never was intended to be! So the research period, I guess, took two years, I would say from 1980 to 1982. And in 1982 I started writing in terms of getting it out.

*HL:* Was that after you finished your degree in creative writing?

*JA:* Oh yes, I'd been out of the program for two years! I graduated from the University of Victoria in 1978. So in 1980 I started the research for the novel. And two years down the road, I completed the research, and felt ready to write. And by then I had some essence of what we wanted to talk about, during that period, what the focus was! And I also had some essence of the layers that I wanted to uncover, that I wanted to speak about. Not just the personal development in terms of his transformation through that circle, but the political movement through that. And also the group and community thinking, and changes in thinking, through that whole time! I had a pretty good idea of how it should move, and how it should work. So I started writing in 1982. That again was about a year and a half of writing, before I completed the first draft. It was in 1984 or sometime.

*HL:* Did you write full time at any point?

*JA:* I wrote full time for about six months, to complete the draft. I did what was called a skeleton of the novel. I did 20 pages, I guess, and about five pages of each chapter. Just basically saying, "This is what's going to happen in the chapter." Then I vaguely sketched in characters, but not in any descriptive or intense way, or whatever. And then I took each of those chapters, and I worked! I worked at writing them!

They weren't written successively or progressively, like chapter one, chapter two, chapter three. The way my mind works is, if there's something in chapter one that's going to relate to chapter two, I would have to see it as a thread all the way through. So I developed those pieces in that thread, all the way through. So it's a different way of developing a novel. I understand that people don't usually develop a novel ...

*HL:* But that makes it into that fabric!

*JA:* And so there is a fabric of the writing there. And there are threads that go there, that are there all the way through, and they sort of weave together, rather than writing in a linear fashion.

*HL:* That also is something that you have in a lot of women's literature: the weaving. And it's used in feminist literary criticism. They say "we weave." There is not this linear development that way, but there are so many strands of this holistic thinking. The way women think, as it has been analyzed, is so much more complex.

*JA:* And it is true! It's keeping hold of those threads right from the beginning all the way through, and bringing them back around again. And the threads involve different aspects.

As I mentioned there are about four or five layers to the novel that I wanted to talk about. And I had to keep those layers all the way through into those threads, making sure that they were woven together with the other ones, and that they fit together and work together without any discomfort.

There were phases where the fabric was weak. As a first novel writer I couldn't see it, because it happens when you're writing. When you're writing, you're so involved in the character, the character becomes so real, and the people, the scenario, the scene, everything else becomes so real that it's hard to be self-critical about it. I think it's that way with any writer, unless you're really disciplined, and I am not.

But I did try in a sense to do that. We cut out quite a lot of the novel in the second draft. I sat down and pulled out a lot of things that were not necessary to the threads in the novel, but that I really wanted in there. (LAUGHS) We did some of that. Some of it got left in there! And I was

23

saying, "Why, you know, I'm going to make a decision here, it's going to stay." And I was sorry later, of course, after going back reading, and I say, "Oh shit, I should have listened!" (LAUGHS) But anyway, that was a good exercise for me! It was a tremendous, painful exercise.

I remember one point when I was writing the worst part of Slash's life, really, actually living, myself, in that headspace. And it was a difficult time that I went through, because I was really emotional, I was really sensitive, I was really angry. And I was really afraid and fearful. And at that point I didn't know if I was going to make it, to finish the novel! To write it, to actually put it down on paper, to pull it together, to pull *him* together! I didn't know if I was going to be able to do it.

And it had an effect on me, a profound effect, that at some point I would like to document for other writers. Because, I remember writing, and writing, and writing, and writing. And the guy I was living with at that time was a pretty understanding person but I remember he wanted to take me away out of town, to go and do some R and R. And we were going to go to Vancouver. There was this play in Vancouver. And he thought it would be a good idea and, I guess, knowing me, he knew I was getting into this state where I was feeling really wretched. Anyway, he wanted to pull me out of this writing, and take me to this thing. And I had agreed, because I was feeling myself that I was really stressed. We said, "Well, we'll leave Thursday evening. And if we leave Thursday evening, we can drive part way there. And if we leave about five o'clock in the afternoon, we can have dinner on the road, and we can be part way there, and we can get a room. And the next day we can get there, rest up, and shop, and then we can see the play. That way we won't be tired!" That sounded fine to me. But I was writing, and I was writing, and I was writing, and I was writing, and I wrote, and wrote, and wrote, and wrote, and wrote. And the next thing I remember was, that he was walking, you know, pacing, and he was saying "Jeannette, please, please! Leave it, leave it!" He was just begging me. And I was saying "I've got to do just this one! One more sentence. I've got to finish this paragraph, I can't leave it now!"

Oh god, it was terrible. And then I looked at the time! It was 12 o'clock Thursday night. We were supposed to have left at four or at five! And there was no way that I was going to leave it, even at that time. And I'd been writing straight for about 28 hours. I didn't sleep, and I didn't eat. I was a mess.

*HL:* Did you handwrite, or—

*JA:* No, I was typing! I was a mess! I was with those characters, inside that world! And I couldn't leave them at that point. If I did, well—it probably wouldn't have happened, but I felt that if I left them at that particular point, if I didn't get it down at that particular point, that I was going to lose the whole thing and I just couldn't ...

Finally I just said, "Look, I just can't, I just can't do it! I can't help it. I can't understand it, and I can't tell you about it. But you are just going to have to accept it!"

So, we didn't go out that weekend. And he ended up forcing me to sleep some, rest some. But I remember the terror that put me through!

As I said, there were things that we did cut out! There were things in that period that I didn't leave in the novel. They didn't need to be there, but I had to work through it myself.

So I guess in terms of the novel, it is four years, three-and-a-half years. The final editing and stuff took about six months, but four years for the novel.

I don't think, for myself, it could be done in less time. Maybe something that I already knew about I could do in less time. If I knew the subject and everything, all the information, if I knew all the stuff, I could probably do it all within a year, the writing of it.

But I still am fearful about doing a second one. I know I will, I know that. I know what it will be about, because I've been working on this idea. I haven't found the courage yet to approach it. It's not the time even, it's space to do it, to work at it. So I'm working at all these other things preliminary to it, that may be part of it.

*HL:* You said, when you were doing research, you were also reading literature by other Native authors, novels. Are there some in particular that you found fascinating, or that to you seemed unique, or moved you?

*JA:* Well, I'd read Bobbi Lee's, Lee Maracle's, book before that.[4] As I have said, it was an influence in terms of my own thinking. And it had an effect and impact on me!

And Maria Campbell's,[5] while I was still at the University of Victoria, came out. And I remember, when her book *Halfbreed* came out, she was visiting, and I was trying to get an interview. I didn't get to talk to her. She was on the radio program, and she was talking. And I remember listening, and listening to her voice, and listening to her thinking, and then going back to the book, reading the book, and trying to imagine what it was like for her. For me *Halfbreed* was an important book in terms of Native literature, even in the way it was presented.

*HL:* Any comments about authors from south of the border? You mentioned Joy Harjo?

*JA:* Yes, Harjo. And mostly articles, political articles. Stuff that was being written by people either in the movement, or people against the movement.

*HL:* I was thinking of Momaday, or Welch, and Silko.

*JA:* Yes, I didn't read Leslie Silko until after that. It wasn't up here in Canada. You couldn't buy it in Canada. But I had read *House Made of Dawn* and I read *The Way to Rainy Mountain*. And I was very, very intrigued by that. I still am. I'm a great admirer of Momaday's writing.

But James Welch I didn't read at that particular period. I don't think it was because he was unavailable, it's just that I hadn't heard about James Welch until much later, when I was reading.

When I said, "I was reading for the research of *Slash*," it was mainly historical stuff. I was reading all kinds of newspaper accounts, and Indian newspaper accounts, and Indian commentaries, political stuff! I would start looking at the political goals, the history of the people, rather than literature.

*HL:* Howard Adams?

*JA:* Yes. Since then, I've been doing more appropriate reading in terms of literature, looking at the development of Native literature, and the development of Native voice, and how various people had approached it. And in particular, I'm really concentrating on poetry. I really had my mind focused on poetry in these last five years since *Slash*.

Just recently I've been looking at short stories, but I'm so afraid of that form of writing, at this point, that I haven't approached it. I submitted one short story to Thomas King's new anthology, *All My Relations*, and he's accepted it. But I'm so afraid of that format, because it's not as easy as telling a story.

From my point of view the Native short story differs in a really fundamental way from what we understand short story to be. And I've seen examples of Native short stories, good examples of Native short stories, and I'm excited about that, but I don't know enough about it.

*HL:* Do you know this anthology, *The Man to Send Rainclouds*? That title story! It's so wonderful!

*JA:* Yes, oh I know. That's one of the books that turned me on to Native short stories! And what I need to do for myself is some critical thinking around short stories, in the same way that I've been doing with my poetry and novels.

*HL:* Having heard you read your poetry the other night and then on tape, you should always write poetry and then *read* it!

*JA:* I'm publishing a book of poems this year. A collected version.

*HL:* If possible, it should also be made available in sound, because you've got a way of reading that is very precise, and also very mellow and soft. It sounds very good.

*JA:* Thank you! Did you get the second tape? We have three tapes! I gave you one.⁶

*HL:* Shall we talk about En'owkin?

*JA:* Sure!

*HL:* I was really excited when I got a flyer from a friend in Lethbridge about En'owkin. And I thought, "I must go there and check that out," because it's the first program of this kind. On the other hand, I'm aware

26

of the School of Native Journalism at the University of Western Ontario, where Alan Chrisjohn is director. I talked to him in 1987. But this is really new!

How did you pull this together? Because I understand that it is mainly you who was pulling it together.

*JA:* Well, it's a natural progression, from my point of view. Not from everybody else's point of view, who said, "What are you doing? Wow!" (LAUGHS) But from my point of view it's a natural progression out of what the work was in terms of the En'owkin Centre we were involved with and what it has been originally set up to be.

If you look at the objectives of the society which governs En'owkin, we want to record and perpetuate and promote "Native" in the cultural sense, in education, and in our lives and our communities. It sounds pretty open-ended, but in terms of En'owkin itself, in terms of its evolving, it has always been in the area of words. We've always been involved in the passing on of information, as correctly as possible, to those people who require that information, whether they're children, our old people, or school teachers, or whoever. And that was always the essence of En'owkin.

The curriculum project was the original founding reason. It was to develop a curriculum for schoolchildren that carried the history and the content in a correct way, and a dignified way, for use in the schools, so that Okanagan history could be read. The history of who the people were, and being proud of that, proud of the contributions, and being proud as an Okanagan person. That part of the founding of the En'owkin Centre was called "The Okanagan Curriculum Project." And a lot of research, and a lot of writing, and a lot of involvement of the Native people, the elders of our communities saying, "Yes, that's important, and that's how it should be presented, that's the correct use of it!"—all was part of the process.

The second part of the process, in terms of putting together the information and delivering it, was the importance of Native people, our own people, doing that work. And that was always one of the ingredients that we insisted on.

Whenever we did a project, it was a political battle, right from the start! Because when we met with the school districts about the production of the curriculum for the schools, right away they wanted to hire non-Indian researchers, anthropologists, historians. They wanted to hire non-Indian writers and coordinators to make sure that the information was going to be good enough to be used in the schools. They were not intending to be paternalistic but that's what it turns out to be. Because that's like saying, "You people can't do that! You don't know your own history, you don't know how to write, you don't know how to research, you don't know how to put material together that's useful, or usable!"

For myself that's unacceptable, and will always be unacceptable!

So that was part of the agreement that we have with each other in terms of the curriculum project. I was on the founding committee for the resources societies, for the Okanagan Tribal Education Committee. And then, of course, we said, "No! We are not going to agree with that. The only correct version has got to be from our people! Nobody else can give the correct version, but our people. And we're going to stick to that!" So, if that means training our people in terms of researching, and in terms of producing information, in terms of developing information and ways to do that, then that's what we'll have to do. So that, if the stuff doesn't come out for 10 years, we're going to work at that, so that the stuff comes out, and it's quality, and it's correct, and it's appropriate and, most of all, is Indian!

And that, from the outset, was a real clear path in terms of how we were to organize, and how we were to work. We've kept that as a guiding force. Always, when we had a project in front of us in which we were going to produce something, Native people would be the ones that were involved in doing that! And so the natural outgrowth of all the other training that we do in En'owkin, and on the curriculum project, was that we developed the Learning Institute, which became a training centre for adult Native people. Giving them skills in writing, and history, and all those things.

We could see that we lack resources, we lack skilled people who have the training that's necessary, that basic and fundamental educational training that is needed to produce and do certain things. So we ended up becoming a training centre to do that. And out of that, Theytus, as a part of the curriculum project, came into being. And out of that, those two dynamics in terms of training people, and in terms of Theytus as a publisher needing people who could edit, and write, and typeset, and people who could contribute, it was a question of, "okay, where do we get these people from? Where do we find these people? Who is training these people? Where the hell in the country do you find a school which talks about Native literature, Native genre, and Native voice? And where in the heck do you get the people who can be skilled in those areas to edit, to publish, to write, to script?" There is no place!

People are doing it in a hit-and-miss method on their own, going through great pains to reach skills in one area maybe. And you have them all over the country! And it seemed to us just a natural outgrowth of that question that Theytus had in front of them. Well, if there aren't those people around, and there's no place they can go, the thing we have to do is develop a situation in which people can gain those skills, and in which people can collectively work together. And we can have Native people who have a variety of skills that can plug into those areas, not just for our needs here, but in the communities out there, for schools and for universities, for their own children and for the non-Native people.

*HL:* So this is really a development from the bottom up?

*JA:* Yes!

*HL:* And not as it happens in the US: people went to university and stayed mainly at the university level, as teachers of English or American literature who are Native persons, and then write.

*JA:* Yes. It comes from the community need! It comes from a real gap there in terms of not having those people to fill those gaps.

And so, I don't have any fears about the success of our school, and the outcome in terms of the writers. But like any new thing it's not something that's just going to explode the moment it starts! We realize that! I have enough experience in the working of En'owkin, the building of this institute here, I have enough experience to know that it's perseverance, and it's work, and it's your heart that matters, and how things are going to be successful. And nothing comes easy that's good!

*HL:* You think En'owkin will function without you? I mean the writers' program? I can't imagine that it could. I know about how it was set up. I should also mention that when I got this booklet of En'owkin, I also got some torn-out-newspaper job description, and I thought, "Oh that seems to be a job for Jeannette Armstrong!" From what I knew about you, and had read.

*JA:* That's really a strange one! It was never my intention, it never occurred to me to teach the writing school programs! I wanted to be a part of it in terms of some of the workshops, because I know that I have done some thinking and some research. I have some understanding about some of those questions I bring up, about Native voice, and the Native in literature.

*HL:* That's what I mean! If you're here, and it's from this community, you are the link between the teaching program in Native writing and the community.

*JA:* You know, what I'm saying is: it *never* occurred to me, that that was the way it was!

I saw that we could set up the program, and could bring in a coordinator, a Native person like Joy Harjo, or Thomas King, or other Native people who have the academic credentials, who would come in and would act as a coordinator and also act as an instructor, and bring in other writers-in-residence.

That's how it was set up. It wasn't set up so that I would teach the program! I really actively wanted to take the time off to write! My intention was to set this thing up, taking time off to write, and do some part-time workshopping with the program.

*HL:* So that would be your ideal for the future?

*JA:* That's my ideal for the future! That's my ideal for myself, you know, as an individual!

But this past year, when we sat down collectively, the writers that we brought together, to look at the curriculum, to look at the focus, the objectives and the outcomes, the learning that we wanted to happen for these doings, the facilitation of that—what happened was: I began to see some of the things that you just mentioned, that it was going to be important to have someone who knew what he or she was talking about. And it was important to have someone who had already done some thinking around that, and some research and so on, and could articulate it. There are pieces of that in all of us as writers! There are pieces that are lacking in me, and there are pieces that are lacking in others. But when we set out to hire coordinators and instructors, we just couldn't find one. We got a lot of response from both Native people and non-Native people.

*HL:* Yes, and I know it's handled together with the University of Victoria's creative writing program, directed by Derk Wynand. I met him last Saturday.

*JA:* He was one of my instructors at the University of Victoria. And so, when we went through the applications, there were three Native people who gave us resumes, whom we wanted, any one of those three. In the end, they decided not to do it. For various reasons they couldn't come to the program.

That left us in the position of making a choice between those others who made applications, who didn't quite fit that profile! So, it should be understood that there isn't just me who can fill this profile. It could operate without me, but it would have to be coordinated more closely.

I think that the way the writers-in-residence are structured, if there is a clear path for them to work through, for the writers to be able to relate from one workshop to the next, that's important. And I think that could be accomplished without me.

The plan for it is that we all workshop together. There was Lee Maracle and Margo Kane, Minnie Freemann and Joy Harjo, Don Fiddler and Henry Michel—the guy that was there in the pink shirt! We all sat down and worked very hard at the thinking. It's not true that it couldn't operate or function without me. This year, probably that's true! But in terms of the school itself, I don't believe that's true.

This year in particular, because we couldn't find an instructor, I stepped in to instruct with an agreement with the University of Victoria that I would only be doing it until we got an instructor. I would do some of the instruction, but I would rely on other writers to fill in those gaps. And so that was agreed on. I'm comfortable with that, and I like doing it. I like covering that ground.

And this summer, when I went to fast in June, I was very concerned about the appropriate person coming to the program, and being the instructor here for the first year. And so, when I went through that ceremony, I said, "We really need the right person that's going to make this program become alive, and real, and give it the strength that it requires to continue the next year. Because of the importance of it for our people, and for all of our communities, and for all of mankind in terms of what contributions can be made by Native writers!"

I was really sincere about that. I really, really prayed for, and asked for, the right person. And it never dawned on me, until Don Fiddler went down to Victoria and met with Derk, and came back and said, "Well, we talked about this whole thing, about the instructor, and we are not satisfied. Once those three people that we wanted declined, we were not satisfied with those, we think you are the best person for it!" And I was flabbergasted! I mean really, I sat here, and I couldn't say anything. I didn't know what to say to Don. I just said, "Well, all I can say is, I'm overwhelmed. I never thought about it, it never occurred to me!" And I really have to be honest in saying that, because I was praying so hard for this right person! And he said, "Well, obviously you're the right person! We will have to do it with you!"

And this was maybe two weeks after I came back from my fast, and I was expecting some magical person to land here! (LAUGHS) So, it was so strange! And I went back that night, and I talked to my dad and my mom, and they said, "Well, when you are praying, you know, when you pray for things, if you pray with a sincere mind, you never really can presume or understand what and how those things are answered. But it's obvious to us that you got what you asked for." And then they laughed (LAUGHS) and told me, I should be careful what I prayed for, you know.

*HL:* Because you don't pray for yourself.

Is there something that you would like to add?

*JA:* Sure! One of the things that I'm very, very, very concerned about, one of the things that I'm really fearful of, is the state that humanity is in right now. I am really fearful of it because of the dehumanization process that has been happening to our people! You can talk about governments, and bureaucracies, and so on—and all of those things act on it—but beyond that, it's a loss of our basic humanity, a twisted ideal in terms of what quality in life and living is all about.

And it's become evident in terms of the natural world around us, and what it looks like. The sickness of us as human beings has become evident in the destruction of the world, in the destruction of our atmosphere and other life forms, and our rivers, and our lakes! And it's *not* a natural occurrence, it's not a natural outgrowth. And what I see happening is the disease of man, not a disease of the Earth! It's a disease of our spirit, a disease that's killing us.

31

It's not a matter of making more laws, and more legislation, or political actions. It's not a matter of that! We can fight for taking nuclear weapons out of there, cleaning up the rivers, and stuff like that! But what we need to talk about and what we need to look at is our humaneness, our compassion, and our love, and how we need to rebuild that! How we need to put that back together, so we can come back to a wholeness and health! So we can be what we were meant to be as a healthy human population. And it's frightening and fearful to watch that process. It's frightening and fearful to turn on the television, to read the newspapers. It's frightening and fearful every day.

For me, as a Native person to see that process, it's like a horror story. You are sitting in the middle of a horror story, when you know things could be different. When you know things could be like the paradise that people describe. And it's so sad, and it's so frightening, and it's so terrible, and I don't know how to put that across!

To me it's important that Native people be brought to health. It's important for me, as a necessary process for all the people, that Native people be brought back to that process, because it's here that I've been able to see help, and wholeness in spirit, in balance with all the other things. And it's here that I know the work has to be done among all of us. And it's here that Native people's words, and their thinking, and their process, and their system, their philosophy, world view or whatever, need to be understood, and looked at, and assimilated by other people. That's so important, and so critical, and so necessary, because we all deserve—we all deserve—the happiness, and the joy, and the cleanness, and the purity. We all deserve that! And we are, I guess, being bereft by our own actions, by our own unthinkingness.

That's what I see as important between us from other countries of the world, the basic love of each other and all things around us, being the most important thing that we need to talk about.

That's what I see.

---

## NOTES

1. Hum-Ishu-Ma (Mourning Dove) *Cogewa: The Half-Blood*, 1927. Repr.: Lincoln: University of Nebraska Press, 1981.
2. Vine Deloria, jr., *God Is Read* (New York: Dell, 1973), 203.
3. Hartmut Lutz, "The Circle as a Philosophical and Structural Concept in Native American Fiction Today," in: *Native American Literatures*, ed. Laura Coltelli (Pisa, Italy: Servizio Editoriale Universitario, 1989), 85–100.
4. Bobbi Lee, *Indian Rebel*. (Vancouver: L.S.M. Press, 1975).
5. Maria Campbell, *Halfbreed*. (Toronto: McClelland & Stewart, 1973).
6. "Poetry Is Not A Luxury" (1987); "Theft of Paradise" (1988); "Your Silence Will Not Protect You" (n.d.), available from: Maya Music Group, 341 Military Trail #43, West Hill, Ontario, Canada M1E 4E4.

# BETH CUTHAND

▼

*Beth Cuthand (Cree) grew up in Saskatchewan and Alberta. She has taught at the Saskatchewan Indian Federated College, University of Regina, and was a journalist for 16 years. Her poetry has been published in magazines and anthologies, and two volumes of her works appeared as separate monographs,* Horse Dance to Emerald Mountain *(1987) and* Voices in the Waterfall *(1989). She is currently doing graduate work in creative writing at the University of Arizona in Tucson, where she is also working on her first novel.*

*The first part of the conversation with Beth Cuthand and Konrad Gross, a colleague from the University of Kiel, Germany, was recorded on 23 September 1989 in Saskatoon. The second part was recorded on 31 January 1991 in Regina* (copyright: Beth Cuthand/Hartmut Lutz).

---

### 23 September 1989, Saskatoon

**BC:** Was there a Sun Dance in Germany this summer?

**HL:** I don't know. I don't think so, but anything can happen.

**BC:** We heard via the grapevine that there was one planned.

**HL:** There was? Well, I know they had one planned about three, four years ago.

So these things are going on. I've never taken part in any of those ceremonies in Germany, because I feel weird about that. And I certainly feel very unsure about the Sun Dance. Anyway, it's none of my business. But, I think, there are plans.

**KG** (TO BC): To what extent are you aware of what's happening in the United States? Is there some clearing centre where you exchange information?

**BC:** I get it by word of mouth, having friends in the States. I've one good friend in the Institute of American Indian Art. We visit, and write letters. That's how we keep informed. And then I know Joy Harjo in Tucson, and talk with her about it. She keeps in touch with Jeannette Armstrong and Viola Thomas, and we all have this network.

33

And then if somebody like a politician from here goes down there, you hear what's going on. And if I can get hold of something printed, I do. I don't think anybody has a formal setup.

*KG:* And what about communication among Natives in Canada? Do you have some sort of political organization?

*BC:* There's a national association, the Assembly of First Nations (AFN), but the Prairie tribes broke away from it, and they have their association, "The Prairie Treaty Nations Alliance" (PTNA).

*KG:* Why did they break away?

*BC:* Just during the constitutional battle. One big unresolved thing in Indian country is the difference between Aboriginal rights and treaty rights. And the treaty people thought that the Aboriginal rights people were not respecting their treaties. And they thought that overall the AFN's approach was weak, so they broke away in order to protect the treaties. And by the end of the constitutional talks there were two distinct groups, and a rift there. It's frustrating because it doesn't have to be. But people had never really talked deeply about what Aboriginal rights and treaty rights are, and how complementary they are.

*HL:* Do you think that Jeannette Armstrong's novel accurately depicts the things that were going on? And that she gets the feeling of the people in the 1970s and 1980s?

*BC:* Yes, I do.

*HL:* So it's a fairly accurate historical picture?

*BC:* I personally was involved in the periphery of the American Indian Movement, very much in the same way as her character in the novel, Thomas Kelasket. And so were many of my friends. And the trail that Thomas Kelasket follows is the trail that so many of the rest of us followed. When I read *Slash* I thought, "Yes, I'm glad she did this," because the older generation didn't understand what we were fighting for. And the novel humanizes that movement. I think for the older generation, and for the younger generation who haven't experienced that, it's a good historical documentation.

*HL:* I'm glad you say that. I've heard several people comment in the same way. Everybody saw themselves in it.

*BC:* I think Jeannette is at her best as a writer when she's writing about the land. Then it turns into poetry. There's a section in *Slash* where Thomas comes back ...

*HL:* ... and it snows, and he walks for a long time ...

*BC:* ... he's walking along the road ... Oh! That is beautiful. Jeannette writes poetry, too, and she writes very beautiful poetry.

*HL:* If you think of Native writers in Canada, which ones would you recommend, or which ones would you like people in Europe, in the world at large, to read?

*BC:* In Canada? I think *Halfbreed* is a classic. If people are studying Canadian Native literature, they have to read it. *Halfbreed* is standard.

I think *Slash* is important, because it's the first Indian novel in Canada, and *April Raintree*, for its sociological content, is good.

*HL:* And have you read any US Native authors?

*BC:* I like Joy Harjo's poetry, and Lucy Tapahonso's. I'm intrigued by Gerald Vizenor's stuff, and I like Leslie Silko's. Scott Momaday seems to be the grand old man. No matter what you think of him, his book has done a lot for Native writing—the fact that it was accepted for a Pulitzer Prize.

*HL:* He's an English professor.

*BC:* That's right! Never become an English professor! That takes away from your writing.

Lenore Keeshig-Tobias is, I think, another important Native writer in Canada. And there's Daniel David Moses, I met him, he came out and did a reading with Lenore. He's a poet, and I'm impressed with his work. He read a poem about going to a feast on the west coast, an Indian feast. And it was right before supper when he read this, and I remember it, I remember it with my mouth! The way he described the feast, juice from the fruit, and just "Oooh."

Then there is a woman in Nova Scotia, Rita Joe.

*KG:* Yes, she writes in Micmac, doesn't she?

*BC:* And in English. You've heard of Basil Johnston?

*HL:* He's very well known, I think, but in *Moosemeat and Wild Rice* I only read two or three stories, and then sort of thumbed through. I like his *Indian Schooldays*. That's very important about the residential schools. But the stories I'm not too sure.

*BC:* They remind me of Kinsella.

Oh, I just remembered an up-and-coming writer, Jordan Wheeler. He's young, he's only about 24, 25. He's been writing full time since he got out of high school. And he's good.

*HL:* I was going to ask you about another one, Tomson Highway.

*BC:* You've got to pay attention to Tomson Highway, regardless of what you think of him, of his subject matter. He stands alone as a playwright!

*HL:* What do you mean, "he stands alone"?

*BC:* Oh, he's the first Indian playwright to have a play that anybody paid any attention to, and that toured Canada.

*HL:* He stands alone in the whole of North America as that, because there are no other Native playwrights that have really made an impact so far, except him.

*BC:* I know that a lot of Native women, Indian women, are sensitive about the way he portrays women. But I think he was very brave to do what he did with *The Rez Sisters*.

**HL:** Did you see that on stage?

**BC:** I saw it twice.

**HL:** I saw it on stage, and since then I've also read it. And when I saw it on stage, I was really impressed. I thought it was a wonderful play!

I know that women are upset about the portrayal of women, that they are stereotypes, and that they are not strong. But when I saw it, it didn't come across like that at all.

**BC:** No, I didn't respond to it that way either.

**HL:** I thought they were really tough and admirable. I really loved that.

Maybe I shouldn't be saying this, as a non-Native and a male, but I had the feeling that some of the very negative reactions came almost in hindsight, after his second play came out. And that, apparently, has been accused of being very sexist and so on. I haven't seen it, so I really don't know anything about it.

**BC:** In *Dry Lips Oughta Move to Kapuskasing*, misogyny is right out in the open. In that play the Trickster is a woman, done up like a whore, and she's always manipulating the men. And in one part, one of the male characters says, "Fuck your woman's power!" But, as a reflection of the reality of our society, I think that he is reflecting the misogyny of some Indian men. And we can't say, "Shut up! Don't talk about this!" I mean, that is not what the artist does. It takes guts to reflect our society as it is.

I was just talking with my dad last night about freedom of speech, as a value. He said, "Without freedom of speech in our traditional society, we would not have survived." He said, "They forget that these days. And they try to stifle the voice."

**KG:** And I think that traditions also have constantly changed. I mean, the changes were so subtle that some people were not able to see. But observers who froze Indian traditions at the point of observation thought, "Well, these traditions are never changing." Whereas, in fact, we are progressing all the time, and traditions change as well.

**BC:** And sometimes we ourselves freeze our tradition, or attempt to freeze it.

### 31 January 1991, Regina

**HL:** Why and how did you start writing?

**BC:** Writing is very important to me. It is something that I started to do very early on in my childhood. It has been the mainstay of my life, and at times it has been something that has kept me sane. It allowed me to get rid of the "boogies," and I am still getting rid of the "boogies" in my life.

My father had a degree in theology from the U of S in Saskatoon, and my mother was a teacher. When we were growing up, we were surrounded by books. Both my parents read a lot, and they were very interested in the world around them. My father "collected" people. He has this curiosity about the world, not just Saskatchewan, and not just Canada, but the whole wide world. We were living in Sandy Lake Reserve up near Shellbrook. I lived there from the time I was 10 months old until I was six years old.

My dad went away with the car one day and brought a black man to the reserve. This was in 1953, and no one in Sandy Lake had ever seen a black man. Dad thought it would be important that everybody see somebody who was not the same colour as them. I remember the man was from Africa. He was a nice man. He was outside our house, walking around, looking at the flowers, and noticing the plants and the trees. There was this little hedge by our house. There were a bunch of kids all lined up hiding in the hedge to get a look at this man. That is the kind of man my father is. He is really curious about the world and always learning and reading. We grew up in a house like that.

My mother thought it was very important that we learn about books very early in life. She bought us children's books, and this was at a time in my father's career when I think he was earning about $100 a month. We did not have a whole lot of money but my parents put priorities on things, and one of the priorities was books. We had *National Geographic* and *Life* magazine, *Time* magazine, *Maclean's*. My parents read to us.

I remember learning the language, learning English very early on. Loving the way words sounded. It was like singing to me. Words were very musical, and I learned words just for the sake of learning words. I just liked them a lot. I had an enormous vocabulary when I was a very small kid, and a lot of people joke today that, when I was a kid, they liked me but they could never understand what I was saying! So I started making up little poems and telling stories when I was about three or four years old. It never left. It was always there. It was just something that was a part of my life. It took me a long, long time in my life to come to the point where I actually looked at those words as being "writing." I actually started to name poems "poems." Before that time I guess I thought that I wasn't worthy enough, or a good enough writer or something, to call poems "poems" and stories "stories." It wasn't until I was in my late twenties that I actually started to accept that I wrote poems and I wrote stories. All the way along in my life, from the time I was three years old when I wanted to write books like *Winnie the Pooh*, I wanted to write more than anything else in my life! That was the one thing I wanted to do. I was really testing it out.

I didn't publish my first short story until I was about 28 and I was afraid of doing that because, what if I published that story and the clouds parted and a voice said, "Beth, you can't write!" Then what would I do with my life? But I had no other desire than to write. So, with the first story I wrote and published, I was just scared. I was really, really scared. And then I saw it on the printed page, and it was a "high" like nothing else. I think it has been a struggle, and a magnificent obsession, to write.

One of the things that happened in my life that really had a profound impact on me was: when I was 20 years old I went crazy, and I was hospitalized. I was in the psychiatric ward for a couple of months, two or three months. I don't remember it, but I had approximately 42 electric shock therapy treatments. In those treatments, they put electrodes on the sides of your head and they zap them with electricity and the electricity goes through your brain. What it does, it deadens your brain, and you don't think any more, and you don't feel any more. It is a way to make crazy people manageable, but I don't think it is therapy.

That had a profound effect on me, because I lost my memory. I was in the third year of an English degree at the University of Saskatchewan at that time, and I lost it! I could not recall that whole year! So I had to, in a way, start life all over again, and learn who I was, because I had no memory of my childhood. To this day, I don't know if my childhood memory is really my own, or the memory of the stories that my family told me to tell me who I was. At this point in my life it doesn't matter. It doesn't matter.

But I went through a period of time after getting out of the psychiatric ward, after being zapped with electricity, where I really grieved. I was very much in pain from the loss of my memory. The most painful part of that whole experience in the psychiatric ward was when, after a period of time in getting the shock treatments, I was allowed to have magazines. They brought the magazines in, and I looked at them, and I couldn't read the words. Those marks on the paper had no meaning to me! When that hit me, I thought my life was over. I couldn't understand how the words could be taken away from me. The thing that I loved the most had been taken away from me.

In my novel-in-progress, coincidently, my female protagonist, Josie, goes through this experience. My own was 20 years ago, and I thought I had done a lot to let go of it, and had done a lot of healing. But when I wrote that chapter about Josie being in the psych ward, it was the hardest thing I ever wrote because I had to go back. That is one thing in my life that I hadn't written about. It was just something I tried to block out, and so there it was!

This fall, down in Tucson, Arizona, beautiful sunny Arizona, there I was in my little apartment looking out the window facing south, trying to find the words to write about this incredible and traumatic experience in my life, and to face it truthfully. I was writing away, and the writing was really exciting, I thought it was a well-written piece about madness.

I was sitting, thinking, "Gee, I am so far away from home! I don't have my family! I don't have my friends! I don't have the prairie to walk on! I can't feel the wind!" My wind, not Arizona wind—it is different. I felt so alone, and it hit me how much courage it takes to write. It takes enormous courage to tell the truth. It was a very testing thing for me to write about that.

I had to stop halfway through the chapter because I started getting the symptoms. My body was remembering what it was like to be zapped with electricity. I started to feel it in my head. I started to feel the sides of my temples being very delicate, and at one point I thought, "I am going insane again." But then I realized that, "No, this is my body's memory that is being brought up by the words, by the potency of these words!"

Soon after, my parents came down to Tucson. I had told them how terribly painful it was to face these "boogies," and they stayed down with me for a week, and we played tourists.

*HL:* The best writing in English today comes from women, and from women of colour especially. Why is that, do you think?

*BC:* Maybe this is a gross generalization, but I think women begin writing as a means of therapy. They write to stay sane. We write to stay sane! We write to let go of the "boogies." I don't know why there aren't more men. Maybe they are struggling to find jobs.

*HL:* I think men may have a harder time to open themselves, lay their feelings open. That again is a very gross generalization. I think you are right.

*BC:* I was taking a Native American Literature class this fall, and Leslie Silko came, and one of the students asked her, "Why did you make the main character in *Ceremony* a man, why not a woman?" And she said, "Because men are more vulnerable, and they have suffered more, and the tale had to be about a man!"

*HL:* I know that Jeannette Armstrong has been asked the same, why Thomas Kelasket is a man, especially asked by women.

*BC:* In my book I have the "creation" story. There are 10 brothers. They are human beings who are on the Earth, and there is no other human being on the Earth. They are out hunting one day, and they come upon a nest high up in a tree. The youngest brother climbs up to the nest, and in the nest he finds a little brother and a little sister. So my novel is told by the brother and the sister. So there are two voices, one is male and one is female.

*HL:* Do you have any other voices besides those two?

*BC:* Yes, I have. The husband of Josie has come into the story, and he is going to come in again. He is a creep, but he is a great character. (Laughs) And he is sort of the metaphor for this machismo gone haywire that a lot of Indian men have adopted in the absence of a deeper, more nurturing male role.

39

*HL:* Is there something that you would like to add?

*BC:* One of the things that I find very, very interesting being down in Arizona is there's something happening in Native American writing, and it has to do with the old stories. There are a number of us who are going back to the old stories and using them, or they are using us, as a means of telling a contemporary story. When you use myths, then the possibilities of the use of time just broaden, because in primordial times it was *times*! It was plural. It was not just one day follows the next, follows the next.

It seems to me that maybe at this time in the history of the world we need to go back to those. Because I see a big change coming in the world itself, and in the way that human beings relate to the Earth, to our existence here. We are going to go through a really rocky time, and we have already started. What I see past the rocky time is something incredibly exciting. I don't see the literal end of the Earth. I see a new beginning, the fifth generation coming into being, or the "Fifth World" as the Hopis call it—"the time of the Fifth World." I also see that down the road, someday, we are going to come to terms with cultural differences, with racism, and it is going to free up humanity to do better things than to kill each other.

# MARIA CAMPBELL

▼

*Maria Campbell (Métis) grew up in a Métis community in northern Saskatchewan in the 1940s and 1950s. The events of her life from early childhood "in the bush" to adulthood in urban isolation and confusion are related in her autobiography* Halfbreed *(1973), which became a bestseller and still is the most important and seminal book authored by a Native person from Canada.*

*Besides raising her family and being an untiring cultural and political activist for Native rights, Maria Campbell has worked with and for Native communities, particularly with women and children. She has facilitated writing workshops and helped other Native authors get published. Her own books include: histories for young readers,* People of the Buffalo *(1976) and* Riel's People *(1978); an anthology of short fiction by younger Native authors,* Achimoona *(1985); and* The Book of Jessica *(1989), a powerful and moving documentation based on her often painful collaboration with non-Native actress Linda Griffiths, and on the latter's attempt to write a mythical dramatization of Maria's autobiography. At present, Maria Campbell, "The Mother of Us All" (L. Keeshig-Tobias, D.D. Moses), is working on a tv-film,* The Road Allowance People.

*The conversation with Maria Campbell and Konrad Gross, a fellow Canadianist from Germany, was recorded on 23 September 1989 in Saskatoon* (copyright: Maria Campbell/Hartmut Lutz).

---

*MC:* I don't think of myself as a writer. My work is in the community. Writing is just one of the tools that I use in my work as an organizer. If I think that something else would work better, then I do it. So it's multimedia kinds of things! I do video, I do film, and I do oral storytelling. I do a lot of teaching. Well, I don't like calling it "teaching," it's facilitating. And I work a lot with elders.

So, I am not a writer, bumping around all over reading and talking about "great literature." I don't think of myself as an authority on that. I get quite embarrassed when I have to speak from the point of view of

41

a writer, because I really don't know what that is.

I know what a storyteller is. A storyteller is a community healer and teacher. There's lots of work in my community, which is important.

*KG:* When you say "your community," where is that?

*MC:* Wherever there are Native people. I don't make a distinction when I am working as to who is Indian and who is Métis. But my really hard core work is within my own community, and that is with Métis people.

We have no money, we have no land base, we have nothing! And so, those of us who are involved have the responsibility to give back to the community. And if anybody else has any money, then they have to pay us.

*HL:* You say you don't see yourself as a writer, but with *Halfbreed* you really started something.

*HL:* Well, I'd never written anything before. That was a letter I wrote to myself.

*HL:* I understand that a large section of the original manuscript never got published?

*MC:* Originally, the handwritten manuscript was over 2,000 pages long. So, part of the decision not to publish all of it was a good one, because I didn't know anything about writing.

I started out writing everything that was bad in my life. When I had finished writing everything that was bad in my life, I thought, "Good gracious, there must have been something good, too!" And that was when I started to write about my growing up. So, the decision to cut a lot of the stuff was good because it wouldn't help anybody.

However, a whole section was taken out of the book that was really important, and I had insisted it stay there. And that was something incriminating the RCMP.

*HL:* Who decided to take it out?

*MC:* The decision was made by the publisher—without consulting me!

*HL:* So you didn't know until it came out?

*MC:* It was in the galley proofs. And when the book came, it was gone.

It was the 100th anniversary of the RCMP that year. The only proof I had to support that part, if the publisher or myself were sued, was my great-grandmother, and she had passed away. So they felt that, if there was a law suit, they wouldn't be able to substantiate it. So they went ahead and took it out.

That whole section makes all of the other stuff make sense. And you can almost tell at what point it was pulled out. Because there is a gap.

*HL:* Do you think there is any chance of you ever getting that out, or getting out a complete version?

*MC:* Some day I would like to re-do the whole. I said it in the book that some day when I was a grandmother I'd write more. Now I am a grandmother, but I am not ready to do it yet.

*HL:* Maybe you have to become like Cheechum, become a great-grandmother first.

*MC:* That's quite possible; my grandson is 15! (LAUGHS)

*HL:* But then you'll know it's time.

You must be aware that there is a lot of interest in your book in Germany, and students write theses about it.

*MC:* Actually I don't know, because I never get any feedback. I'd never heard from the publisher! I don't know how the book is doing.

*HL:* I think it's a publisher from Munich, "Frauenoffensive," right?

*MC:* It's a woman's outfit, yes. But I know nothing about it. I've never heard anything and I have never had my fee. Nobody has ever contacted me from Germany, other than the lady that came and spent a few days with me one time.

*HL:* One of my students wrote a thesis on your book, and Beatrice Culleton's. She'll be happy to learn that we actually met. I knew a little about your activities from Howard Adams and some other Native people I know, and I am very glad that we are here right now.

Two years ago, at Medrig McDougall's house, I saw an eagle feather that you had given him.

*MC:* Medrig was a very special man.

*HL:* In West Germany there are three couples of eagles left.

*MC:* Three couples, really?

*HL:* Three couples of eagles, and while they hatch they are watched day in and day out—and that's a tiny feather of one of those. And that's for you.

*MC:* Ah! You know something? I go to fast very soon. And each time we go to a fast, we have to find one of these feathers to take with us. And that's amazing because you never know where they are going to come from.

*HL:* Well, you've got it.

*MC:* Thank you!

And I have no tobacco to give you, but here's a cigarette. So you can put the tobacco where the eagles dwell.

*HL:* Okay, thank you!

Where are you from, originally?

*MC:* Originally I am from about 80 miles northwest of Prince Albert. That's where I grew up.

The village isn't there any more. It was a road allowance community. But our church and our graveyard are still there, and we still use them. There are no people left there, no Métis people.

*HL:* What happened instead with the plots, or the land that the Métis people had? Is it privately owned?

*MC:* It's owned by people that came in and bought the land for farming.

*HL:* From the government?

*MC:* Yes! And they also built a road in there. I don't know if you understand what a road allowance is.

*HL:* It's a strip of land set aside on either side of a planned road, and it is crown land.

*MC:* But when there is no road, it's quite a large piece. Well, it's set aside to build roads. And then we would use the land that wasn't occupied around us. But as the farmers came, we ended up squeezed into that narrow piece of land, about the size of this building. And then, eventually, if you don't move, they come and move you out.

*HL:* Who does that? The RCMP?

*MC:* Usually the priest comes and gets the people ready. And then, if the people refuse to leave, then the RCMP come, but they have to get a court order.

I have just finished working on a four-part television series. I finished a script called "The Road Allowance People." It's dramatized. It's the story of Métis people in Saskatchewan, but I have used one community where this actually happened. And it's a community probably about 60 miles outside of Regina, and this was in 1948. The priest came and told the people that they had to move, and prepared them for the move. And he convinced most of them that they should go, because the government was giving them land in Green Lake, Saskatchewan. I don't know if you have heard about the Green Lake farms, or the Métis farms in Saskatchewan? There were five farms set aside in Saskatchewan in the 1940s, and the people were told it was a land settlement for them.

*HL:* Oh yes, Howard spoke about that.

*MC:* Cumberland House, Île-á-la-Crosse, Green Lake, and Lebrett—I mean, in the Lebrett area.

So the people believed it, and they were prepared to move. But the priest convinced them that it was going to be their land, all 22 townships of it. And so, a train came with box cars, actually cattle cars, and the people were loaded up with all of their bags and stuff, their bedding, whatever! And as they were driving away, as the train pulled out, their village was burned behind them.

They were taken to Green Lake, well, actually to Meadow Lake, about 40 miles from where Green Lake is, because there were no roads during the 1940s. They were not allowed off the train that whole trip, and there were no facilities for them, or anything. And it was November, so it was cold. Some of the people got pneumonia and were really sick. Some babies died. When they got to Meadow Lake, they were loaded on to big trucks that would take them to Green Lake, and they were left there.

And they were told that there would be houses when they arrived, but there were no houses. And so, a lot of the people lived in tents all winter, with their families. There were some people who already had

44

houses there, and they shared their log cabins with them. A lot of people got sick and died, just from flu, and pneumonia, and other diseases. In the spring a lot of them moved back by wagon, back to some of their communities, and then tried to rebuild again. But they were scattered. The communities were never the same again.

The story, the script that I wrote, is based on those communities, but I use the oral stories of all the people, and all the dispersals, and give it to one community, and particularly one family.

The last dispersal was in 1963. It was just outside of Yorkton, Saskatchewan. See, you can't convince Canadian people that these things happen. They don't want to listen to it, and in particular in Saskatchewan. Most people don't even know that history. There were no communications of any kind.

And we didn't have people that were educated. We're quite different from treaty Indian people in that Indian people were forced to go to school, we weren't. And so we had no spokespeople, other than a handful, and nobody would listen to them because they were considered political agitators. So, most people don't know that history.

That's what this four-part series is about. Each part is two hours long. And right now I am working with a producer who is trying to raise the money. I don't know, it's an ugly story. But the story of the people itself is very beautiful and powerful.

It's a story of survival. And no matter what happened, the people never lost. They should have been wasted with that last dispersal in 1963, but they weren't. Throughout our whole history, we have been packing and moving, and everybody would say, "Well, here we go again!"

*KG:* You say you're looking for a producer. Does it mean that you have also approached CBC?

*MC:* No, but when you work with CBC, there's a lot of major changes. And I don't want the changes.

*KG:* You mean in the story?

*MC:* Yes, because they say, "Well, it couldn't have been that bad!" Nobody ever believes that things are that bad. I have an independent producer, and we are looking for people to invest. I don't mind the rewrites if it's to make the story stronger, but not to cut key parts of the story out because they might upset somebody! It might take a while, but we'll get the money!

I have a good instinct! I believe in the Grandmothers! And I know it'll be okay. It might take us a while, but I know that we'll tell the story. I feel that way about books, about projects—I know when this is the right one. I think we'll find the people to do it! I also know a lot more about looking for money. More than I did 10 years ago, because I've been involved in film production for the last five years. And I know more people.

45

*HL:* And more people know you.

*MC:* More people who are courageous film makers and investors. So I feel like it'll happen. Who will air it, I don't know. It's a television film, it's not a big screen movie. And the reason I want it for television is the video part. I want that to be accessible to the people in the communities.

CBC was interested, and other producers wanted it, but they wanted me to do a 90-minute feature. And you can't tell that story in 90 minutes. I mean, you probably could if you wanted to do a commercial film, but it's not a commercial film.

*KG:* But even commercial films can be quite effective, you know, and they probably get more publicity than television series.

*MC:* Yes, but it's really hard in Canada, unless you can go to Warner Brothers or somebody. Canadian films just don't go anywhere. You might see them in a little theatre for two nights, and that's it. There is no distribution because the distribution is owned by the big film companies. A television film has longer life, and has more impact for what I want to do, than a feature. Not all our people can go to a movie. And there are no movie theatres. But everybody gets video tapes.

*HL:* I was going to say, you go to St. Louis ...

*KG:* ... and it's got a video library.

*HL:* But there is no cinema anywhere!

*MC:* I come from a family that is involved in film, video, and television. My adopted brother has been a film maker for a long time. Films and books are the way to go. And newspapers.

One of the things I am really excited about is the job that I just started with *New Breed*. I'd never have taken it, because I am used to free-lancing, but everybody reads the newspaper, and you can do so many things with a newspaper. I am not thinking in terms of a newspaper, like the city papers which cover the news, but you can do all of the other things: you can develop writers, you can really educate and inform people.

*HL:* So you would include poetry, etc., as well?

*MC:* Oh yes! Poetry, creative writing. That was never done before in *New Breed*.

*KG:* Coming back to "The Road Allowance People," what is so incredible in the story that you told us is that the people seem to believe the powers that be, just by word of mouth! We are living in a society in which everything has to be testified and documented on a piece of paper. But then, your community believed just what the priest said!

*MC:* Right up until about 20 years ago, the priest had total power in the community. In the last few years that had been getting shaky, and now the priest has very little power. It is still there, but not the kind of influence they had before. That's been our history—with Métis people, it's our priest.

*HL:* I don't know, but to me it seems as if that is the dilemma of Métis people, compared to the Indian people, who have got their own traditions, their own religion, and not somebody who tells them.

*MC:* But you have to remember, when it comes to traditional and Indian spiritual things, that's been more alive in the Métis communities in the North than it has on the reserves. We were never forced to go to school, so we never lost the language. It was almost as if we were the keepers of a lot of things that were our Grandmothers'.

Mind you, Indian people get really upset with me for saying that, but it's true. The language is almost pure in some Métis communities, where you don't find that on Indian reserves. Because there you had the power of the church, you had Indian Affairs. With us, we always had political activity, always a conflict between the church leaders and the political leaders, and no one bothered us. We were forgotten people.

My personal opinion is that when it comes to Aboriginal people in Canada, we have the church to "thank" in all areas, whether we are Métis, non-status or whatever, for the dilemma that we are in now! Certainly the church has always been the "man coming in front of" the oppressor, the colonizer.

The interesting thing in the last five years is that what the church was responsible for outlawing, the church is now incorporating into its own ceremonies. You have the priests doing ceremonies, they are going to sweat lodges.

But that's the history of Christianity. When you can't completely oppress a people, if you are losing them, then you incorporate their spiritual beliefs. And that's even uglier than the other way, because then people think "Oh, well, now it's okay, because the priest is now doing our ceremonies."

So the priest ends up becoming the shaman in the community. And then we have a whole other battle to take on. And it's hard because our old people have been conditioned.

\*     \*     \*

*HL:* Would you like to rewrite *Halfbreed* sometime?

*MC:* Yes, some day. I don't think I'd make changes. What I would do with the book is, I would only put in that piece that was taken out. I wouldn't want to touch what's there, because that was the way I was writing then, and I think that it's important it stays that way, because that's where I was at. And now, a lot of my thoughts have changed. I don't think that I've changed as to where I was at, but my vision has changed quite a bit! I think I have more tolerance—not tolerance, but more patience than I had then. And I really fooled myself when I was writing that. When I look at my ending I say: "I am no longer idealistic," but really, I was still idealistic when I wrote that.

    Like I said, my grandmother was 104, and goodness knows, I might be 104 ...

*HL:* I realized that Native writers, and particularly Native women writers who are also politically active, seem to talk with each other a lot. There's a lot of webbing and connections.

*MC:* Writing from Native women has always been very exciting, right from the beginning, because that's where the political writing, and the really analytical writing, is.

*HL:* That's true!

*MC:* The writing that's coming from men is still stuff like, "There's Wesakeechak wandering through the forest, and this is how his coat turned red"—that kind of thing! Men are not prepared to be vulnerable in their writing. Part of it is the kind of oppression that we've been under.

    But I am certainly excited about the stuff that women have been doing. There are some really powerful women writers, young women. The kind of writing I do can hardly be put in the same category. I am constantly struggling with the language. I am articulate enough when I am sitting here talking, but when I am writing, it's another thing.

    I've been working with dialect for about 10 years, and a lot of my writing now is in very broken English. I find that I can express myself better that way. I can't write in our language, because who would understand it? So I've been using the way that I spoke when I was at home, rather than the way I speak today. And the way I spoke when I was at home was what linguists call "village English"—you know, very broken English. It's very beautiful, but it took me a long time to realize that. Very lyrical, and I can express myself much better. I can also express my community better than I can in "good" English. It's more like oral tradition, and I am able to work as a storyteller with that.

*HL:* There's so much good writing done by women. That's not just Native women but ...

*MC:* All over!

*HL:* All women, and all minority women certainly! Black women, Chicanos, who are *really* writing. And again they also use their own language, "Spanglish," or they switch codes, and all that is very powerful.

    Jeannette Armstrong was talking about that, too. To use in literature the English that Native people speak, if they speak English, which is *not* the Queen's! That's a new development in Native literature.

*MC:* Each time I wrote a book, it *had* to come, there had to be a reason why I was writing it. The two books that I wrote for children, I wrote for my children, because they were at school, and there was no material for them.

    The last book that I wrote, *Little Badger and Fire Spirit*, was written because my grandson wanted to know where we got fire.

After that I couldn't write. I tried and tried, I mean I had lots that I wanted to say, but when I put it down on paper it sounded as if I was lecturing. There was something missing. And I went around for four, five years, really frustrated. I could articulate it, but it had no spirit in it! I blamed the English language, because I felt that the language was manipulating me.

So I went to the old man who's been my mentor, my teacher, my grandfather, whatever you want to call him. It was the first time I'd ever talked to him about the struggle I had. I had talked to him about storytelling, but I never talked to him about what I felt the language was doing to me; going to him as a writer to another writer.

And he just laughed, probably thinking, "Why didn't she come here a long time ago!" "It's really simple," he said, "why you have trouble with the English language, it's because the language has no Mother. This language lost its Mother a long time ago, and what you have to do is, put the Mother back in the language!"

And then I went away, and I thought, "Now, how am I going to put the Mother back in the language?" Because, in our language, and in our culture, as well as Indian people's culture, Mother is the land.

So I tried, but what I ended up sounding like was an evangelist minister. Talking about the Mother, the Mother, constantly. So that still didn't do it.

And then, one day, my dad came to stay with me for a weekend. And my father is always telling me something. He'll be making something, and then he'll say, "You know, I just remembered." He has an association, and it reminds him of something. So he told me a story and I listened to him that night. I woke up about two o'clock in the morning. I had this most incredible inspiration that I had something I wanted to say. So, I went to the typewriter, and I started working. This was the first time that I've been struck with total inspiration—when they say "the muses," I call it "Grandmothers" coming. I really know what that means. I worked about five hours, and it felt like an hour.

I had the story in my father's voice, or somebody's voice. It was all there. I could smell the community, I could smell the old people, all those familiar things were there. And what I had been trying to say, over and over again, in rewriting and everything else, I said in this broken English. And it was eloquent, it was full of humour, it was full of love, and yet it was hard. It was all there. And that was when I understood what the old man said about the Mother in the language.

My father is very close to the land. If you asked him about Mother Earth he wouldn't know how to answer you, because he doesn't know how to say it. But he lives off the land, he's been a hunter and trapper all his life. He respects the land. He's one of those old people who puts tobacco out before he goes out in the morning, sings his song in the morning. But if I asked my father, "What's our culture?" he'd say, "We don't have one," because he doesn't know what "culture" means. And he wouldn't understand if I tried to explain it to him.

*KG:* It's too analytic!

*MC:* Yes! And I had never thought of it. When I'd say, "Dad, don't we have any stories? I mean, don't we have any stories about culture?" Even when I said it in his language, he'd say "No, I don't know any!" I've been deaf to him. All these years he had been telling me stories, but I was expecting something profound.

You see what happened to me was that I was thinking English. It's really hard to explain what that is. So now I have the old man's voice. Sometimes, when I am doing a story, or sometimes when I'm doing a poem, I think, "I'll write it in English, the way I talk." But I can't get it. And then all of a sudden I'll start to type. And the poem will come, I almost never have to rewrite, because it all comes. And sometimes it's just saying something in real broken English, like, "Boy, you know, that man, he talks to the eagles, too." That will say what I would spend an hour and 10 pages trying to explain, just saying that man looks like he talks to eagles, that will tell everything.

But I can't control it. This voice is really inspired. And it doesn't, he doesn't, always want to come. I'll think "Gee, this will make a good story, me sitting, having dinner with these people who are German, and I am exchanging this. I'm going to go home, and I am going to write it in the old man's voice." There is no way! He won't come in! He decides what he is going to talk about, and I can't manipulate him at all. And he's a man, but his voice is the Mother.

I have another voice, that's the old lady. But the old lady is very masculine. She tells the men's stories. I can't get her to tell the women's stories, and I can't get him to tell the men's stories! So it's like opposites, the contrary, or whatever. So I don't question it any more! I just know it works.

*KG:* When you say "my language" does it mean Cree or ...?

*MC:* Both, Cree and Mitchif. I speak both fluently.

*KG:* French?

*MC:* The old lady's voice is Indian. And his voice has got lots of French in it, but it's Mitchif.

*KG:* And do the young people still speak both, Mitchif and Cree?

*MC:* Not exactly the way the old people spoke it, because there's a lot of new things. It's like on Indian reserves—nobody speaks Cree the way the old people spoke it, because there are new things. You know, cultures and words change. When I do the rewrite, if there is too much French, I take it out and I reword it in broken English, or else I just put a little dictionary in one.

*KG:* What about writing in Mitchif?

*MC:* It's not taught, and so my readership would be limited.

*KG:* I know! But would you say that the older generation has also read your book?

*MC:* The older generation doesn't read and write. It's only my generation that reads and writes. With the exception of a few people like Medrig.

You know, Indian people went to school, my people didn't because we weren't allowed to go to school until 1951. We couldn't go to Indian schools, and we couldn't go to white people's schools, because we didn't pay taxes, we weren't landowners.

We had well-educated people until the Resistance in 1885. We had people that had university degrees, but then after that — it was like when they use the words "Forgotten People," we really were. Until the late 1800s and early 1900s, our people didn't say very much, because they really believed that the soldiers were still out looking for them. You know, it wasn't till the 1920s and 1930s that political leadership started to emerge again. But my great-grandmother's and my grandmother's generation were always afraid of the police, because they felt that the police would still charge us for the fighting that the grandparents did. We were all people that had run away from the soldiers.

*HL:* We were amazed or even saddened by a lot of people who obviously were Métis people, and the first thing they would tell us is, "I'm French!"

*MC:* Yes, but you don't find that in too many places! You find some of that around Batoche and St. Louis.

*KG:* But for what reason?

*MC:* The church again. In order for the people to be able to survive, they had to pretend that they were French. And the church encouraged that, because they wanted them to let their culture go. Because with our history, if we hang on, if we believe in nationalism, or we believe in ourselves as a race of people, there is no way that we cannot be political. You know, our lives, every day of our lives is political, just being alive is political. And so, in places like St. Louis, part of it is, the people suffered so much discrimination that they didn't want their children to suffer that.

But in communities like where I came from, there were so many villages, and the people lived off the land, and they were hunters and trappers, and so they were real nationalists. But in places like Batoche and St. Louis, the people pretended they were farmers, they tried to farm, they learned to speak French fluently and tried to get rid of all of the Mitchif. They talk more French, and change the spellings of their names so that they would sound French, or would sound more English.

*KG:* It's a pity, really.

*MC:* It is a pity. But that's part of the colonizer's way of doing things.

It was very disturbing for the priest in the 1960s when Métis people in Batoche and St. Louis started to get political. When they started to have a sense of nationalism. That's when the priest started to lose them! At that point people like myself, people like Howard [Adams], became enemies of the church. There is certainly no love for us among the priests in that area, because they have always seen us as a threat. For every Métis person, young or old, who says, "we read your book," as far as the priest is concerned, that's, you know ...

*KG:* That's a deadly sin, isn't it?

*MC:* It's a deadly sin. I'm sure that if he could get away with burning our books, he'd do it. But you can't get away with things like that any more. So he has to pretend, and he says, "You know, you're lucky, you have some people that can do this." But, at one time he would have told them not to read it. In the last 20 years that doesn't work any more, so he finds other ways of doing it.

The priest has never openly attacked me or said anything to the people, because people are very protective of me.

Maybe it sounds egotistical, but whenever a book is coming out, like now, I'm really afraid. I think, "Maybe the people will be angry this time." And the same with Howard. But the people look after us. They wouldn't allow anybody from the outside to attack us. I really believe that. Even if they agreed. It's like, "It's okay if we say that, but don't you come and say that. Because these people belong to us." And the priest knows that. We are social with one another. But I am the enemy as far as he is concerned, and as far as I am concerned, he is the enemy, too.

\*       \*       \*

*HL:* Would you mind telling us roughly what you've been up to since the end of *Halfbreed*? Where that leaves off?

*MC:* What have I been up to? I've been raising kids, writing, studying. Studying with old people, with the community. I work with women's groups, with kids. A lot of work with women in conflict with the law. Mostly with women coming out of prison, women working on the street. I couldn't even tell you how many workshops I've done, in communities, working with young writers. Not teaching them, but trying to help them feel good about the place that they come from. And not to be afraid to use that. Oh I don't know, I really don't know what I have done.

The last three years I've been politically involved for the first time. You know, where I've actually taken part in Métis politics again. I ran for president in February. I decided at the annual meeting that I was going to run for president. I had three weeks before the elections. So, my campaign came together in three weeks, but I came in third, and that really quite surprised everybody. It surprised the men who were running against me.

52

**HL:** And the editorship of *New Breed* is your first regular job?

**MC:** This is the first time that I am getting paid enough money that I don't have to worry about whether I am going to starve or not. It's always been free-lance money.

When I say I really believe that the Grandmothers look after people: about 1972, 1971, I had a dream. And this voice told me that if I listen to them I would never be without food, that I would always have a good place to live, and that my children would be okay, and I would have good health. They told me I would work with people who would write, and paint, and sing songs. And I said, "Come on, I don't know how to do any of these things!" And that was when they told me not to worry. That if I did what they wanted me to do, they would look after me, and that this was my work. And they have.

When I started to write *Halfbreed* I didn't know I was going to write a book. I was very angry, very frustrated.

I wrote the book after I had the dream! I had no money, and I was on the verge of being kicked out of my house, had no food, and I decided to go back out in the street and work. I went out one night and sat in a bar. And I just couldn't, because I knew that if I went back to that, I'd be back on drugs again.

I always carry paper in my bag, and I started writing a letter because I had to have somebody to talk to, and there was nobody to talk to. And that was how I wrote *Halfbreed*. Two thousand pages later, friends of mine who just came back from studying in England stayed at my house, and they used my bedroom. He's now practising law in Vancouver, and she teaches. And all of this, piles and pounds of paper, handwritten, was sitting there. He got up in the morning, he had it all in a big bundle, and he said, "I want to take this with me, you've got a book." And I thought, "Oh, sure I do."

Anyway, about three weeks later I got a phone call from Jack McClelland, asking me if he could publish the book. And that was when I remembered what I had been told in the dream. Without my knowing it, they had created the situation for that to happen. The book was a bestseller, and I think that they decided that. And so that's what I've done with my life. I might be going this way, I might be going over there with you, but on the way out the door, if they tell me to go this way, then I listen to them. And maybe it sounds crazy, but my kids have always had lots to eat, we've always had a home, just like they promised.

My direction to go to the Crossing[1] was the same thing. I dreamed that I was to have that land, and that it would be a place where Native people would be together, and create things. That it would really be a crossing. And so I got the place. I didn't have any money. I put a deposit on it. And they told me not to worry about it, the money would come. And it did.

*HL:* The previous owner wasn't in the Dumont family?

*MC:* No, it hadn't been in the family since after the Resistance. It had been burned to the ground, and Gabriel never came back there to live.

*HL:* And that little house there?

*MC:* The little house is about 80 years old, it's not the original house. A part of it was the house that was built after. And it was used as a ferry.

But what have I been doing? I don't know!

*HL:* A lot!

*MC:* I've been writing. I write a lot. I like working in collectives, with other people. I write poetry, but I am not a poet where I sit down and I write poetry every day. And it's writing that I don't always like to show people, because I don't always understand it. But I work with the one language. And then I do other writing that's contemporary. It's very different. One is me the single mother, the contemporary woman, fighting male structures and stuff. The other voice is somebody who is very protective of men and tries to see that part.

There was a time when I used to think I was schizophrenic. Maybe I am crazy.

*KG:* Who were the storytellers in your community? Everybody, or just the family?

*MC:* Just about everybody. Everybody was a different kind of storyteller. My dad was a storyteller. There was a young man when I was growing up, and he was a hunting-story teller. Then there were particular stories that were told only by certain people and at certain times of the year. Stories belong in their season, you know.

My great auntie and my grandmother were midwives, so there were certain kinds of stories they told. And then there was the fiddle player who was a storyteller. There was a sort of village fool or idiot, whatever you might call him, who was also a storyteller, who had his kinds of stories. I never really appreciated or saw those things until I was much older. Really, until I started to work with the old man, and with the language, that's when I began to think, "My god, this guy was a storyteller," because these stories they told were a part of our everyday life.

And when you come out here, everybody has special words for things. Nobody started to use the word "storyteller" until a few years ago, then it became fashionable. You were either a writer or a poet. Well, we never had writers and poets in our community.

One of the things that I try to do when I work with young people, or with anybody in the community, when it comes to writing or any of the arts, is not to let them get caught up in "the mystery." Because the mystery makes you powerless. You don't have to be educated to write, you don't have to be any of those things. But we think we have to be, because we are conditioned to believe that there have to be experts. That there has to be somebody always at the top, who knows, who will give us the information, and then you'll have the power to teach everybody. It was never like that. Even today in communities it's not like that.

I just came back from La Ronge last night, and all the way home in the car, all through our workshops, having dinner last night with the family, the storytelling, it's just rich. And yet, if I asked any of those people, told any of those people, "you are a writer," or "you are a storyteller," they would say "no, not me." But there's so much richness. The way they use the language, the way they say things. Writers would kill to be able to do that.

*KG:* There must have been a lot of "gossip," too.

*MC:* That's all part of it! My people are the world's worst gossips. We've been called that in history. But we're not gossips. When you look at the history of Métis people that's been written by other people, they say that we're very sociable, we're very idle, we love to gossip, we love to dance. It's like we never did anything else.

*KG:* But this is also a stereotype, it crops up in literature as well!

*MC:* I know, and yet on the other hand all of that is true.

*KG:* It's only part of the whole!

*MC:* That's right. In fact, Howard and I laugh about this sometimes. It's the two of us who are the two worst gossips in the world. We visit, and then somebody else will join us, they will bring a whole bunch, and the next thing we've been sitting there for hours. But we've been storytelling, we are just having a really good time. Even Indian people think that we're very irresponsible, yet we get lots of work done.

*KG:* And what about the stories in the book *Achimoona*? Who are the tellers? I mean, what kind of people are they?

*MC:* The people that are in the book are young Native people—when I say "young," I mean between the ages of 19 and 35, 38.

All of them have incredible storytelling abilities. They don't speak their language, with the exception of one, and one other speaks a little bit of it, but that doesn't matter. It doesn't matter if you speak your language or not, because your spirit speaks the language. You just have to find the way to touch it.

I'm excited about En'owkin Centre, the School of International Writing for Native students in Penticton, and about the kinds of workshops that I've been involved in, and what other people are doing. It will help the young writers to feel good about where they come from, because for many Native people it's been a struggle to reclaim that. It doesn't matter how educated you are, you have to make a journey in yourself to reclaim your own language, even if you don't speak it, so that the manipulation will stop. Sometimes, the more education somebody has, the harder it seems to be to overcome that.

Am I making sense?

**HL:** Yes! Definitely!

**MC:** The road home isn't easy. You don't have to come through the kinds of things I did to have a hard road home. There are different kinds of pain and struggle.

I believe that all of them will be great storytellers. They just have to decide that's what they want to do. Maybe they want to do something else. In our community everybody is a storyteller, but not everybody would choose that as an occupation.

**HL:** The way I understand the oral tradition is that it tells people who they are, and where they are headed, where they come from. If you read about it, or if storytellers are asked, that is more or less what it seems to come down to: the oral tradition tells people who they are, gives them identity.

And I know also that some people who are very traditional and who know their own language say, "The oral tradition is oral only! The stories are only to be told *orally*, and in the language." On the other hand, you have creative writers, or you have people who publish stories from the tradition, like the book by Alexander Wolfe, which I think is a wonderful book ...

**MC:** Yes, he's a wonderful man.

**HL:** Oh, I'm sure he must be, yes. I see that as within the tradition as well. So, how do you deal with that? What is your opinion?

**MC:** I would love to be able to preserve the stories in the language. But that's not possible, and if we don't start to record the stories, and find a way to be able to do that without the language manipulating us, we are going to lose them, and if we lose the stories, we've lost the people.

**HL:** The identity. That's what keeps the essence. But it also means that if you write the stories down and publish them, you've got to share it with other people, because anybody can buy the book, right?

**MC:** I also believe that culture constantly changes. It doesn't stay in one place. We didn't have horses, then the horse came, and became a part of our tradition. So much so, that we have horse spirits and horse dances. We didn't have beads. The beads came, they're now a part of our culture.

We have to understand that the new tools for our young people are writing, painting, dancing, singing in English. There'll always be, I think, some people like myself. I'm probably getting to be one of the people who will be the storytellers one day, because I have the language.

The stories have to be written down, they have to be recorded, but not all the elders agree with me. For younger Aboriginal people, this is the real struggle, because when you decide to do that, you really are being a warrior. You might not have the support of your community, but you have to do what you believe is right. And, certainly, the elders don't always agree, they say, "That's not to be recorded, that's sacred!" And I say, "Well, a dog was sacred once, too, but you accepted the horse."

And then it's, "Don't question what the elders say!" And I say, "We have to question what the elders say, if we don't, our generations are going to lose!"

I don't believe that those stories should be recorded by anybody except us. I don't think that you have any right to come into my community and tell my stories for me. I can speak for myself. I share them with you, and you can read them. And if you come into my circle, and I tell you the stories, then you should respect that you're invited into the circle.

You know, when you go to visit somebody, and they make you tea, you don't walk off with the tea-set—the stories are the same thing. Either you are a friend of the people, or you're not. And if you're a friend of the people, you don't steal.

The book that's coming out is all about that.[2] Because, you see, I did that! I worked with a non-Native writer, and I'll never do it again. On a play. And what ended up happening is that I had to take her on a journey with me. And maybe that was meant to happen, must have been, otherwise I wouldn't have ended up in this eight-year relationship with this woman. The story is that very thing. And it's been very painful. There was no respect for the place that I came from. You don't go walking into somebody's personal places and pick through their stuff and decide what you're going to walk off with! It doesn't matter what culture you come from, it's bad manners to do that!

But people in the world are hungry for truth and for spiritual things. And there are some people that exploit.

I believe that in your culture, there are the same beautiful things that are in mine, and that we should be sharing those things. And as artists, writers, if we really are healers and teachers, and we're committed to that, then we have to be responsible for the things that we give back to our community. Otherwise, why are we talking about trying to create a better world for ourselves?

That's no different than having uranium mines and building reactors and stuff. It's the same thing. The change has to come from respect. It means respecting Mother Earth. It means sharing. Being able to be honest with each other, and to say, "Well, there are some things in the culture, in our way of life, that are not always good." But the way we can change that is to have a dialogue that's meaningful and honest.

*HL:* Have you ever read Margaret Laurence?

*MC:* Margaret was a good friend of mine.

*HL:* I always admired the way she treated the history of the Tonnerre

57

family. For years I did research in Indian stereotyping in US and then European literature. That was my main research. And here in Margaret Laurence, I thought, there was a writer from the mainstream, who wrote with respect. Would you agree to that?

*MC:* She was a respectful and spiritual woman. She was like that with all of her writing, regardless of what culture she was dealing with, her own or anybody else's.

\*        \*        \*

How can we know if we're Canadian? I mean, how can we know what "Canadian" is, unless all of us develop what we have. I would never attempt to write about German people's beliefs. Maybe I would write about an experience I had with a German writer, like Margaret did with the experience she had with the people. But I couldn't tell you your people's story. And I don't need you to tell the story of our people to other white people.

How can somebody interpret or tell? How can a white person tell you, another white person, about my community and my people, when he's only coming from half a place? He has to believe the other half, too. He has to believe it's there. Not up there, but all over.

Non-Native writers tell me that writers have to write what's there. I think, maybe, that's a different kind of writer. That's not the kind of storytelling place I come from. The bear doesn't try to tell the deer's story.

*KG:* What does that mean? I don't get the message.

*MC:* The bear doesn't try to tell the deer's story. The tiger lily doesn't try to tell the dandelion story. It's a full-time job just looking after your own stuff. And if you look after your own stuff, then you can look after the world. You can't look after the world if you are being busy looking after everybody else's stuff.

Save me from people that mean well!

Canada's history, the history of Canadians, is that they are killing us with their liberal gentleness. Helping us, being kind to us. "We don't have horrible racism in this country," is one of the things they say. They tell us, "We never had slavery here, we never had this," but some of the horrible things that have happened are worse, or every bit as bad. Because the kinds of things that have happened to Aboriginal people in Canada are things that were so "nice" that nobody's ever bothered to record them because they were done in such a "nice" way, or if they were recorded, they were changed.

It's okay to report the atrocities of other countries, and what they do to their peoples, but heaven forbid that Canadians would ever do something like that!

We were busy in the 1940s hearing about the horrible things Germany was doing. Nobody ever would believe that in Saskatchewan at the same time people were loaded into cattle cars, not having bathrooms or facilities, and were carted off, hauled some place, and dumped off in the middle of the snow—and some of those people dying. We never hear about things like that because Canada doesn't do things like that. We need to write those stories ourselves.

*HL:* And what about Japanese-Canadians, until Joy Kogawa wrote that book?[3]

*MC:* That's right. And then, even then, people have the excuse, "Well, that was war!" We haven't even heard of half of the atrocities that have been committed in this country. For me, and I'm sure for a lot of other Native people that are doing the kind of work that I'm doing, I feel that we have choices! Do we want to educate white people? Or do we want to go on about the business of working with our community?

*HL:* The way I see this reeducation, or what I do in Native Studies, and have done, there are two things. One thing is the decolonization of the European minds. To learn about the kind of history that we've committed, and that didn't enter the books. And the other thing is to disseminate information about Native people, or translating them, or whatever!

I know it must come from ourselves, and there are some people working on that. But, in some cases that are very specific, and often very recent, it's very difficult for us as non-Natives to really get into that process, unless what we say is backed up by Native people.

*MC:* Yes, but you see, you are German. Your culture is German. Those are your people. What happens when people come to Canada and immigrate here—is that how they become Canadians?

But what is a Canadian? It's as if, somewhere between here and whatever country they came from, they dumped all their stuff in the ocean, and they're starting from scratch again. They really don't look at their history. They look at it, but it's the history of the pioneer. They don't ever really think about it or feel. Somehow, they lost something coming over here, the connection, maybe, to why they came here, the kind of oppression that they were fleeing from.

It's the same thing here. If they would somehow have kept that connection! And there are writers here who could certainly do that. I believe in memory, and reaching back, and touching. They could do that and if they did that, then you would have a voice emerging. People would start to understand each other, maybe.

You know, the kind of oppression that many immigrants fled from is no different. Their oppression isn't worse than my oppression. But if you sit across the table from me, and you say, "You poor thing, you've been oppressed. You live under colonization," and everything else. What you do is, you cop out from what your people came from. And we're no longer equal sitting across the table from each other. What happens then is, I become the poor oppressed person, and you have power over me. But if both of us acknowledge that our grandfathers and grandmothers came through great struggles, then we can talk to one another. Then you can appreciate and value what I have to say, like I can appreciate and value what you have to say, and there's a place to start from.

That doesn't happen here. I mean, "we are the poor Native people." We are not poor. We are the richest people in this country. My people are rich. We might not have lots of stuff, but we're rich. Anybody that can come through what we've come through and still be able to laugh and smile is rich.

I don't need to read books written by white people about my people that show me as being oppressed, and poor, and colonized. I know that, and I can talk about that. It might take me a while, but I can do it, thank you. If you really are my friend, then get out of the road and let me do it. And if it takes 20 years, it'll take 20 years. We will tell our own story.

I don't know if Jeannette told you we went to Baffin Island last winter for a month, Native writers. One of the amazing things that I experienced was that all of a sudden, I knew what it felt like to be a foreigner. I know those were Aboriginal people, but I felt so inadequate. This is what it must have been like when white people first started coming here. This must be what my people were like. People were so fragile, so innocent, and the country is so incredibly powerful. You think, standing there, the wind is blowing from the North Pole, and there's nothing between you and it. It was really overwhelming.

We were Aboriginal people coming there to work with the Aboriginal people. But what we were talking about, they couldn't really believe it. When we talked about what can happen to the language, and about how the language can manipulate you, even if you speak it well, they smiled, and they'd give us more food. They know, but they don't know. And it was the first time that I had empathy for non-Native writers. I thought, "This must be what writers sometimes feel, why they think they have to speak for me."

The only thing that, as a Native person from here, I could give them, was to share my own experiences. I was asked to come back again. In fact, I just got a phone call about a week ago. I said, "No, not this year," because I feel they can do it. They have Inuit writers, they have Inuit storytellers. And if the people in Toronto feel like they want to help, then my recommendation to them is, "Get the Inuit writers who have published. Get the carvers who are well known to come in and work with their people. Don't bring us in from the outside!" There are many similarities, but I didn't grow up in the high Arctic. And the recognition, and the teachers, should be their own people.

*KG:* Excuse me if I come back to it again. Don't you think that white authors who try to write from a Native perspective are necessary? I mean, I see the step that you have been taking. It's certainly the last and final step, the most important one. But I think that those white writers may have some sort of, perhaps "mission" is the wrong word, even though they may come from a Christian perspective.

It's similar when you come across Anglophone-African writers. Tania Blixen's work, for example, which was made into a film just a few years ago. Her experiences on an African farm, as a colonizer, as a woman with a colonizing background, and how she dealt with people. That book was written in the 1930s and 1940s.

Of course, according to our standards today it still reveals much of the colonizer's mind, but if you look at it historically, it was a step away already from the old colonizing spirit, even though the colonizing mentality was not completely given up. But it was one step in a process that suddenly has come to a stop.

*HL* (TO KG): Would you feel comfortable writing a novel about, say, a Jewish family being transported to Auschwitz?

*KG:* No.

*HL:* Would you feel that you could do that?

*KG:* No.

*HL:* I wouldn't feel like I could do that, either!

*KG:* Perhaps somebody would feel comfortable, you know, in a hundred years. But I think I couldn't.

*      *      *

*MC:* It's the way things are. We are told, people write. Writers write about whatever. And perhaps there is nothing we can do to stop that, but it's wrong.

The really tragic thing for me is when I go to a Native community and I see children reading white authors' stereotyped books about "Indians," or reading non-Native's studies of Native cultures, or high-class literature about Native people. I think that's really sad; we don't have enough of our own people writing. And our people are very hungry for stories of themselves. They are surrounded by books, they are surrounded by television, that have precious things about everybody else. Not that I think all the things that are written or shown on tv are precious.

*HL:* Is there anything that you think non-Native people can or should do with regard to Native writing?

*MC:* Teach it in their classes! Use it in their classes! Make the institutions available to those writers to come in, and storytellers to come in! Help with translations! Find good translators. You see there are translators and then there are translators! And I have to tell you, I don't know what the translation of my book is like. I know the lady who did it. And she is a good lady, but I don't speak German. Help to find publishers who are sensitive, in the countries they come from.

I don't know what else.

**HL:** That's plenty, and we are working on that!

**MC:** If I invite you to come to a workshop that we are doing at the Crossing, as in the case of *Achimoona*, come and share your experiences with us. Not about writing about Indian things, but to share your experience as a writer, or a storyteller, and your history. I think those things are important. But that's all.

The two of you have a lot of power. You're teaching in a university. Those institutions are not easy for us to get to. You work with a lot of people. And so, we have this, you have that, and in that way we help each other. To me there is no other way, really, as a storyteller. Just the storytelling, and the writing, that's all I need from you! I don't need anything else! The other things have to come from me, they have to come from my community.

**HL:** You said earlier that the English language has lost the Mother as it's spoken here. And that made me think of something I've talked to Konrad about before, and he may think, "Oh, he's always on about this!"

The English that is spoken here came from England, of course. I don't know, but are you aware that English, or a lot of it, originated in the region, the Jutland Peninsula, where Konrad now lives, and where originally I come from? Around 400–500 A.D. some of the tribespeople living there, the Anglians, Saxons, and Jutlanders, rowed across the North Sea to England and settled there. And our traditional language, south of the Danish border, "Plattdütsch"—a "regional dialect" it's often called, but it's actually a language of itself—is still spoken in that area. It is quite different from the written German that you'll find in books. It's very close to English.

Now I just realized, if you tie the language to the Mother, the land, and you think of those removals, over and over again, it makes a lot of sense to me! With each move, the people and the language got further away from the region where they originated, further and further away from the Mother.

There are still some stories in that area about the "little people." There are also stories about giants. And a lot of these stories show a culture conflict.

You get stories about this giant who tried to throw a rock on a church because he couldn't stand the bells any more, they were driving him crazy. So giants were driven off the land.

The same with the little people! There's one story, where this ferryman woke up at night, and he saw all these lights out there, and somebody was throwing rocks at his window pane, or whatever, to wake him up. He walked out, and he saw all these lights there, and all the little people with little horses, wagons, cattle, young, old, everything. They were going north across the Eider River—that's where I come from. And he took them over, the whole night. And then, in the morning they had left him gold in his hat. So they are gone. That's the story.

Now, we've got churches.

*MC:* I've never been in any other country, other than the States, and for a bit of time I went to Mexico. But I believe that, in every country, the language of an area must not be any different from here, where the Cree that's spoken by the river, five miles up the road, is a little bit different. I would think that it's the same in other countries ...

*HL:* Oh yes.

*MC:* ... that the language changes from place to place. But also, in the country that you live in, the past is always there. The voices, even if they are 5,000 years old, a million years old, are there. But when you leave that place, and you come to another place, then it must be harder to be able to hear those voices.

And I guess a part of what the old man told me about the voices, that the language has no Mother, that people have no Mother—part of what he meant was, that Christianity took that away, not just Christianity, but going back to Judaism, too, when changes started to happen.

I don't know enough about that, to articulate what I feel, other than my own feelings about that. But that makes a lot of sense to me, because I have met people who come from countries, some of them have been Catholic for centuries, and maybe your family has been Catholic for centuries in Germany, but still, the voices will come through to some of the people, because of the power that was there, from the land before.

But when people come to another country it's the same Mother, it's the same land, but there is something that's a little bit different. I know what that is, but I don't really know how to explain it. So, somehow, people have to be able to bring that memory with them, or try to nurture it, or midwife it, so that it's here.

And I believe that can happen. My great-grandfather was from Scotland, and his mother was Irish, and in the last few years I've heard their voices. There is this circle that says, "Well we are your Grandmothers, too, we are your Grandfathers, too." And I have never been to those countries.

So, I believe that the people who come to Canada, or who have been in Canada for generations, who say "this is our land" and "this is our culture" and "this is where it is," if they are really artists and writers, how can they not hear those voices? How can they not hear them?

And, maybe they hear them, and if they do, why do they shut them out? Why do they not listen to them? I believe that the purpose of an artist or a writer, regardless of how afraid they are, is to not be afraid to go. The whole idea is to climb one hill, and then to climb another hill, and to climb another hill, or to open a door. And once you open a door, there's another door, and there's another door. And if you're really committed to what you're doing, no matter how afraid you are, when the door is there, you have to believe that it's real if you've come through all those doors. I mean, surely, you can't believe that you've opened them yourself.

So you have to be brave enough or foolish enough, one or the other. Because both, the idiot and whoever, know that the power is there and that you'll be okay. There's also some kind of excitement to opening the door, finding out what's there. And believing that what you came through already gives you the right and the power to be able to open that door, and will protect you, that that's your protection.

So, I guess what I am asking is, "Why don't they hear the voices?" I would like to know that.

I can sit with Native writers, mixed-blood writers, or storytellers, people who have never been able to read or write, who will say, "Yes, my Scottish grandfather talked to me last night," or, "The eagles from Scotland talked to me," or whatever, from Ireland, and, "There was a funny 'little person' in our ceremony last night. Don't know where they came from," or "I heard a song, and I don't know anything about Ireland, don't know anything about what the songs are, or anything else." And they'll sing you a piece of a song that they heard. So if we can hear them, and we've never been over there, why can't Canadian writers hear their voices?

I think it's a cop-out. Being a writer is very romantic. You can be somebody, being a writer. You can be a person of power, so you write for or about "the poor, or the oppressed" ...

*KG:* I invite you to come to Ireland! My wife is from there.

*MC:* I would love to go to Ireland. That's something that I want to do. I want to go to Ireland, Scotland, Wales, and France.

*KG:* Come over then, and stay with us!

*MC:* Ireland and Scotland are the two places that I feel ... like they are my home. And I felt that long before I ever knew anything about any of them. And it amazes me especially with Scotland, how the history of Scotland and the colonization of the people—whatever you want to call it—is so similar to the history of our people. And how a people could come through that kind of stuff, and be a part of doing that to another people.

But, I think it's because they don't hear the voices, or they refuse to listen to the voices of their ancient elders. It's much easier to wave flags about what's happening in Guatemala, or wherever, than it is to really look at what's happening right on this block. Because right on this block it means that you've got to roll up your sleeves and do something. But any place else than the Native community. It's easy to contribute by doing things for a far-away community, because it's not in your yard, or in your immediate community.

Anyway, I've really been talking. I'm very opinionated.

*HL:* I've always wondered. I spent a year in California, working within Native Studies at UC Davis, and at a small college, DQ University. We had discussions about this all the time. And it's something I still haven't figured out. You say, it's not listening to our voices. But this process through Europe, the colonization, the destruction of the old beliefs, how that has affected the whole of the world. And if you look at the centre, where did all this start? It started in northern Europe, maybe it started earlier even, started in Rome. Maybe it started in the Palestine. And it has gone on, and on, and on. And wave after wave, the people have suffered from that. Maybe it's what you call the loss of the Mother. And we have just collaborated, one after the other.

However, I think things are changing, and I should be saying that. There are a lot of young people, not only young people, old people, who are really concerned about what is happening to our Mother, and fight to protect her. And that's the only way. And we get a lot of help from Native people. There are young people coming over here to learn. There are some Native people going over to Europe to teach. There are also some "instant medicine men" trying to make money, but I'm not talking about those.

*MC:* I know what you're saying. And I have to tell you, I'm very optimistic. I feel that a lot of good things are happening. I feel good, and I feel strong every day. And I constantly run into people that reinforce that.

I think there are many people from many cultures that are going in the same direction. Some of us are halfway up the hill, some of us are partway down, some others are walking together. But, I feel good. I just hope that I'm still able to dance, when ...

---

## NOTES

1. Maria Campbell owns a small property at Gabriel's Crossing, the exact place where Gabriel Dumont, general of the Resistance of 1885, operated a ferry across the South Saskatchewan River, south of Batoche.
2. Campbell, Maria and Linda Griffiths, *The Book of Jessica* (Toronto: Coach House Press, 1989).
3. Joy Kogawa, *Obasan* (Markham, Ont.: Penguin, 1983, 1981).

# JORDAN WHEELER

▼

*Jordan Wheeler (Cree, Ojibway, Assiniboine, Irish, English, Scottish, French) was born in Victoria but grew up predominantly in Winnipeg. One of the few full-time freelance Native authors in Canada, Jordan dedicates his time to writing stories, novellas, plays and scripts for video and film — and to raising his family. He is co-founder of the Indigenous Writers Association of Manitoba and the* Weetamah *newspaper. His stories have appeared in anthologies (*Achimoona, 1985; All My Relations, 1990) *and magazines. His first monograph,* Brothers in Arms, *came out in 1989. It contains the novellas "Hearse in Snow," "Red Waves," and "Exposure." "Hearse in Snow" became a half-hour drama for the CBC, written by Jordan, called "Welcome Home Hero." Though based in Winnipeg, Jordan gets around in Canada.*

*The conversation was recorded on 30 September 1989 in Winnipeg (copyright: Jordan Wheeler/Hartmut Lutz).*

---

**JW:** I was going to say that the *Achimoona* stories were not my first—I had written a story, a fiction story, after I got out of high school, and I wanted to be a journalist. I joined an exchange program, "Canada World Youth." It's with a Third World country. I went to Indonesia, and in the Canadian half I worked with a newspaper in St. Paul, Alberta. I didn't like the experience. I didn't like the constraints of writing facts.

When I was in Indonesia, I was lying on the beach one day, and I just started writing a story. And I wrote a novella. Still to this day, it is my favourite piece of writing. It'll never be published, because it's basically about the sexual fantasies of a 13 year old.

But after that, I came back home and my mom was going to this workshop that Maria Campbell was holding, and she said I better come. So I thought I'd come along and just sort of hang around and watch. But Maria said, "Of course, you've got to write!" So I wrote. And I wrote three stories, and after that they were going to get published. I found out that my three stories had all been published, whereas everybody else only had one. I thought I was ... well, the ego rose. And I thought I'd write a novel.

And I started writing a novel, and I wrote, and I wrote, and I wrote for three years. And when it was finished I shelved it. That was it! I didn't like it. It wasn't doing what I wanted it to. And I didn't write for about two months.

I was working at a bar, just down the street here, as a door person and at the front desk. And I just started writing a story. I had no expectations that it's going to be a novel, it's going to be this or that. I started to write a story, I thought maybe 25 pages long. And I wrote, and I wrote, and I wrote, and it ended up about 65 pages long. And I liked it. I called it "Hearse in Snow." It's about two brothers, their father dies, and one has been living in Vancouver, and one has been living on the reserve looking after their father. And there is a sister. They come back for the funeral, and the two guys just don't get along.

It's based on when my grandfather died. It was the first time in my life that I saw all my aunts and uncles at one place at the same time. And the four aunts had always been feuding. They were sitting down at the table, and there were a few of us cousins there. They were talking about family unity, and what's happening, you know, and it's a shame that the family is disintegrating. And we told them, "Bullshit! It's you guys that are fucking it up!" So, it's sort of based on that whole experience.

And the way my grandfather's funeral worked: there was a ceremony in the city, then we took his body out to the reserve for a wake, for the funeral. So that's it, the story is like that. There is a ceremony in the city and then the two brothers are in the hearse, and they take the body to the reserve. And there's a blizzard, and they get stuck in the back of the hearse with their father overnight. That's sort of where the crux of the story happens, that's where they have to come to terms with their relationship.

That's one of the novellas in *Brothers in Arms*.[1] I finished it, I took it to Pemmican, where at that time Beatrice Culleton was manager. You know, she wrote *April Raintree*.[2] She is the fourth person that has done a lot for my writing.

**HL:** I was going to say, those two brothers in your novella seem to be a parallel to the two sisters in *April Raintree*.
**JW:** Yes!

I took it to her. She had written this book called *Spirit of the White Bison*, which got heavily criticized, but I loved it. And I thought, well, it's sort of that length. And she said she couldn't publish it on its own, maybe I could make it longer. And I thought, "Well, the story is finished, that's where it begins, that's where it ends. So I'll write two more."

"Okay, when are you gonna have it finished?" "Oh," I said, "in a couple of months, no problem!"

It took two more years! But then I wrote the next story, and it was a bit different.

Two brothers again—all of these stories have two brothers as the central characters. The book is called *Brothers in Arms*. But the second story is set sometime in the future, maybe in the late 1990s, when the optimism that I have about economic linking of reserves, like the linking in communication, satellite communication, and the connecting of Native society in a Native network, where all that is in place—computer linkages and a Native-owned transportation network.

In the story, one of the brothers is a journalist, working at a Native multimedia, and the other brother is a terrorist. They are both older, and the one brother is older than the other. He was in Wounded Knee, and they were both in the occupation of Anishinabe Park in Kenora, which my sister was at, and all this stuff. It's the revival of Red Power. And I started writing this about a year-and-a-half before the E 12 issue ever came up, and this rallying which now is beginning to happen. The brother that is a terrorist is with a group who've blown up a church and a brewery down east. And in Winnipeg they've blown up the Hudson's Bay Company. You know, those three oppressors, the major oppressors. And the one brother is figuring, just putting two and two together: "Hey this might be a Native group!" So, as a journalist, he gets on the chase, you know, let's dig the story.

And it's his brother. He doesn't know it's his brother. So there is a whole detective side to it. And their mother—well, it's all fiction, but when they went to Anishinabe Park in Kenora, the mother got raped and killed by an RCMP officer, and the older brother saw it. There is a scene in there where, while she is being raped, she reaches for his gun and tries to pull it out of the holster, but she can't.

The reason I put that scene in there is because of the J.J. Harper case, because the policeman said J.J. Harper pulled out the policeman's gun to shoot him. Well, the older brother saw all this, but he didn't tell his younger brother. And also, the police officer only worked as a policeman in the summer, and otherwise he went to law school. And later he went into politics. And at the time the story was happening, he was the minister of Indian and Northern Affairs.

*HL:* Sounds like Janklow in South Dakota! He was governor of South Dakota. He raped an Indian girl when he was an advisor on, I think, Rosebud Indian Reservation.

*JW:* Really?

*HL:* A legal advisor, he's a law-man. And during the height of AIM activities he said, "There's one solution to the American Indian Movement, and that's a bullet through the heads of Dennis Banks and Russel Means." That's why Dennis Banks jumped bail, I guess. He knew that if he was going back to South Dakota, that's *it*! But later he went and did his time.

*JW:* He did? He served the sentence?

*HL:* Yes, after Janklow wasn't around any more. But he was on political sanctuary in California for several years. And then on the Iroquois land at Onondaga, that was later on. He was in California for five or six years. He was chancellor of DQ University. I was teaching there in 1979/80, when he was chancellor.

*JW:* Well, that's funny! The guy who edited my book said, "I don't think this is really believable."

*HL:* It is! There is a case like that. That's William Janklow, ex-governor of South Dakota. It's documented. The Rosebud Tribal Court treated this, and all the law stuff. They wanted him to appear, but, of course he didn't appear. But he has been found guilty by the tribal court in his absence.[3]

*JW:* There's a guy who is doing time, serving a sentence for life in Sioux Falls. When he first allegedly committed murder, he was convicted very easily, and at that time the governor's side had also murdered so many and got out scot-free. But he told me once that he thought Janklow was a pretty straight kind of guy. "He doesn't like any Indians, and he admits it," that's what he said about him.

*HL:* Yes, I wouldn't call that "a straight kind of guy."

*JW:* But there's another aspect of the story, too. I thought of Native terrorism. This was a couple of years ago, again, but I was talking to one of the writers I will be meeting tonight.[4] She knows people in Ontario, Native people, who are serving time for blowing up Pickering. They set a bomb at the Pickering Nuclear Station. Why Pickering, I don't know, but that's already happened. So there are all these facts, and I thought: "Hey, that's a story!"

So the crux of the story happens when CSIS breaks in and shoots everybody except for the CSIS plant, who was in the group. And the older brother gets away and goes back to his brother's place. While there, the news flashes over the air and his editor calls him to get his butt down to the centre to cover the story. And his brother finally tells him the story about his mother. And then he goes to Indian Affairs loaded with dynamite, to meet up with the minister. And his brother is taken down, later on in the day. He is taken down there by CSIS. So, that's what that story is about.

And the third story is: two brothers again, they've been apart for a long time. One of them is dying of AIDS, and he wants to die on the reserve. And he phones up his brother and tells him this and wants him to help out. He wants to fix up the house they spent time in when they were really young, before their father died, before their mother was committed to an asylum because she lost her sanity. And it's a struggle. His own personal struggle, although I don't dwell on it, the homophobia of the one brother, and then with his other brother against the reserve and their homophobia, and a bit of the physical and the emotional things that AIDS patients go through as they die.

And for that one I interviewed a guy who's gay, and his close personal friend had died of AIDS. And that's a lot of the stuff that he went through — I have based it on that.

*HL:* And that was a Native guy? And he had the same kind of problems on the reserve because of his friend's AIDS?

*JW:* Yes, maybe more dramatically than in the book. He went home, he was from The Pas. His name is Paul P., and he went home to the reserve, and nobody accepted him because he's gay. Nobody else knew he had AIDS except his mother. And his mother turned him away. And he was dying in St. Boniface Hospital. At this point he knew he wasn't leaving the hospital any more — this was it! And shortly before he died his mother came down, and sat with him and accepted him. And that's what he died with. So that's in the book, too. That's in the story.

The first one, "Hearse in Snow" — I've dedicated each one — is in memory of my grandfather. The third one is in memory of Paul P., and the second one, "The Red Waves," with the terrorists that is, I dedicated to the memory of Buddy Wolf and Anna Mae Aquash. So that's what I did. There are so many people that have been killed.

*HL:* That's terrible, yes.

\*          \*          \*

Have you read *Slash*?

*JW:* No. Who wrote that?

*HL:* Jeannette Armstrong. Her first novel. *Slash* came out by Theytus Books. It's a wonderful book.

*JW:* I've heard about that.

*HL:* It's about the last 20 years of AIM and related Native movements, seen through one character. But there are all kinds of characters coming in. So it's a whole mosaic. It's a wonderful book.

*JW:* I heard about it, yes. I don't read as much as I should.

One book I'm reading now is written by Jeffrey Goodman, *American Genesis*. He's an archeologist, and he is suggesting that the Bering Strait theory is real, but the migration was modern man developing in North America and going the other way!

*HL:* Right, that's something that, years and years ago, Floyd Westerman told a German audience. He said, "Yeah, yeah, the archeologists find tracks on the Bering Strait. And each time they find them, the tracks are getting older and older. One time you people will have to acknowledge we went across backwards." So it's coming that way! Oh, definitely.

*JW:* I think his whole theory was dependent upon a new dating technique.

They tested the polarization of the mineral acid crystals.

*HL:* The radiocarbon?

*JW:* Beyond radiocarbon! Radiocarbon only goes back, is only accurate, I think, to 40,000 years ago. And there are digs in North America that are much older.

*HL:* Oh, I see.

*JW:* And he suggested one dig was about 500,000. There are others, and there is one in the northern Yukon, which, believe it or not, was never dug up by glaciation, it was untouched. I think it was the Old Crow Dig. It was about 140,000. But this whole theory is dependent upon the archeological community accepting this new dating technique.

*HL:* You know what intrigued me about the Bering Strait theory? Why, to begin with, did the theory show that what was here came from somewhere else? If it came from Eurasia, maybe there was a chance it came from Europe? Is that the reason? I don't know. It's weird.

*JW:* I've always thought that it is because it justifies them colonizing and saying ...

*HL:* Oh, yes, saying that Indians are also "newcomers"?

*JW:* The conquest, justifying the conquest.

*HL:* That's pretty stupid. Yes. There is no justification.

*JW:* You know the Spanish, all over they burned all the Aztec and Mayan libraries.

*HL:* And the Inca, too.

*JW:* They had mathematical systems that would far surpass ours today.

*HL:* The Mayan calendar, I've heard, is the only one that can really handle the leap year without adding an extra day. I don't know how they do it, but they have a calendar that is far more advanced.

There is a wonderful little book about things like that. Also put out by Theytus, I forget the author, but it's called "Indian Giver." [5] It was written by a white person in respect of what Native cultures have given the world, and he just lists them, you know, for example in medicine and astrology. And one thing that I find is very important, and I talk about that a lot, is foodstuffs! Out of the four staple foods of the world, two of them are Native, potatoes and corn, right? And most people in Europe don't know that. They think potatoes ...

*JW:* ... they're from Arabs! (LAUGHS)

Oh, and there's wild rice!

*HL:* Yes, sure. That knowledge is always displaced. For obvious reasons. So we don't feel guilty.

*JW:* The people ... there's still that old colonial attitude, too, that Native people suffer from. We've been colonialized so much that a lot of Native people disinherit the past: "Let's not harp on negatives!" But my feeling is that it can't be overstated. So much has been ripped off and destroyed, polluted, that it can't be overstated—the injustice is so immense! There is so much, I'm sure, that is still alive, but the time isn't right. I don't know when or how, but I do believe it! The philosophy of Native people is going to become a universal thing.

*HL:* It has to, if we are to survive on this Mother.

*JW:* In conjunction with the philosophy of all Aboriginal, all land-based people. There is so much, in the richness of the culture and the medicine, that I hope can survive. I don't know, but the optimist in me feels that we haven't lost it, that it is still there. People have it, and they are, for obvious reasons, not showing it. But my feeling is, the time is to be. I think that more people, like yourself, are willing not so much to "admit" but to share, and realize, and understand, and have not sympathy but empathy.

*HL:* I think, if we manage—if I say "we," I mean mainly non-Native people—if we manage to get across respect of human beings, or creation, that would be enough. But we are not brought up that way to respect others.

*JW:* I know. That's such a struggle to attain that state of mind. But I think there's a lot of it growing. It's occurring to a number of people.

*HL:* I think so, too.

*JW:* It's not the people of power, and that's the problem.

*HL:* No, sure. It's always the poor people, and the outsiders, the underdogs. That's true!

*JW:* The people between the cracks.

*HL:* That's right, of the borderland!

Now that you mention that, it's living in the borderlands or on the fence. That's a concept you also find among other people, like Chicanos. Chicanos write about that. Living in the "borderlands"—that's, first of all, the geographical borderlands of the US-Mexican border. But it's also the cultural borderlands. The borderlands of gender. There's one book by Gloria Anzaldúa,[6] who is lesbian. She writes about her personal borderlands.

And there are others who write about it. Some black writers call it "Meridianism," like Alice Walker's "Meridian."[7] It's a life that does not admit being categorized from the outside, "you're this, or that, or that," but being a person sharing in a world that is to come and that people are struggling for. They say, "it's the borderlands, I've got the options!" There is something positive, not the "neither/nor." Or, even, there are whole theories about "liminality." *Limes* is "the border" in Latin, and liminality denotes the possibility of relating to various sides or halves, but still remaining a whole person.[8] And not be categorized, and to reject outside definitions.

So, when you said this was "borderlands," because I had that in mind,

I thought I should say that. And it's the borderlands people who are more perceptive.

*JW:* The awareness and acceptance. But it's not something we learn, it's something we have to evolve intellectually at this point. Maybe if a child grows up in a vacuum this might be natural, I don't know. For myself, it's something that you have to evolve on your own, develop in your own mind. And often it's the luck of the draw, who your parents are and who you are in contact with, because the hardliner of North America is generally a bigot and wrestling-fan type. And they are really scary. Like this whole Aboriginal Justice Inquiry thing happening here, it's bringing a lot of the bigots out of their closets.

*HL:* You know that in Maria Campbell's book, a large section she had on the RCMP was never published! Did she ever tell you that? That book originally, the manuscript for *Halfbreed*, was about 2,000 pages.

*JW:* Holy good one!

*HL:* The publishers cut that down and said, "We can't publish that," and she is not very happy about that. She got the proofs. There was a large section on the RCMP, but when the book came out that part had been removed. So, she said, one day she'll sit down and write that again and get that published.

*JW:* She talked to me, well, she talked to a lot of us, about the climate when she wrote that book. That was a successful book! I think it still has a record as the bestselling first book by anybody in Canadian history. It was at a time when Native nationalism was rising and that was becoming more of a forefront issue in society, and people were interested. That was after *Bury My Heart at Wounded Knee*, and all that, so it was the right climate for a book like that. And she didn't have a lot of say. The publisher told her how to dress, what to say to people at conferences, what to do. And she knew that she couldn't rock the boat at that time. She just went along. But I think now with places like Theytus and Pemmican, you have greater control over the whole process.

There are so many Native books that you can't get a hold of anywhere.

*HL:* That's right, because they are in limited small editions.

*JW:* Like *American Genesis*. I can't remember the term the bookstore gave me , but apparently the publisher has sold off all the remaining copies to one company, to do with what they wanted, and you can't get it any more! And another one, *The Life and Times of Anna Mae Aquash*.

*HL:* Is that out of print?

*JW:* I don't know if it's out, I can't find it.

Also, I have aspirations as a film maker. Right now, I am writing a half-hour drama for the CBC. It's based on the first story in the book that I'm writing. But I'd love at some point to do a film on Anna Mae

Aquash. Something like the Silkwood type film, or the one about the crew in Chile where the American was killed after he found out too much information. Something of that genre, about Anna Mae Aquash, but I'd have to do that years down the road.

*HL:* You know, in *Slash*, that novel by Jeannette Armstrong, there's a character like that. I thought immediately, "Oh, there's Anna Mae Aquash." And I asked her, she said, well, she didn't really have her in mind. She's been asked this again and again. It's probably like you. Writing about stuff that does happen, and then later on you find "Oh, yes, that is a specific case!" Because the structures that you describe, the political structures, ideological structures, or whatever, that you write about, are the same that surround you. So even if you dream of the case there's bound to be something very similar, because you have a clear perception of what the structures are, I guess.

*JW:* I'm really excited about Native writers, because historically it's always been the artists of any people that have made change. They have always been the persecuted ones, and the ones who are always broke. Well, maybe they're trying to give us more to do than we should have, but it's not going to be the Native politicians that do anything for us!

*HL:* Usually professional politicians only work for themselves.

*JW:* So does the bureaucracy.

*HL:* That is the same in our societies, I think.

*JW:* You know, I know some nice guys that are chiefs and all that. But their vision only reaches this far. They are too safe now. Twenty years ago it was different. Guys like Dave Courchene, Senior, and George Manuel, when they went to Ottawa, they'd take the cheap train fare, and sleep in people's living rooms. Now it's "Why, if I can't get a hotel room, I can't go to Ottawa!" There's a totally different level of commitment now.

*HL:* During this whole trip I was once put up in an expensive hotel. That was right here by the Native Studies Department. That much money! I didn't say "No." I suggested going to a cheaper one. "No, no, you have this. That's a fine hotel!" Sure it's a fine hotel.

*JW:* Where?

*HL:* That's the Ramada Inn.

*JW:* You should have gone to the St. Regis. That's where all the Indian people go.

*HL:* Yes, I saw that. I was in the breakfast room there. That's nice.

*JW:* We call it "the Embassy."

*HL:* Is there a Department of Indian and Northern Affairs somewhere near?

*JW:* Yes!

*HL:* You know, that's what I thought. There were so many Indians that

75

I thought the DINA must be somewhere close, because I never saw so many Native people in ...

*JW:* ... in suits?

*HL:* ... Indian business, Indian politics.

*JW:* There are a lot of them, yes.

*HL:* Okay, that's what I thought.

*JW:* Actually the night J.J. Harper got killed he started out at the St. Regis.

*HL:* You tell me about that. I know nothing about it.

*JW:* In my party days, this was the same route I'd take. After work, you go to the St. Regis Hotel for a few beers, and then you meet some friends. You always meet somebody, you know. Then you go from there to the West Brook. And at that time they came out with a new bar called D.J.'s. It used to be, you'd go to the Club Marocco to close down the evening. But he went to D.J.'s with friends and he left D.J.'s just before closing time and was walking down Logan Avenue towards his house.

And there was a stolen car. The description was: two young Native people had stolen a car. The description was shorter and lighter than J.J. Harper. And what that policeman says is that he saw Harper walking down the street. The only reason he stopped him was because he was Native. So, he came up to him, said he tried to talk to him, and Harper turned around and was aggressive, went for his gun, pulled it out of the holster. And they struggled with the gun, and the gun went off, and hit Harper in the chest.

I don't know the exact physical description of the struggle, but one of the columnists from the *Winnipeg Free Press* tried to recreate it. And he said it would take an acrobatic act, you know, somebody from China might be able to do this. But the guy died, and the police launched an inquest into the death, an internal investigation which lasted two days or something like that. They exonerated the officer, no wrongdoing at all! Like that! That death sparked outcries, and at the same time there was the murder of Helen Betty Osborne and the pow wow that happened in 1971. Nobody was ever convicted of it until last year. They convicted one of the four youths at that time, now they are middle-aged men. They are just serving time for second-degree murder. But it took 15 years for that to come forward. So those two incidences sparked this Aboriginal Justice Inquiry. And it happened at a time when the Donald Marshall case was happening in Nova Scotia. And the whole policy of the Winnipeg Police Department came under scrutiny.

*HL:* Is that where one of the officers was in charge of the inquest?

*JW:* One of the officers was in charge of the investigation of the Harper shooting. And he was also in charge of another—a cab driver got killed about two years ago. This guy had 17 or 19 years on the police force. And at one point two Native men were charged, and he had a Native woman as a witness to this slaying, or whatever. And under cross-examination she broke down and said the police had forced her to lie. So now they got somebody else up on that charge. But he was in charge of that investigation. And the morning that he was to testify before the inquiry, he killed himself.

*     *     *

But there is so much! A lot of Native people made presentations, and it's nothing that I haven't heard before. The accusation sort of put a burr up the rear end of the city and the RCMP for treatment. My cousin, when he was living in Winnipeg about 10 years ago, got taken out to a seldom-used road in the northern city, and they beat the crap out of him, and left him there.

My mum's ex-husband once was at a bar on Main Street. He had $800 in his pocket. The police picked him up, beat him up, dropped him off at Main Street Project, and when he woke up, the 800 bucks were gone.

And there is so much of that! That is always happening! You know, we know about it, and it took something like this to bring that out.

---

## NOTES

1. (Winnipeg: Pemmican, 1988)
2. (Winnipeg: Pemmican, 1983ff.)
3. Mario Ganzales, Chief Justice, Rosebud Tribal Court, Rosebud, South Dakota. *Judicial Opinion* (date of signature: 31 October 1974), Portland, Oregon: Olive Press, n.d., 6 pp. chapbook.
4. Later that day, 30 September 1990, Jordan Wheeler took me along to the founding meeting of the Manitoba Native Writers Association at the house of Cybil Courchene. Besides her, Jordan, and myself, the following people were present: Marguerita Roberts, Stan Manoakeesick (of Pemmican Press), and Duncan Mercredi.
5. Warren Lowe, *Indian Giver: A Legacy of North American Native Peoples* (Penticton, B.C.: Theytus, 1986). See also another book about the same issue with almost the same title: Jack Weatherford, *Indian Givers: How Indians of the Americas Transformed the World* (New York: Ballantine Books, 1988).
6. Gloria Anzaldúa, *Borderlands/La Frontera: The New Mestiza*, (San Francisco: Spinsters/Aunt Lute, 1987).
7. Cf. Melba Boyd. "The Politics of Cherokee Spirituality in Alice Walker's *"Meridian,"* *Minority Literatures in North America: Contemporary Perspectives*, eds. W. Karrer & H. Lutz (Frankfurt et.al.: Peter Lang, 1990), 115–127.
8. Hartwig Isernhagen. "Literature—Language—Country: The Preservation of Difference and the Possibility of Relation." *Zeitschrift der Gesellschaft für Kanada-Studien* 6.1 (1986), 81–94.

# LENORE KEESHIG-TOBIAS

▼

*Lenore Keeshig-Tobias (Ojibway/Pottawatomi) grew up on the Nawash Reserve on the Bruce Peninsula. She graduated from York University with a BFA, emphasis in creative writing. As a storyteller, poet, and cultural activist she has served as an editor of* Ontario Indian *and* The Magazine to Re-Establish the Trickster. *Her poetry has appeared in various magazines and anthologies, including* Seventh Generation, *ed. Heather Hodgson (Penticton, B.C.: Theytus, 1989). She has made a lasting impact on the Canadian writers community by her many presentations and subsequent articles against the appropriation of Native stories by non-Native authors.*

*The conversation was recorded on 9 October 1989 at Lenore Keeshig-Tobias's home in Toronto, in a half-hour squeezed in between her arrival from one speaking engagement and her dashing off to the next* (copyright: Lenore Keeshig-Tobias/Hartmut Lutz).

---

*HL:*  Your name has come up recently on press releases, etc., with criticism of producers of Native materials by non-Native authors.

*LKT:* Yes, I think I've gone on record a number of times for saying that I don't think that non-Natives should be telling Native stories. And, of course, the immediate reaction is: "You are censuring my imagination!"

Which makes me wonder why God has given the white man such a broad, all-encompassing imagination? If it's so broad why can't the white men just make up their own fictional cultural society? Why draw on Native society? They show us nothing new. They make no new discoveries. They simply embellish and prop up old stereotypes.

*HL:*  What writers do you think of in particular?

*LKT:* Well, I think of W.P. Kinsella, and this horrid series of books coming out of the States by the author Lynn Andrews. I think she has done *Medicine Woman, Jaguar Woman*, and I don't know what other woman.

So she sashays in with her designer jeans and what not, and basically confronts her own Christian psyche under the guise of being a Native storyteller, tapping into Native spirituality. Our spiritual teachers, our elders, are not as harsh as Lynn Andrews or even Carlos Castaneda make them out to be. They are patient, almost infinitely patient, and very gentle. But at the same time they are forthright! They'll tell you if you're making a mistake! They'll tell you if you are making an ass of yourself. But other than that, they are very gentle and very, very patient.

*HL:* What do you think of Anne Cameron?

*LKT:* I'm ambivalent about Anne Cameron's work. On the one hand, there is a need, and there has been a desperate need, to have these stories saved, or retained, or revived. On the other hand, I don't like, nor do I think it's right, how she has used these stories to give credence to her white feminist politics. Those stories were not created for feminists at all.

*HL:* I've asked this question of a lot of people all along. When I first saw those books by Anne Cameron, I thought, "Oh yes, they have been produced for the general interest in spirituality, and they cater to the feminist market." I was wondering how the people, the women in the community who told her all these stories, would feel now.

*LKT:* We are ambivalent.

*HL:* But there are also Native women who think very highly of Anne Cameron.

*LKT:* I think very highly of Anne Cameron, too. I think she is a wonderful writer, and I do appreciate what she has done to foster and to promote a greater understanding of Native cultures.

I can also say that for writers like Rudy Wiebe and M.T. Kelly, even though I don't think that either of them is capable of assuming a Native voice. That is what a lot of people don't understand. Why don't they understand? After all, we've all grown up to view the world, and have been taught to view the world, from a particular point in time, a particular position in the universe.

For example, if you and I were sitting around the campfire: there is this campfire and it's beautiful. But you look at it from that side and I look at it from this side. How could you, unless you come and sit right on top of me and knock me out of the way, sit down and tell what my side of the campfire looks like? The sun may be rising behind you or setting behind you, and I have that perspective. Likewise, when you look across at me, you have a different perspective, too. Sharing that, I think, is what it's all about.

*HL:* Can you think of any non-Native writers that treat Native people with respect or in a way that would be acceptable?

*LKT:* Okay, I would say M.T. Kelly, his book *A Dream Like Mine*. I read it, and, to me, there was a big hole in it, and that hole was the Native voice.

*HL:* Do you know Margaret Laurence?

*LKT:* No.

*HL:* Well, I always felt that she manages at least to treat Native people and other cultures with respect.

*LKT:* Well, I think M.T. Kelly does, too. He has respect for the cultures. He has the respect of intelligent Native people, and he has talent. Kinsella doesn't. Kinsella is reaping scorn!

*HL:* You said earlier that you think there is a need for writing down and saving the oral tradition, the stories that might otherwise get lost. On the other hand, there are traditional people who say the oral tradition is *oral*, is in the original language, and is not for publication. But I see that, in Canada in particular, more and more Native people themselves are writing down the oral tradition.

*LKT:* I am not saying that writing is better than the oral tradition. I really don't think it is, because you lose that intimacy of contact. But what it does is that it allows you to reach a larger number of people.

The other unfortunate thing about writing is that it handicaps your memory, your mind. But at this point I don't really have any fear that these stories might get lost. Our storytellers are coming back to us.

And this is one reason why I go on saying that I don't think non-Natives should tell Native stories. I think when the day comes that there is equity between First Nations people and Canadians, *then* we can sit down and we can talk about this issue again. Then, perhaps there are some people out there who can effectively tell Native stories.

*HL:* Well, it's a question of unequal power!

*LKT:* Yes, it is!

*HL:* And as long as the power structure remains as it is now, there is never a free dialogue.

*LKT:* Exactly! The people who have control of your stories, control of your voice, also have control of your destiny, your culture.

*HL:* I'm very glad you say this. There's one book in particular that struck me, by Margaret Atwood. She is so widely read throughout the world, and in *Surfacing*, when the nameless narrator is sort of—I don't know whether you read that book—

*LKT:* Yes, I have, but years ago.

*HL:* ... where the central character goes back to "Indian roots," that aren't hers. Two, three hundred years of colonization and dispossession just disappear in this one person's quest to find a meaningful way of worshipping at sacred places. And I thought that's not honest, because it leaves out and displaces the whole historical process, and just acts as if *any* culture that there is, is for the having, and can be tapped into by whoever feels a need for that culture's spirituality, regardless of history and the politics of oppression.

*LKT:* That's right! It's like this vast wonderful Canada we have! White Canadians look at it, and they say, "Oh, this is an unused national resource! Let's go and cut down the trees! Let's go and mine! Let's bring out the uranium! Let's take out the nickel, and whatever! No one is using it. Look at this wild rice here: it's an unused natural resource, we'll have our commercial harvesters come in!"

They never think! They never think that this is someone's home.

*HL:* It's true! And it's not just the sort of national resources that are *out* there, but now it's Native people becoming a natural resource!

*LKT:* Yes, right! Exactly, exactly! They have our land, and now they want our stories, our voices, too. And I say, "No!"

*HL:* For a long time I had a hard time understanding the very strong resistance of Native people against this. But then somebody told me, "It's going for our very essence, because the oral stories convey identity and tradition!"

*LKT:* Of course, I think all stories do.

*HL:* And if that is taken by the colonizers as well, what is there left of Native identity?

*LKT:* I think that goes for any country. It's your storytellers, your storytellers! And I don't know what it is about the storytellers, their attention to detail, cultural nuances. Those things that give life, or give credibility, to what people call universal *motifs*.

I mean, we all cry, but some of us cry for different reasons, and some of those reasons are cultural reasons. Only the people who know most intimately those things are the people who should critique. Those are the people to interpret. Not someone who just comes in cruising through your culture. (LAUGHS)

*HL:* So, what do you say about non-Native people taking an interest in Native literature? People like me, "cruising" through Canada, meeting with Native writers and presses?

*LKT:* Well it depends. I think I always give people the benefit of a doubt, first. And if you prove yourself to be (LAUGHS) an arsehole, I'll tell you!

*HL:* Sure!

*LKT:* The way things operate in Native society: if you are doing something, and you are doing okay, you are not going to hear anything from anybody. They are just going to let you exist and go and do what you have to do. But as soon as you make a mistake: watch out! That's how it works. So, you'll know.

*HL:* I know. I've been working with Native people for 14 years.

*LKT:* That's good.

*HL:* So, one of the reasons why I come over here is, because, unless I am able to talk to people, I never get feedback. Otherwise, I may be miles and miles away from the issues that Native people *really* convey in their

82

writing, and I'm just making a mere exercise in academic literary criticism. That's not what I want, but that's what's happening all the time.

So, when you look at Native writing coming out of Canada now, who, besides yourself, are the authors that you would recommend that people should read?

*LKT:* I would recommend that people read everything! And I think one of the most important things I want people to know is that just because something is "Indian" or Native, doesn't mean it's good.

You know, there is bad writing, there is good writing, you make up your mind. I have a preference for the authors that I like.

*HL:* Authors like ...

*LKT:* ... well, like Daniel David Moses and Maria Campbell.

*HL:* Oh yes, I met with Maria in Saskatoon.

*LKT:* Daniel calls her "The Mother Of Us All."

*HL:* She is, actually! She is!

*LKT:* She is. Of course she is. She has really struggled.

So, I guess, that's the way we all feel about her. It's unfortunate, very unfortunate, that PEN didn't see fit to ask her to present at the PEN Conference this past month. In fact, she could have presented here in Toronto and in Montreal as well.

*HL:* Whose decision was this?

*LKT:* I have no idea! You know, I don't belong to PEN, and I'm ambivalent about PEN, especially with the most recent events that have taken place.

*HL:* I heard from Ruby Slipperjack, she was there ...

*LKT:* Yes, she was.

*HL:* ... and Margaret Atwood met her there, and passed her around, and introduced her also to the head of the union of writers, and he said: "Are you a member of our union?" And she said: "I can't afford those $160!"

*LKT:* Dan Moses and I belong to the Writers' Union, we are the only "Indians" there! (LAUGHS) I guess it's a good organization to belong to if you want to know the business of writing, because that's all it deals with.

You know this issue of voice came up, this issue of racism in writing and publishing. The motion didn't pass! Because Canadians, and I have to say Canadians, don't want to think that they are racist. The racism in Canada is insidious.

Nobody likes to think that. People are afraid to think that they may be harbouring racist sentiments, racist feelings. And they should think! I mean, for heaven's sake, there is no equity in Canada for Native, First Nations peoples, none whatsoever!

*HL:* That's true!

*LKT:* I'm not a lawyer, I'm not a politician. I'm a storyteller. I've always been a storyteller. And now, I am in a position where people do take note of what I say. And this is my contribution.

This is probably the only contribution I can make to my society: to be a storyteller, and to defend the authentic Native voice, to speak up for the Trickster. To tell people: "Keep your hands off! If you want to hear stories then you come to me. And you go to my grandmother or my grandfather. If you want to hear stories, don't you go over there to W.P. Kinsella, or Lynn Andrews, or even M.T. Kelly for that matter, or Rudy Wiebe."

*HL:* So you see yourself primarily as a storyteller?

*LKT:* I think we're all!

*HL:* ... And the poet is part of that?

*LKT:* The poet is part of that. We are all storytellers. Writing, theatre, poetry, etc, these are just forms of storytelling, and writing is just a tool. That's all, that's all!

*HL:* But isn't there a big qualitative difference? If you think of the storyteller and the listener: they're together in one circle. Once you put something down on paper, and it gets published, you have no control over who reads it, and what they do with it.

*LKT:* Again, this is that issue of voice. Stories and words are powerful, and we as storytellers, as writers, must take the responsibility for the words that we put out there to the public. For the words that we put into the air! We can't just throw them away carelessly!

I think we all try to be subtle. We all try for the subtlety, the impact of story either through the oral tradition or the written tradition. The impact of a story that's going to hang onto a person long after they put the book down, or leave the storytelling circle. We all strive for that. Because it shows we have influence, and we do! We just have to be careful with it, it's power!

*HL:* The way I understand the oral tradition, from what I've read about it in autobiographies, fiction, and critical writing, and from what I've heard about it from Native people, is: the stories are told so that people know who they are, where they come from, and where they are going.

*LKT:* Exactly, exactly.

*HL:* The oral tradition is embedded in specific cultures and languages. Now, if Native writers are sharing that with the reading public in general, that adds a new dimension, doesn't it?

*LKT:* Well, I think what it does is give identity to Canadians! Canadians think that the founding peoples were French and English. But there were First Peoples, too, you know! Had it not been for the First People, the explorers would have died of scurvy, right?

*HL:* That's right!

*LKT:* It was Native people who showed them how to get from A to B. And when they found out that they could do it by themselves, and the bears weren't going to gobble them up, then the relationship between the white man and the Natives, as allies, began to change.

*HL:* Or they've been displaced from history. You know, we've also tried to displace certain facts of our history, like concentration camps, because it's shameful to remember, it hurts and is humiliating, even for coming generations. But we must remember, so that the same won't happen again.

*LKT:* Exactly! And this is why the Trickster tales are so wonderful.

*HL:* Was that your idea, founding the Society for the Reawakening of the Trickster?

*LKT:* The Committee to Re-Establish the Trickster. You know, this is to learn from your mistakes. The Trickster, the Teacher, is a paradox: Christlike in a way. Except that from our Teacher, we learn through the Teacher's mistakes as well as the Teacher's virtues. I don't know if it's the same with Christianity?

*HL:* No, I think, but Christianity seems to be something very special. If you go back to original beliefs in Europe that are pre-Christian, for example you may take the Greek gods, you may take the Roman gods, or you may take the Nordic gods ...

*LKT:* They are Tricksters, too.

*HL:* They have Tricksters! They have pretty mean characters, and they have good characters. They are all striving and trying to be human, trying to stay alive and teach, trying to show which roles are the wrong ones. By their mistakes. I think it's the same concept.

*LKT:* Yes, I think it's the same.

*HL:* It's not this "being on a pedestal," and you just fall down and sacrifice everything.

*LKT:* Yes, that's true.

*HL:* We, our ancestors way back, were colonized. Christianity was crammed down the throats of our ancestors, too. This was long ago, but it's the same process.

*LKT:* Yes!

*HL:* A lot of people forget that.

*LKT:* Isn't that unfortunate! And I think this is why we're struggling so hard to remember.

*HL:* Native people are also teaching other people. Some Europeans, like myself, learn through contact with Native people. I know a lot of Europeans who, after contact with Native cultures and talking to Native people over here, then went into their own history and asked themselves: "What is it that we had?"

A lot of it is destroyed, though. But we are very grateful for the help we get from Native people. Also in ecological issues, or through the Native American Peace Delegation. The Aboriginal Peoples' International Uranium Delegation came over some years ago.

*LKT:* And I am dealing with this issue of racism! And I think sometimes,

"Oh boy, what am I doing here? Why am I dealing with this? Why don't I just go off somewhere and just write?"

**HL:** When did you start writing?

**LKT:** When did I start writing? I guess, seriously, when I went to university. I did a degree in Fine Arts with the emphasis on creative writing at York University. But I've always been! I can truthfully say that I've always been a storyteller, even as a child. Because, I could look around, and I could see stories happening there. And I always listened to my father and my mum with their stories, and then my grandparents with their stories. And when I could read, even though I was reading nursery rhymes, like "One, two, buckle your shoe," I used to wonder "How come there are no Indian children in these nursery rhymes? How come?"

So I think it started then. From my father, I think we got mostly the traditional stories. From my mother, we had traditional stories as well, but she has a high school education, and she read to us. So, I guess that's the balance, the connection with the old and the new.

**HL:** So you were brought up with both traditions at the same time?

**LKT:** Yes, yes!

**HL:** Did you grow up in the city?

**LKT:** No, I grew up on the reserve.

**HL:** Where is that?

**LKT:** This is on Cape Croker, on the Bruce peninsula. So I consider myself very fortunate that I've had that upbringing.

**HL:** You mentioned Daniel David Moses and Tomson Highway, people that you work together with. Is there a network of Native writers? Are you in contact with other Native writers throughout Canada?

**LKT:** Yes I am. And since we're all sort of working artists, we don't keep regular contact, but we do meet every so often, here and there. And there is a group of Native writers here in Toronto.

**HL:** So that's a regional or local group.

**LKT:** A regional group.

**HL:** Do you think there would be a need for a larger organization, or possibilities of meeting, nationwide? I mean, Canadian-nation wide.

**LKT:** Yes, I think so. I would like to. I would, shit, I wouldn't go just with Canada! I would go with the States, too! And, as well, the hemisphere, if we could manage, and then, of course, the world.

But, yes, I would like to see that. I would like them all to become members of the Committee to Re-Establish the Trickster.

**HL:** Could you tell me some more about that committee?

**LKT:** We founded it the summer of 1986. We had been meeting, off and on, for maybe four or five years. Just coming together in groups of people with some of our poetry, and sometimes we just sat around, played scrabble or talked—but just to make that connection.

We had found through our own experiences in a number of workshop situations that there were times when we came out of a workshop and wondered what the hell had happened. Because issues, or forms, or symbols, or structures that we were looking for, were not there. And if we presented one, then no one understood it. They didn't understand what we were working from, or what we were drawing from, and what we were trying to do with the stuff that we were creating.

And I guess that out of that frustration, to know that "we are not crazy!," we decided to get together. And this is our committee! And we thought, well, Committee to Re-Establish the Trickster.

*HL:* It's a program, too.

*LKT:* Yes, it's political. It is, of course.

*HL:* I was wondering, because I was in Winnipeg and somebody by the name of Jordan Wheeler ...

*LKT:* Oh yes!

*HL:* ... he took me along. We met for an interview, and he said, "Well, there is a meeting tonight. We're trying to put a book together, short biographies of famous Native Americans as role models." There were five or six young people, or young writers—well, some of them weren't that young—and they just founded the Manitoba Native Writers Association.

*LKT:* Oh, good for them. I have to get in touch with them.

*HL:* Yes, that's what I thought, and I've put that address here. And there is also a group in BC. There are initiatives like that in Saskatchewan. So the same thing seems to be happening all over at the same time, and I wonder how much networking there is?

*LKT:* Not very much because we are way, way away.

*HL:* I'm very privileged, because I started out in Vancouver, and I am travelling for five weeks, and I'm meeting all these wonderful people. And then I sort of zoom on. But, there are connections.

*LKT:* That's good!

*HL:* Maybe I should write down some addresses?

*LKT:* Oh I'd appreciate that if you could.

*       *       *

I don't read a lot of Canadian literature. I read Native literature, everything and anything I can get my hands on. I also read Native history books, and sociology, and anthropology, and stuff—things Native.

One of these days, when I know who I am, inside out, with all the stuff I'm reading, then I'll venture on to Canadian stuff.

I made it a point in university not to do English literature. I didn't mind Canadian literature or American literature! It was closer to home in what I was looking for. But, no, no English literature!

It's the feeling, the purpose of what I am. Even though I use the

English language, the metaphors and the symbols I use are not English.
**HL:**   Now, if you read Canadian literature I think the writer that you probably will like — and a lot of Native people that I talked to, including, for example, Maria Campbell, like her — is Margaret Laurence.
**LKT:** I have read Margaret Laurence. I'm not saying that I have abstained totally, but every once in a while I pick up a book.

# TOMSON HIGHWAY

▼

*Tomson Highway is Canada's most prominent and internationally recognized Native dramatist. He has published two very successful plays,* The Rez Sisters *(1988), and* Dry Lips Oughta Move to Kapuskasing *(1989), which won him several prestigious awards (Dora Mavor Moore Award for Best New Play, 1986/87 and 1988/89).* The Rez Sisters *was selected to represent Canada at the 1988 Edinburgh Festival, and Tomson Highway himself has been to Europe on several occasions, both as a student and as a lecturer. He is the director of Native Earth Performing Arts, a Toronto-based Native theatre and arts agency. Together with his late brother, the dancer René Highway, Tomson has done more than anybody else so far to inscribe Native drama in the international literary canon. The conversation was recorded at Native Earth Performing Arts, Toronto, on 10 October 1989* (copyright: Tomson Highway/Hartmut Lutz).

---

**HL:** Maybe you could say how you got started in writing?

**TH:** It was always one of my dreams to write things like that. I like novels. I like beautiful novels, beautiful plays, and beautiful movies. I always wanted to do something like telling stories.

**HL:** So you see yourself as a storyteller, in that tradition?

**TH:** Of course, but not in any desperate way. I suppose I look at it more in a way of, "I'll try to learn how to do that."

**HL:** When you say you like beautiful books, beautiful novels are there some novels, or plays, or other texts that have influenced you particularly, or that you admire a lot? And that you could name?

**TH:** In terms of novels, I suppose among my favourites are the novels of William Faulkner and Fyodor Dostoyevsky. Those are the two novelists in particular that I have a tremendous admiration for. And a lot of the Southern writers in the United States: people like Katherine Ann Porter, Eudora Welty, Carson McCullers, Flannery O'Connor, and those people, because they wrote about working-class people—well, grassroots people, very ordinary people—and turned their stories with the art of storytelling and great technique into major visionary works.

*HL:* Can you think of Canadian authors?

*TH:* In terms of Canadian authors, the two playwrights who influenced me most are James Reaney and Michel Tremblay. Both use a lot of religious imagery, and James Reaney ...

Well, first of all, they write about working-class people, really grassroots people, basic people, street people from many places. And both superimpose—particularly in the case of James Reaney, he superimposes the level of mythology on top of his stories. Well, Christian mythology particularly because that's the mythology that has most affected the thinking, you know, the workings of mainstream society. And, just the superimposition, the combination, the marriage with hard-core reality, the miraculous, or a universal mythology. And even in opera, for instance Richard Wagner, the way he used Teutonic mythology to tell his stories about ordinary or supposedly ordinary people. Although in his case, of course, he wrote about royalty, and a kind of superhero mythology.

*HL:* You know that this has been spoiled and misused in the Nazi period in Germany? So that now it's very, very difficult to go back to it without sort of ending up with very strange associates. But a lot of people are doing that.

*TH:* Yes. It's the technique of doing it that I admire.

*HL:* Well, it's one way of trying to, sort of, decolonize our own minds to go back to what was before, and a lot of people are doing this right now in Germany.

Some of them have been influenced by Native people asking: "Why do you come here looking? Why don't you go and look at your own things?" So, a lot of people are doing that. Maybe the approach is different. If Wagner went to Odin and the leading gods, a god that was much more down to earth was Thor. He was *not* a comic figure!

*TH:* And, of course, the Greeks!

*HL:* If you think of Native literature today, in Canada, or in the US as well, do you see something that is specific, that you could put into words, regarding Native literature as opposed or compared to mainstream literature?

*TH:* You mean the difference between the two?

*HL:* Yes, what is specifically Native? How would you describe that?

*TH:* Well, we have a mythology that is thousands and thousands of years old, which was almost destroyed, or some of it obliterated, by the onslaught of missionaries and affected by Christian religion.

But, I suppose, when you do that to something, inevitably, the spirit of it survives even more strongly, and the mythologies too. It's coming back, it's still very much alive. It just went underground.

It's still very much alive in our spirits, although it's not an intellectual thing necessarily. But the spirit is still infused with it—our people. And the vitality, and the relevancy of it, and the immediacy of it are very much with us. Whereas we have people—and the way our writing is coming on proves it—that you know there is this connection with God. There is a spirituality that still is so powerful and beautiful and passionate! Whereas, in the case of mainstream culture here on this continent, both American and Canadian, we find that the mythology that they came over with is—their relationship to that mythology is really an academic relationship. It's not a living thing any more. So it was lost along the way.

*HL:* That's right. So, it doesn't come from the heart, but it's reserved for Sundays or for museums.

*TH:* Or for death ...

*HL:* Yes! Are there any authors in particular that you think of when you think about Native literature today?

*TH:* Well, there are a lot of young ones, particularly, coming out ever so little by little, that are eventually going to make quite an impact.

We have a writer here called John McCleod[1], whose play is the first one we are producing this year. He is an Ojibway man, 39 years old, who has written a lot of short stories, and up to this point in time, has primarily made his reputation as a short story writer. I think he, for one, particularly has a very unique vision, and he comes out with these stories. He's certainly made a tremendous and admirable effort to go back to the ancient Ojibway mythology and storytelling tradition, and to apply it to the 1980s and 1990s Toronto.

*HL:* That's what you do, too.

*TH:* Yes! And the process questions the existing system. And, for instance, in his play *Diary of a Crazy Boy* he comes out talking about the "little people" and the purpose they serve in Ojibway mythology. And there is a little person in this play, as a matter of fact. And should anyone question the existence and the relevancy of this mythological figure, then he has written into the script that the questioning psychiatrist, who takes care of this boy who is under treatment at a psychiatric institution, is asked, "If we don't believe in these 'little people,' in Ojibway mythological figures, then, who are the angels? Do you actually drink the blood of Christ?," you know, and all that!

*HL:* Oh yes, I've asked that too! The cannibalism in the Christian Church has really intrigued me. In some classes when we talk about Native people and some use the term "savage," I always ask, "oh, what do you mean by 'savage'?" So they sometimes answer, "well, perhaps cannibals," and I say, "no, you've got the cannibals right here! If you think of Christian mythology, and eating the body, and drinking the blood!"

But another thing! In the region I come from, there are lots of stories about little people.

*TH:* Where you have the "troll," up in Scandinavia?

*HL:* That's right. Where I come from between Scandinavia and Germany, on the Jutland Peninsula, north of Hamburg, Schleswig Holstein, that's where.

*TH:* That's where you come from? I've been to Jutland.

*HL:* Oh yes? But I'm not on the Danish side, I'm on the German side, there are still about 100 miles ...

*TH:* Are you close to the train that goes from Hamburg to Copenhagen? That line.

*HL:* That's right, yes! Well, it depends on how you go, if you go up Jutland and then over to ...

*TH:* No, I went by ferry.

*HL:* Oh, okay! No, then you bypassed it, because I'm north of that. If you draw a straight line up to the border, it's right in the middle. It's Rendsburg, it's on the Kiel Canal, and there is a large railway bridge that turns in a circle so that it descends slowly into the station.

And the Eider river is there, which was the old borderline between Denmark and the German tribespeople. There are lots of stories about the little people. And I believe that farmers, both in Denmark and where I lived, are supposed to leave some food for them, you know, so that they thrive.

But there are also stories! One I told Maria Campbell recently, and sometimes it just makes me very sad telling it because it's about the exodus of the little people.

And there are stories also about the giants who used to live there. They couldn't take the ringing of the church bells. So, sometimes you find large boulders, and large rocks, near the churches, and they are called very often in folk mythology "devil's rock," or whatever. Some of the legends say these were thrown by giants to knock out the bells because they couldn't take the ringing any more. And then they left.

So it's even reflected in the story, this process of displacing the old.

*TH:* The Europeans use their ancient mythologies, like William Butler Yeats for instance, and what he did.

You know, all the pre-Christian mythologies in the European countries were eradicated. It would have been interesting to see how the European civilization could have developed if all the mythologies had survived.

*HL:* Well, this is getting off the track, but what has intrigued me, and I still don't have an answer—What was it that made everything turn so bad? That people from Europe went out to conquer and spread Christianity.

*TH:* I think the faith and the vitality of Christian mythology and the spiritual use of Christian religion were still very much alive up to a certain point. You only have to look at the paintings of the Renaissance. Look at those paintings and the sculptures in Florence, for instance, and all over Italy. The faith and the love, the kind of belief in these icons. The symbols and the hymns of praise, the works of beauty, exquisite beauty, they came up with. I figure that the Industrial Revolution certainly had a lot to do with it.

*  *  *

Anyway, so there are a lot of languages like that. I mean, it's a frightening prospect to be faced with, a world where nobody speaks any language but English. I think that would be very boring, you know.

***HL:*** I think that would take a long time, though.

***TH:*** If it ever happens! Well, in North America—but not in Europe, thank God! What I admire so much about Europe, the northern European countries, particularly the Danish, they speak four languages!

***HL:*** Yes, often, the smaller the country in Europe, the more languages people tend to speak. I admire that!

***TH:*** It's so wonderful to be able to speak several languages. There are Native languages, but in my generation ...

***HL:*** Do you write in Cree or in English?

***TH:*** Both. My plays are ...

***HL:*** Do you use the syllabics?

***TH:*** No, I just use the Arabic letters.

Anyway, how envious the younger people are of us! I mean, our generation, we just rattle along in Cree like nothing. And it's such a funny language. Such a good-time language. They are missing out on a good time.

***HL:*** Also, if you have two or more languages, it makes you more aware of language. You know, in teaching English literature, especially poetry, I tell students, okay, you take that poem, and you translate it at home. That's the closest reading you can give a text. If you have a second language, and you try to put it into it, you may not come up with a good product, but you'll come up with a good understanding of the text itself. So, that can be used really to advantage.

Why is it that in Canada, as opposed to the US, there is so much more going on in Native performing arts?

There's hardly anything at all in the US. If you think of publications, there is Geiogamah's *Three Plays*, and that's about it. And here, there are your plays, there was the anthology *The Land Called Morning*, and ...

***TH:*** There are several differences between the Native experience in the States and in Canada. One of which is that we have a huge, huge—for lack of better words—"Hinterland." Most of the urban centres are all strung along the southern edge, the border. Then there is this huge land which is basically, for the most part, still ours. And there is nothing surrounding us. Whereas in the States, we are completely surrounded by urban centres.

And the second is that, historically, there hasn't been that bloodiness. We haven't been ...

*HL:* Yes, not the bloodiness, but everything else.

*TH:* We haven't been massacred. We've been moved.

*HL:* Well, the only difference is, maybe there wasn't genocide but there is ethnocide all the time. If you think of that as the destruction of the culture of a people, which destroys them as people as well.

But you are right, it's not that bloody.

*TH:* And, in America I think there is this ... one of the central tenets of American society is this idea of the melting pot, where everybody just becomes American, whereas in Canada there is still the option of the multicultural mosaic, and it's encouraged ...

*HL:* You think that helps drama?

*TH:* I think so. And I think that our funding, certainly, through the Canadian government and the Ontario government, bespeaks the fact that there are efforts to be supportive. And on top of that, well, I don't know Indians in the States that well, but it seems to me that our languages, that Cree, is very much alive. But who, in the States, speaks Delaware, for example? Well, Navaho! The Navaho are in a class by themselves. Maybe the Sioux as well. Like I say, I don't know the States too well.

But here we have my generation, who speak Cree, English — and French, in some cases, as well, on top of that. We are the first generation of Indian people as a group to have university degrees, to take a good long look at the "other" side, its literature, its storytelling tradition, its mythology, its philosophy, and still are able to go back, and mix the best of both, the Native and the white. And we are at a point in our history where the "American Dream" is not so beautiful any more. And we question it. We see that it is not going to work very much longer, and so we are looking for a turn of awareness. We are looking at the world, relating to the world. And I think, as time goes on, we are realizing that we just may have, if not the answer, but at least, an indication as to where the answer lies.

So, it's a combination of those facts that's made our work so dynamic.

*HL:* Yes. And with regard to drama, in particular, do you think it's also the difference of cultural politics of the Canadian government, like helping theatre productions and so on, that helps?

*TH:* Well, with this current government it's not very ... but it was, yes. And the reason I gravitate so naturally to the theatre — I used to write poetry but I write more and more plays — it's very natural for me to go to the theatre, instinctively. But I'm not trained. It's all done through the help of friends, God bless their souls!

**HL:** I think, probably, its strength is that you are still rooted in the culture that you come from. You haven't lost that. And if you think of other good Native writers—well, one I think of is Jeannette Armstrong, who impressed me a lot—she is deeply rooted in her Okanagan ways, and I think she draws a lot of strength from that.

**TH:** Oh, it's fantastic stuff.

But what I was going to say about the theatre, why I took the theatre as my medium, is because to me it's a natural extension of the oral storytelling tradition. You still hear the words.

**HL:** And there is contact with the audience!

**TH:** Yes. It's an extension.

---

## NOTES

1. John McCleod, *Diary of a Crazy Boy*. Directors: Tomson Highway and René Highway. Native Canadian Centre of Toronto, January–March 1990.

# BEATRICE CULLETON

▼

*Beatrice Culleton (Métis) grew up in and around Winnipeg in various foster families as a ward of the Children's Aid Society. After the suicide of her second sister, Beatrice began writing. Her first novel,* In Search of April Raintree, *came out in 1983, followed a year later by a slightly edited school edition. The book was a great success and remains one of the most favourite Native novels in Canada. It follows the lives of two Métis girls caught between assimilation into dominant white society and cultural self-definition as Métis. Her novella, "Spirit of the White Bison" (1985), is the fictional biography of a white female buffalo at the time of the near extermination of the bison in North America. It is a powerful indictment of the ruthless exploitation of natural resources for profit. She has also written an unpublished play,* Night of the Trickster *(1990) and has completed a filmscript, "Walker," for the National Film Board. Beatrice Culleton is presently living in Toronto and is playwright-in-residence of Native Earth Performing Arts.*

*The conversation was recorded at her home in Toronto on 10 October 1989 (copyright: Beatrice Culleton/Hartmut Lutz).*

---

**HL:** Maybe you can start by telling something about yourself, and how you came to write *In Search of April Raintree*?
**BC:** Okay. I decided to write the book after the second suicide of a member of my family. I have two sisters and a brother. Both of my sisters committed suicide at different times, and I just decided that I was going to write a book after the second one. And what I would use in the book was what had affected our lives. And part of that was being raised in foster homes, because of the alcoholism of my parents. I think the effect of growing up today, all these Native people growing up in urban Canada today, is that there is a lot of pressure on you to assimilate and forget totally what you are as a person, what your heritage is, and everything!

So, as a child I never thought about all that was going on. But as an adult, I didn't think about it either. If I watched tv, and the news, and there were Indian problems happening somewhere, it didn't really concern me because I've grown up in white foster homes. And, you know, that's what I really fell for.

So it was after the second suicide that I really thought, "Why are my family members alcoholics?" And "Why do we have so many problems?"

I grew up with a lot of other foster kids, you know. They came in and out of the home where I was mostly raised, and they all had problems coping as adults. They all had problems, and so did I. But not as bad as that, because I never became alcoholic. So that wasn't a problem with me. But most of my foster sisters, even those who weren't Native, they had problems, too!

*HL:* So there was the foster situation on top of the racism?

*BC:* Yes, so this was two things. Everybody was having problems.

So, I decided, "If I write it, maybe I can figure out some of the answers," or something. At least, rethink the way I've been living. Kind of blind, with my head in the sand, or something. And eventually it came out as a book. As I wrote, it wasn't going to be about a search for identity. But while I was writing that's what I realized about myself: that I had to accept my identity, not to make everything right or things like that. It doesn't happen like that! But it gives me, I think, a strong foundation. I'm not so wounded by what's happening with Indian problems, and I can get more involved in it by understanding more of their side of the situation, as well as the white side of the situation. The white side, I say, because it's the dominant society. And then, I think, I kept writing.

Well, when I first wrote, I wrote three rough drafts before the actual book was published.

*HL:* When you were writing, were you writing part time or full time?

*BC:* I wrote full time. I wrote during the month of April 1981. I wrote the whole month, day and night almost, on the first rough draft.

*HL:* That was right after the event?

*BC:* My sister had died in October 1980, and I was going to start writing then. But then we had a house fire, and we had to relocate, and things like that. So I didn't really start writing until after I did our taxes, you know?

*HL:* Was that in Winnipeg?

*BC:* That was in Oakbank, which is close to Winnipeg. First we lived in Vita, Manitoba, which is about 80 miles south of Winnipeg. We lived on a farm. That was with my first husband. George is my second husband. That's why I got the "Culleton" name.

*HL:* What was your own family name?

*BC:* It's what I've taken back now, it's "Mosionier." It's a French name. So if I write any more books I'll be writing them under "Mosionier" rather than "Culleton."

*HL:* You said that originally the book wasn't going to be about establishing identity or finding identity?

*BC:* No, not when I started. It was about alcoholism. It wasn't about any foster homes, because I didn't want anybody to think it was about where I grew up.

*HL:* But I think you made that very clear, because there are various places where the two sisters grow up. Some of them are good, and some of them are horrid.

*BC:* So, eventually, that's what I decided. To make one really good family, and if anybody wanted to identify, and say, "This is what they were like," or something, the good family was more easily identifiable to my own foster family, although they weren't the people.

Then I wrote about the bad foster home. Because I felt people ought to know about those homes, too. Because I had heard about them. Foster kids that came to our place had been there.

I don't think it's unusual, but people kind of just close their eyes to it. They don't really want to get into it, they don't want to know about it.

*HL:* It's the same in my country as well. My wife used to work in foster homes. She helped, actually, to close one of them down, because it was so terrible.

*BC:* Yes, and that's awful, you know! Like they have this thing going on on tv.

*HL:* Yes, that's about religious homes! That's from out east, right?

*BC:* Yes, and that kind of thing has happened a lot to Native kids.

They used to adopt them to the States or to other provinces like Manitoba.

One boy killed his father. I think his name is David Cameron, but I'm not really sure about that. His father in the States, in North Dakota or South Dakota, had been sexually abusing the kids that he was adopting.

Now the boy is in jail. I don't know for how long, but he was in Stoney Mountain when I was there, but I didn't get to see him. You see, a lot of times you don't know all those influences that are on you. And you kind of wonder why you are bad.

*HL:* If I look at your book, I mean, there are several books that came out of Canada, but also out of the US, by Native people, where the protagonist is in a search for identity. And usually he or she goes through a circle. First, away from the origins and the roots, and into a lot of conflict, and then there is a return. And very often there is a ritual or a renewal to reestablish the Native identity.

And if you look at your book, it's there, too. Or you could also say, it's two circles, because the two sisters together form a unity.

**BC:** Yes, yes! So one goes too far one way and the other goes too far the other way.

**HL:** But they overlap, because they start off. In the beginning, they go two different ways. And then there is an overlap where they don't meet, and in the end they almost change sides, right?

Or is that a wrong interpretation?

**BC:** Well, Cheryl doesn't change sides.

**HL:** No, but I mean, her way of life changes.

**BC:** Oh yes.

**HL:** I don't mean "sides" politically.

**BC:** Yes. Her ideals and everything are on a fragile foundation. So it's easier to shatter her idealism, and out of that comes hopelessness. And the fact that she, too, is an alcoholic. So her foundation — although she has identified very strongly with the Indian side — is not a true foundation. And I always think in terms of foundation. If you have a solid foundation, you can do a lot from that.

April had experienced a lot of hardships in her life as she was growing up. So she was more capable of handling future hardships because, a lot of times, if you have hardships in your life as you are growing up, it kind of prepares you for future ones.

**HL:** If it doesn't destroy you!

**BC:** Yes! And I was looking over a comment calling April a "survivor."

**HL:** How come she survives?

**BC:** I think it's just in her, (LAUGHS) in her blood.

When I look back at my own life, at my parents ...

My parents were both alcoholics, but still, in spite of that, they are fantastic people. I am not close to them, because I grew up in foster homes from the time I was three. So, I'm not at all close to them. I'm not close to the main foster family that I grew up in either.

I think, at an early age, I rejected both of them, you know, I rejected the idea of family. But my parents are really — to me — very admirable in spite of their alcoholism. Today, they support themselves. I mean, they don't support themselves still working because they are on old age pension, but they take care of themselves. They are not dependent on anybody to take care of them, and they do what they want, and they are self-sufficient. They handle their own finances, and all that kind of thing. So they are very independent, and I admire that about them.

Did I get off the track of writing? I forget where I was at.

There are so many things that are involved in writing the book. I could probably talk again and say something different. Basically the things started because of the suicide in my family. That affected *me*. And in that way, in the book, Cheryl's suicide affects April very profoundly, to where she finally decides she has no choice but to accept who she is. If she can do good for other people in her situation, that's good.

*HL:* You've been talking about foundations—in a way she has very brittle foundations when it comes to, maybe, traditional Native ways, because she is taken away at such an early date. But then, there is the scene where April takes her along to this gathering, and there is this old woman who gives her her hand. The way I saw that scene, I think that's a very important one, because she seems to receive some identity, or some power, there.

*BC:* Yes. See, all her life she's grown up, and Natives are very disrespected, in the West especially. There is a lot of contempt and even hatred. But people are very polite and they say they're not prejudiced, or not racist, and all that stuff! But when they start patronizing you, you know that's a sign that they think they are superior. All that kind of thing.

And as a child, growing up, you are very aware of all that. Nobody has to tell you people are prejudiced or racist or they are patronizing you. You know it's phoney! And I think it begins to build an anger in you, but at the same time, people react differently. People, like oppressed people, people who feel the prejudice, a lot of them react differently to that thing.

Some people become anti-white and hate whites. There are all different ways to handle it. So, anyway, April's way and my way was to also look down on Natives, and not want anything to do with them.

*HL:* She was quite brainwashed, in a way ...

*BC:* Yes!

*HL:* ... believing in the white success story, in the "Knight in Shining Armour," and then getting everything much worse ...

*BC:* ... and want everything white, you know!

*HL:* Yes, yes, and then really being hit much more profoundly, because of the hypocrisy.

*BC:* And so, when this woman touches her, it's the first indication that—it's a very simple truth, but—not all Native people are drunks, and good-for-nothings, and all that!

It's just the power that you can feel, sometimes, from a person, like encouragement or something. "I like you because you're you, not because of your money, or your, say, education or whatever, but because you're a person!" And that's the kind of thing that happened there with her.

And, I guess, another part of the story, the way I wrote *April Raintree*, was to make Cheryl more lovable than April. When she died, she could have attained a lot if she had gone all the way through with what she could do. Even if she became a social worker, she wouldn't stop there, she could do a lot of good for Native people. She has the brains and the possibility of doing it, of going through the whole thing. And, plus, she was very likeable when she wasn't drunk, when she wasn't drinking, you know?

*HL:* Yes, she was very creative and exuberant.

*BC:* So, I wanted people really to get involved with her over April. So that they'd really feel the pain when she died.

And April, well, she was the main character, but because of the way she thought, and because of her feelings and everything, she wasn't going to be all that likeable, once she got older.

So I had to build her in when she was very young, and let her see what she could be. And then, for the rest of the story, she goes through what she does. And then, at the end, she comes full circle. So, in a way, I kind of felt that way, too.

And one of the things that happened, like I'd always been pretty much neutral in my feelings about Native people and white people as an adult. So the feeling was old, it wasn't recent or just before I wrote the book.

After I wrote the book, that's how I got to start working at Pemmican, because I submitted the manuscript there. And then I got the opportunity to work there, and eventually become manager. And when I became manager, I, of course, got involved in a lot of Native things going on. I'd never ever been involved.

*HL:* With the Manitoba Métis Association?

*BC:* Yes, part of that and other things that were going on, too. And there, for a while, when I learned all the things that had been done to Indians, and then to the Métis, I felt a real anger towards white society, you know.

And it takes a lot to try to be neutral and objective, because, as a writer, I think I should be objective, in the way that I'm not condemning all whites, you know, running around condemning white people. It would be so easy to do, because ...

*HL:* And very understandable, sure!

*BC:* ... there is a lot of truth in it! But as a Métis, I feel that somewhere in my background there is white blood in me. So I'm part white and I'm part Indian.

So I try! And, if I'm going to write any more books, I want to be objective, and fair, but still honest.

*HL:* Even if you are fair and honest, it's devastating for the white side, because if you look at history there is no beating round the bush.

*BC:* Yes. It depends on what you want to concentrate on, too. You can concentrate on a lot of the bad stuff, and it'll be all true. But I think there are some good aspects to it, like, if the whites hadn't come along, I wouldn't be here! (LAUGHS) And I mean, that's the good part of it. (BOTH LAUGH)

*HL:* I was going to ask you, but in a way you've answered that already. If you look at the history or your experience, or the experiences of your sister, and at the way you transform that and use it in the book, there must be a lot of hatred and anger. And, if you write, does that help you, personally, to cope with the hatred and the anger?

*BC:* To tell you the truth, I never knew, I never realized I had hatred or anger.

*HL:* Maybe you don't, I don't know!

*BC:* I don't know, people haven't told me that it shows in the book.

*HL:* No. I'm not saying that, but it would be ...

*BC:* So that's what I want to keep writing like. I've been fair and honest in the book and that's the way I want to keep writing. I want to look for good sides, too, both parties, so to speak.

*HL:* No, I didn't mean that anger shows in the book. Sometimes it's amazing how little anger there is! But the facts speak for themselves. And if I said, "students cried or sometimes they got so angry," I mean it's just the text that evokes that. It's not preaching in this or that direction. No, certainly not!

*BC:* See, probably I have a leaning towards preaching, so I have to try to avoid that. I don't know if you've read "Spirit of the White Bison"?

*HL:* Yes. There is more of that!

*BC:* Yes. When I wrote the first rough draft, there was no white man in it. As if all the white men were bad men. To me it was way too onesided, so I put that white man in there with a Métis sidekick, to represent the good side of the white side. So, that's why he is in there.

But, yes, when I first wrote the book I was angry. I mean, it didn't start out that I was angry. It's just, once I started writing the anger came. At the injustice and the way of controlling another people. That makes me angry.

But I'm not angry at white people. If it were, say, the Indians and they were oppressing the white people, I would be angry with the Indians, of course. It's the injustice that people do to each other! There's just no reason for it! People don't have to be mean to each other to enjoy life, do they?

*HL:* No! So when you write something like "Spirit of the White Bison," do you write that on purpose for young people?

*BC:* I wrote it because I'd been watching this animation on television, *Watership Down*, about rabbits. It's an animation. It's really a unique story, you know!

And I thought Native people should have a classic cartoon, like an animation thing. So I thought about what could I write about, and eventually I decided to write about a buffalo.

*HL:* But then, you used a white buffalo. And there's the White Buffalo Calf Woman in Lakota belief. The one who brought the pipe?

*BC:* I'm not familiar with that.

*HL:* Among the Sioux, there is the White Buffalo Calf Woman. There was a white buffalo calf. There was a beautiful woman, and there were two hunters who met her, and one of them wanted to rape her. And she just made him disappear. But she told the other one, "You go back to your people and tell them I'll be coming to bring you something." So he went back to camp and told them that she would be coming to bring them something. And she brought them the pipe. And then she, I think, where she stood, suddenly a white buffalo calf rose, and she had disappeared. Or it was the other way round, that there was a white buffalo calf first, and then the woman. And then there was this book by Ruth Beebe Hill, *Hanta Yo* or *The Mystic Warrior*. It was serialized on television. And the Lakota people waged a long war against it because they did not want that to be put on. She also uses the white buffalo, but in a very different way. I thought, maybe, you'd been aware of the Sioux and the White Buffalo Calf Woman?

*BC:* No! With *April Raintree*, I didn't do the research till after I had written the first rough draft. First of all, I wanted to write it on my own feeling and what I knew, and not be influenced by other books and things like that. And the same with "Spirit of the White Bison."

*HL:* Do you read a lot of other books?

*BC:* Not really a lot of other Native books. I use Native books for research, more or less. That's when I read books about Natives. But I'm mostly a bestseller reader, you know. "Trash books" is what they're called. I'm not a scholarly type of reader.

*HL:* But some of the books that scholars deal with are a lot of fun to read! And you said you read Janet Campbell Hale, right?

*BC:* I've read those books because I've met the author and I want to read that.

*HL:* Are there other Native authors that you've read?

*BC:* Of course Maria Campbell!

*HL:* Oh yes! Has she encouraged you with that project?

*BC:* When I went on my first book launch, back in September 1983, I stayed at her daughter's place in Saskatoon.

*HL:* Oh yes, I've been there.

*BC:* Yes, and then, after that we went on a tour of northern Saskatchewan together.

*HL:* Where did you go? P.A.?

*BC:* No, further north. All these little towns, a lot of them you had to fly into. And that was scary, because I don't like flying, and it was in a little Cesna plane. They sat at the back and I sat in front with the pilot. Quite an experience, you know! But I don't like it. Now I won't fly at all in the winter. On November 1st I'm coming back to Toronto from Winnipeg. Of course, I think it might still be okay, but I don't like flying in winter! I don't like flying to begin with! I have, but I haven't done as much as I used to.

But I'm hoping to start doing talks and readings in Toronto schools, because I think that kind of thing is necessary here. Not so much because there is a large Native population here, but there is a lot of prejudice and racism that goes on here. People should learn tolerance of each other.

*HL:* Are you aware of any other Native writers here in Toronto?

*BC:* Yes, there is a poet, Lenore Keeshig-Tobias.

*HL:* Yes, I met her last night. And she, together with some others, founded The Committee to Re-establish the Trickster, and I was wondering whether you are somehow connected with them?

*BC:* No! It's not what I am interested in. My shortcoming, I guess, is that I am very lazy. I get involved with other things, and writing isn't a priority with me. I've never been an ambitious writer.

Like *April Raintree*! Before I wrote *April Raintree* I wrote a short story and sent it to an editor here whom I'd met when I came to my sister's funeral. He worked at McLane-Hunter. I sent a short story to him. And I told him, and I started telling people, "I'm gonna write a book," so that I would do it.

*HL:* So you put yourself under pressure?

*BC:* I tried that this time, too, but it still hasn't worked. I still haven't written a book!

But, anyway, he said it was saleable. It wasn't to do with anything Native, it was just an Alfred Hitchcock type of story, a short story. So, once he wrote back and said it was saleable, I started working on *April Raintree*, and I never did anything with that other story. I just let it sit. And if people wanted something written from me, like a story by a Native writer, I would send that to them. But they are not interested, because it is not about Natives.

# THOMAS KING

▼

Thomas King (Cherokee, Greek, German) taught for years at the Native Studies Department of the University of Lethbridge, but in 1990 he accepted a professorship in American Studies at the University of Minnesota because that position will allow him more time for his writing. He has organized numerous conferences and has spoken on many occasions about Native literature in Canada. In 1987 he co-edited The Native in Literature together with Cheryl Calver and Helen Hoy. He published his first novel, Medicine River, in 1989. He also guest-edited a special "Native Issue" of Canadian Fiction Magazine in 1987. The volume contained short stories by Canadian Native authors, many of which were republished in the very substantial anthology All My Relations in 1990.

The conversation was recorded on 2 May 1990, at the Saskatchewan Writers Guild Conference "Writing the Future" in the Ramada Inn café, Regina (copyright: Thomas King/Hartmut Lutz).

---

**HL:** You lived in Canada for several years now?
**TK:** That's right, 10 years I've been in Lethbridge.
**HL:** And, given the reception of your book and the novel you published here, the people would label you as a "Canadian Native Author." How do you see that?
**TK:** There's only a problem in the sense that I am not originally from Canada, and the Cherokee certainly aren't a Canadian tribe. Now that becomes a problem only if you recognize the particular political line which runs between Canada and the US, and if you agree with the assumptions that that line makes.

I think of myself as a Native writer and a Canadian writer. I doubt if I could call myself a Canadian Native writer, just because I'm not from one of the tribes from up here. But all of my short stories, and the novel, and the anthologies, and the critical book that I co-edited, were published here in Canada, and they all have to do with Canadian material. I have done nothing in the US to speak of. So, yes, I consider myself a Canadian writer. I write about the Canadian prairie, I don't write about New York.

**HL:** Do you find definitions unnecessary or helpful to defining Native literature?

**TK:** They are not helpful to me in particular, but I don't mind them. When someone says, "are you a Native writer?," I take it as a description of me, and who I am, and not my work particularly. So, what they're saying is, "you are a Native who writes." And that is a perfectly good description for me. But if they ask me, "are you a Native writer?" and what they mean is, "are you a writer who happens to be Native who only writes about Native things?," that's a poor description because I write about non-Native material too.

**HL:** So would you then define "Native writing" as something "written by Native people?"

**TK:** I think it's the best definition we have, but these definitions are primarily for the academic community. They are not necessary for me. I'm quite comfortable talking about Native literature without trying to define it. And that particular definition is as far as I am willing to go. Because as soon as you start to talk about what is Native in the literature itself, you run into all sorts of trouble. As soon as you start to try to describe who is an Indian and who is not—oh, it's a mess.

**HL:** Yes, I mean, even with the definition "Native literature is literature written by Native people," you end up with this mess of definitions. But at least you could say, "that author is established as a Native author, or can be established, and he or she is noticed as such."

**TK:** Yes, they are recognized by a community. You can say "Native literature is literature produced by Native people," as long as you don't ask "who is Native?" Because that would open a whole can of worms. And it's a pretty nasty can of worms, too.

**HL:** I think it shows that many draw this borderline. The borderline system is sometimes perhaps necessary, but really it creates more problems than it solves.

**TK:** Yes, well I mean you've got extreme cases where you have someone like Jamake Highwater, who, so far as I know, is not Native, doesn't have Native ancestry. The complaining about Highwater was that he was using identity to sell his books and make lots of money and get himself some notoriety, and that could be true. At the same time, Highwater produced two of the very best books on Native art. Now, they will be superseded, no doubt. But at the time, his second book in particular gave young Native artists a real boost because he highlighted many of those artists whom no one had seen before, at least in print. So he provided a very valuable service to that whole field of Native art.

But it is important, I think, to keep those kinds of lines straight because otherwise we begin to have non-Natives doing the same that they have done for years and years, and that is to speak for Native people.

That isn't a role I'm even interested in being involved in. There are enough people from the various tribes who speak both languages, who have very close ties, which I don't, to their tribe, who can do that for each one of the tribes. Everybody tries to hit upon one particular Indian at any point in time to answer all the questions about Indian affairs in the whole of North America. Most Indians won't take that job, so people go looking for someone who will. Most times it's a non-Indian who thinks he knows all about Indians or a social guru like, say, Lynn Andrews. I get fairly appalled when that begins to happen. I don't really care if the person is Native or non-Native. But to put anybody into a role like that, particularly a non-Native, is maddening. Just maddening.

**HL:** When you think of Native writing in Canada and Native writing in the US—is there just a time gap in the development?

**TK:** In the US you have that cornerstone and it's Scott Momaday's *House Made of Dawn*. It comes out in 1968 when, so far as we can see, there's very little on the landscape. It comes just, bang, like that. It wins a Pulitzer Prize and becomes a marker for all the rest of us. And then right on its heels come Welch's *Winter in the Blood* and Silko's *Ceremony*. Well those three become sort of a triumvirate. And they are good models. They are strong novels, not a weak novel among them. And so there is a great send-off for contemporary Native literature in the US.

Now, in Canada, that really hasn't happened. The closest thing that we have to it, I think, are Tomson Highway's plays. And they sort of serve the same function, and probably would have served the function even more had Highway won the Governor General's Award. He should have, you know.

**HL:** Yes.

**TK:** He did win the Dora Mavor Moore Award.

**HL:** Yes, but I think that also points to a different kind of development in Canada. The way I see it is: the inroad for Native literature in general has been made by Momaday, as you say, but there is very little in drama in the US. But in Canada there seems to be a very surprising amount of drama. Do you have an explanation for that?

**TK:** I don't know. I would have thought that drama would come first. Looking at oral literature, looking at more traditional forms of entertainment and ceremonials, I would have suspected that drama would have come first. I don't know why it didn't in the US, but it certainly didn't. The major Native playwright in the US, so far as I know, is Hanay Geiogomah. He brought out that collection of three plays earlier on and has been very active in Native theatre. I know there are other Native playwrights certainly, but they don't get very much exposure in the US. But in Canada, yes. For some reason I think maybe it is the fact that

109

Highway is a playwright, and those plays got lots of attention when they came out, and of course you have a very strong Native playwrighting community in Ontario, and you also have one in Saskatoon, one out in Vancouver ...

*HL:* In Regina ...

*TK:* Oh yes! It's an odd thing, because I was doing a bibliography on Native literature, contemporary and older material. As I was going through that, I would call people up and say, "who is writing?," so I could get their names in there. More people knew more dramatists than anybody else. And I was able to call Native Earth Performing Arts in Ontario. Elaine Bomberry used to be executive director there, and she was able to just go down a whole list of people, playwrights, whose plays had been workshopped, whose plays had been performed.

You have dozens of Native playwrights in every province of Canada. I don't know why that is, but there seems to be more emphasis on drama in Canada.

Now you've got some really great prose writers, too, like Ruby Slipperjack who is a wonderful novelist. Really wonderful, first rate. I think people really don't realize how good she is, and I suspect that Slipperjack doesn't know how good she is either.

*HL:* She doesn't! It's a shame!

*TK:* And the more I read that book, the more I'm impressed with what she is able to do and to accomplish, very skilled.

*HL:* And even this book *Honour the Sun* had been sitting on the shelf years and years. And she never thought about publishing it, and then somebody picked it up and said, "Listen, you are going to publish this! You have yourself a novel."

*TK:* You never know! That's the thing, you never know where these people are going to come from. Because there are quite a few small presses that publish Native work. You just don't know until something pops up. Her novel was a great surprise, a wonderful treat. But there is Harry Robinson, too, and there is Basil Johnston's book *Indian School Days*. They published and sold it as an autobiography. I think of it as fiction. It may have all sorts of autobiographical elements, but I think of it as a novel and a fine novel at that.

*HL:* Yes it is. *Moose Meat and Wild Rice* — that's catering to a very large market.

*TK:* One thing I like about *Indian School Days* and *Honour the Sun* is that both of those books deal with Native community. They don't involve themselves to any great extent with the clash between Native and non-Native cultures. Johnston concentrates on the Native kids in the boarding schools, and Slipperjack concentrates on a family up in northern Ontario. And I think, by avoiding that clash and not getting caught up in the debate

110

"which culture is better?," which many writers are tempted by, these novels are the stronger.

**HL:** Ruby didn't want to get involved in the politics that a lot of Native writers are into. She said, "I'm not political and I'm not interested in that." I think this is what she was expressing.

**TK:** Well, I think once you get involved in "whose culture is better?," and in the politics of Native/non-Native relationships, I think you get suckered into beginning to look at the world through non-Native eyes. I think you run the risk of having to redefine yourself and justify yourself as a Native, and as a Native writer. Johnston and Slipperjack avoid that completely. They simply say, "Here is the world that I want to describe and it's the world that I know."

Johnston has all sorts of opportunities to just blast the Jesuits in the boarding school. Yet, in the end, he comes away with just as much sympathy for the Jesuits who are prisoners of sorts, because they are German Jesuits who were stuck in Canada during the Second World War, and in many ways they are very kind to the Indian students. I mean, they have their problems and certainly they played tricks back and forth on each other. There is that one story about summer holidays in Spanish, where they all go off to the island and just sort of roam around. It's just people on an island making do. The Jesuits have their own way of doing things, and the Indian kids have their own way of doing things—a very powerful story. It doesn't involve itself in making the Indians victims or victors in it. You wind up seeing a very human side of Native life that you don't see in many books.

**HL:** Actually that's also what your novel *Medicine River* is about.

**TK:** I'll let you say that.

**HL:** Yes, but it is true, and I'm very sure!

**TK:** I wasn't concerned about the white community in *Medicine River*. My focus really was on the Native community. Whatever kinds of mistakes the people make in *Medicine River* I wanted to make sure that they were Native mistakes that they made. So, I didn't want to do what Kinsella does, you know, pit Indians against whites. Because I think you begin to lose track of some of the really powerful elements of contemporary Native life. Another thing is that you make it sound as though the Native people spend their entire existence fighting against non-Native whatever. That just isn't true.

There was a guy at Victoria who got up after I gave a paper and wanted to know why I didn't picture Indians realistically as drunks, and down-and-outers, suicides, and whatnot. He had really bought the stereotype. Alcoholism and drugs and suicide *are* problems, but it doesn't mean all Indians are like that. Hell, most of us aren't.

The other thing that I like to point out in my talks is that if things

111

were that bad, if things were really as bad as non-Native writers picture them, and some Native writers too, if we were that bad, we'd be dead as a people. We wouldn't have lasted 500 years. So, there is something that keeps us going. Now as soon as you say that, people say, "well, don't you have alcoholism? Don't you have suicide?" And the answer is, "sure, yes, we have that," we also have a certain cultural tenacity that keeps us going.

I think people like Slipperjack and Johnston are able to show that. I want to show that—that's what I want to look at.

Another thing that is nice about Johnston and Slipperjack is that they don't prioritize Indians. They don't start talking about who is a better Indian. There's no pecking order between full-bloods, half-bloods, mixed, they are all there together. We don't even know if they are all full-bloods or if there's some mixed-bloods.

**HL:** With Slipperjack there's no telling if it's a Métis community, are they Indians, are they white? That's right! That's not an issue! They are people!

**TK:** Even in *Medicine River*, even though you know that Will is not a full-blood, there is really no big deal made, except at one point when the question of status comes up for the kids and for the mother. But it is just something that is so divisive. To enshrine it in literature, I think, is just asking for problems.

And it doesn't help the fiction if all you do is talk about the kinds of oppressions white culture has had on Natives. There are all sorts of other ways to do it which are much more powerful.

I listen to poets. I think, in some ways, poets are the worst offenders! Native poets, especially those who really get involved politically, where the poem itself is simply a recitation about the kinds of oppression. It's not that the oppression does not take place, it's not that it is not true. The point is that, if you are going to enshrine it in the poem, do it in such a way that it has an impact. It has very little impact if you just throw it out there and say: "I am an Indian, I don't like the way you treat me, you brutalize me, etc., etc., etc." After a while it has no impact at all. People just turn their ears off. For me that's not a poem, that's not creative writing, that is simply preaching. I think you have to get beyond that and figure out clever ways to say that. Poetry is, in part, economy of language and, at its best, it is a very skilled thing.

**HL:** When you think of Native poets, are there some whom you think of as writing this "lament"?

**TK:** Yes, "lament" is a very nice way of putting it.

**HL:** Well, there is the traditional poetic stereotype of the "Indian's Lament."

**TK:** Yes, the white man's lament.

**HL:** I mean, this sounds silly, and maybe I shouldn't be saying that, but

112

I think I know which texts and also which authors you are talking about. There are some others that moved beyond that, I think. Are there some you want to mention?

*TK:* Yes, I think there are a number who have moved beyond that. Certainly people like Joy Harjo, and Louise Erdrich, and one of my favourites, Lucy Tapahonso. Tapahonso writes these great poems about Navajo cowboys. They are sparkling things, just sparkling. That kind of poetry avoids that trap, those polemics, that catch you up.

Who else? Let's see. Some of Jeannette Armstrong's poetry is very powerful stuff. Jeannette comes to the edge of that a lot of times, right to the edge, but she very seldom falls over. She does sometimes, but not often. Who else do I like? Well, Lance Henson. I like a lot of Lance's pieces. And again, Lance ignores a lot of the conflict. His poetry is concerned with Native peoples' ceremonies, with ways of thinking, if you will.

*HL:* Yes, and even when he makes some of those statements, it's not a political statement, but just raises the issue of race, or ethnicity. If you think of the one, "another song for america," about people living in cardboard boxes, carrying banners declaring their hunger, things like that! It's the race issue, it's the poverty! Or the one about "Kent State," that is raising the Vietnam issue. It's true.

*TK:* Then you have Maurice Kenny, Peter Blue Cloud, Joseph Bruchac. A lot of people would be on that list. It makes a huge difference, because if you want to talk about political or moral issues, the best way is to sneak up on people and scare the pants off of them! If you run down the street yelling and screaming they are just going to step aside. The mask comes on, and they say, "Yes, it's true! Yes, it's true! Good bye! See you later," and that's it. I think probably that bit of advice is good for any writer. Not to let the message, if you have a message that you want to play with, get out of hand!

When I came back from Victoria after that confrontation with that one guy out there, I sat down to write a short story. It was called "A Seat in the Garden," which was about this little bench the guy supposedly built, so that drunk or stoned Indians could sit on it. I had to say to myself, "Okay, I'm really angry with that guy. I'm really angry with that kind of racist stereotype that he's conjured up. And I want to do something about it." So I started writing. But what I started writing wasn't worth the effort because I was still upset. Then, finally, I got around to where I could see the humour in it, and the irony, and once I could do that then the short story just came like that. It was a good short story.

But some people just wrap themselves up in these ideas. Sometimes they use it as a blanket to wrap themselves in, I think. It's a way of providing them—well this is a horrible thing to say—but I think for some Native writers and probably more for Natives raised in urban areas, it's one of the things they think gives them an Indian identity. They *are* Native. They don't have the connections to tribe and community that they would like to have, so they wrap themselves up in this particular blanket. But it doesn't serve anything. In the end it does not serve literature very well and I don't think that it serves Indian people in general. I'm more taken with Ruby Slipperjack's description of an Indian community than I am with some other writers who really bang away on the oppression. Probably because much of Slipperjack is positive. I'm tired of negative descriptions of Indians, whether Indians develop them or whether non-Indians develop them, and I'm tired of romantic images too! So, I would like to see some very calm, very ordinary images, Indians doing ordinary things.

*HL:* If you had to teach a course for somebody on Native literature which books would you include?

*TK:* Well, I am more comfortable with fiction than I am with poetry or drama. I might take Erdrich's *Tracks*, which is my favourite of hers. I would certainly use Scott Momaday's *House Made of Dawn*, Welch's *Winter in Blood*, and Harry Robinson's *Write It On Your Heart*, Slipperjack's *Honour the Sun*, Basil Johnston's *Indian School Days*, probably Leslie Silko's *Ceremony*. Then Gerald Vizenor. And it would be problematic which book I chose there. I would probably choose *Darkness in St. Louis Bearheart*, or his autobiography, *Interior Landscapes*.

*HL:* D'Arcy McNickle or Mourning Dove?

*TK:* Yes, I would have to use those if I was teaching a year-long class. Certainly McNickle, Mourning Dove, John Joseph Matthews, John Oskison.

*HL:* Would you teach short stories?

*TK:* Sure, there is *Earth Power Coming*, which is the best collection of short fiction by Native writers in the US. And I suppose *All My Relations* would be the anthology to use for Canadian writers.

*HL:* How do you like *The Man to Send Rainclouds*? I mean that's 20 years old already.

*TK:* The trouble with *The Man To Send Rainclouds* is that about half the stories are by Simon Ortiz and Leslie Silko. So it is an anthology only in the most general sense of the word. It really is the Silko and Ortiz show, and they are both good writers, so it doesn't hurt the anthology at all. But many of the other pieces in that anthology aren't as strong. *Earth Power Coming* is more balanced.

*HL:* What would you use for Canada?

*TK:* Even my anthology is going to take a little bit of heat, because I have a couple of writers in there who are very marginally Native, but whom I wanted to include. It allows the stories to range from traditional to the very contemporary and even the experimental. But I know I am going to have people who are not in the anthology complain that they should have been in it instead of these other folks. So, it's going to be a problematic anthology, I think, as all anthologies are.

*HL:* What about poetry?

*TK:* Well, the guy who has done a great deal in the States is Duane Niatum. Those two volumes are a major contribution, and of course Joseph Bruchac, who is the godfather of Native poetry in the States.

*HL:* I always use *Songs from this Earth on Turtle's Back* by Joe Bruchac.

*TK:* Well you have those two, certainly, Niatum and Bruchac. They have nice collections. In Canada you don't have anything.

*HL:* There is *Seventh Generation*, but there are just very few.

*TK:* Yes. Yes. My mind is beginning to pack up.

*HL:* And I think it is a group of people who know each other and worked on this together. So it's not representative for the whole of Canada.

What about autobiography?

*TK:* Autobiography is, oddly enough, one of the major genres for Native writers. Partly, I think it is because if there's one thing that non-Native readers love to read, it's how real Indians lived. They love to read about the oldtime Indians and how they managed things.

*HL:* And even today.

*TK:* And even today. Oh yes, it's a great draw. Even if it's really one of those as-told-to biographies.

*HL:* In Canada there are some that are mainly written by the person her- or himself. I know that Maria Campbell has done it herself. This is what she told me. Again, there are some who say that she didn't even write it.

*TK:* I don't believe that. I've met Maria, I know her. There is one book that is quite interesting. I think that I will be using it in my history courses next year, and that's Percy Bullchild's book called *The Sun Came Down*. He's Blackfoot.

*HL:* What is it about?

*TK:* Well, it's the history of the world as told by Blackfoot elders. So it is a very interesting book. It cuts across a number of genres. And it's got very little play! I mean, it's there, it's been published already, it's been out for three years, something like that. It's in paperback now, so I can use it for my class. It's a history, sort of a narrative history. It starts at the beginning of the world. It doesn't start with colonialism. The nice thing is, this stuff is not even taught in classes.

*HL:* I might be using parts of this interview in class back in Germany. What would you say to people in Germany?

*TK:* I suppose the only thing I might say is to watch out for the romanticism contained within the images of Indians. It will do a couple of things. The biggest thing is that it will disappoint you. If you come, let's say, to America thinking that we have long hair and that we ride around on ponies, you're going to be disappointed.

115

**HL:** A lot of people in Germany now are interested in Native stories. But then, there is so much rhetoric from Native people about Mother Earth—and I strongly believe in it!—but we also see Native people not thinking twice about the environment.

**TK:** I don't think it's so much that Indians are environmentalists. Okay, in a way. Indians are not so much ecologists as we have a land ethic, and it's important to know the difference. You could say, well sure, but North Americans have a land ethic too. And I would say, "no they don't." What they have is an ability to rise to a crisis. When that oil spill happened in Alaska, everybody gets outraged. They want to hang the captain. They want to hang Exxon. They want to get up there and clean up the coast. At the same time, they continue to throw plastic bags in the garbage, they keep using disposable diapers, they are running their cars up and down to go to the store. They have really got no concept of what a land ethic is all about.

**HL:** They believe everything can be solved.

**TK:** They believe everything can be solved by science. Whereas with a Native society there is the sense that everything is part of a living chain and you have to pay attention to what happens with the animals, with the environment. The world as an organic flow. Now, that begins to sound very clichéd. And unfortunately it is a cliché, because it's been used and advertised so much, but it is true! It is true. It's not so much that Indians are environmentalists, because we make the same mistakes that non-Indians make about the environment, but we have a particular sense of that physical world that is so much a part of culture and so much a part of the ceremonies and everything else. They are connected. It's a hard thing to describe now, because advertising firms have started to use Indians to connect products to the environment, products that won't do the environment any good at all.

**HL:** It's just an extension of what you were talking about.

**TK:** But if you go down to a place like the Southwest, for example, or even if you're in Canada, there are specific ceremonies that are still conducted that are reminders for the community as a whole of their place within that world, and their obligations as human beings in the world. The non-Native world does not have those kinds of things. It doesn't happen within the various religions, it doesn't happen within the society. We don't really spend much time teaching the kids about it. They see it on television, they read it in a book. We have this superficial concern with the environment. And then, too, modern human beings think of themselves as being above everything else. Very smart, able to fix anything. In actual fact, human beings can destroy a lot easier than they can fix. They may do that yet. Then we won't have to worry about literature or anything else for that matter.

116

# GREG YOUNG-ING

▼

*Greg Young-Ing is one of the most creative and widely productive young Native poets and cultural workers in Canada. His poetry has appeared in* Seventh Generation *(1989) and* Gatherings *(1990), and he has been instrumental in publishing Native poetry and song on cassette tapes. In this, he has worked together closely with Lee Maracle, Jeannette Armstrong, and other artists of colour.*

*Greg Young-Ing is a master's degree student at Carleton University in Ottawa, but he is also active in many Native organizations promoting the Native voice. Presently, he also teaches and learns at En'owkin Centre in Penticton, British Columbia.*

*The interview was recorded on 13 October 1990 at the Palais de Congrès in Hull, at the CINSA Annual Conference in Ottawa* (copyright: Greg Young-Ing/Hartmut Lutz).

---

**HL:** Native people here are making great efforts to produce stuff on tapes. Maybe you can explain why that is. Why on tapes, why not books?

**GYI:** Music is something that is more entertaining than straight reading, and something that you can listen to at leisure while you are carving, or cooking, or whatever. I think it is also something that young people listen to a lot. A lot of people probably will not be so likely to pick up a book and read, as they would be to put on some music. When music is added to poetry, it also enhances the experience of the word, and it adds another dimension to it.

**HL:** So that is an effort to reach young people?

**GYI:** I guess so. It's just a way, also, of getting the message in a different format and accessing other media like radio.

**HL:** How did you start writing?

**GYI:** I guess I started when I was forced to write poems in the Canadian public school system. I didn't really enjoy that, of course. And I got back into it when I was 19 or so, on my own.

By that time I had come into my own, and I wasn't trying to imitate any of the British writers that we had been taught in English classes in school, the classical poetry. It was to me a release. A way of releasing some of my ideas, and some of my anger sometimes. It's a therapeutic way of expressing yourself and getting things off your chest, so to speak.

*HL:* So, when you just mentioned the public schools, or British culture, I guess, in your poem "I Am Mixed Blood," where you have this passage with the pink fingers stretching eyelids in "a metaphor of narrow vision," is that autobiographical? Your experience in school?

*GYI:* Well, I think almost all poems are autobiographical in some way. They may not tell a specific story of one's life, but they are all rooted in our life experience. And as far as the school system goes, I went in the Canadian public school system. I never went to school on my reserve. I lived in the cities most of my life.

That line you mention is, of course, about racism. And I can say that I experienced a great deal of racism in elementary and public school, totally from the white kids. And one thing that bothers me now is that in high school the incidents of overt racism decreased a bit. But I know it is still there, and it just became covert. And what I didn't like about high school, and the current situation now, is: you can't tell. You can't point your finger, and say, "That's racist," whereas little kids had not been taught to cover up their racism.

The government is trying to push this idea of multiculturalism and ethnic harmony in Canada, and I think that is a bunch of bullshit! I don't mean ethnic harmony is not desirable, it's just not a reality. But the effect that the multiculturalism propaganda does have is to teach people to cover up and hide their racism.

*HL:* Well, Oka brought everything out very much in the open, eh?

*GYI:* Oh, definitely.

*HL:* Did the fact that you are part Native, part Asian, make your experience any different from the experience of other Native kids?

*GYI:* I don't think so. I am part Scottish too. I don't think so. I think that all that matters is that you're not white.

*HL:* Are there writers who influenced you?

*GYI:* If I had to mention some writers who influenced me, I would mention Lee Maracle, Jeannette Armstrong, John Trudell, to a certain extent, Linton Kwesi Johnson, Gil Scott-Heron, and I guess those are the only people that come to mind.

I would have to say also that I was influenced by some of the musicians who wrote lyrics that I think are poetry—like Bob Dylan, Ian Curtis from Joy Division, Mike Scott from the Waterboys, and Bob Marley. Bob Marley was a big influence on me.

So, I guess those are some of the influences that I have, but I haven't really thought about it too much before. I haven't been interviewed as a poet before.

*HL:* If you had to devise a course on Native Literature in Canada, what texts would you want to include?

*GYI:* I could think of a few books that I would include. *Slash* by Jeannette Armstrong, *I am Woman* by Lee Maracle. I don't know what the precise definition of literature is, but some of the political books that have been written like *The Fourth World* by George Manuel, *The Unjust Society* by Harold Cardinal, *No Foreign Land* by Wilf Pelletier, *Prison of Grass* by Howard Adams.

*HL:* Poetry?

*GYI:* I'm not allowed to say *The Seventh Generation*, or *Gatherings*, right, because I am in there. (LAUGHS)

*HL:* (CHUCKLES) Yes, those are the ones that I include in the class that I teach.

*GYI:* In terms of historical materials, I think it would be good for the young Indian students to read Pauline Johnson too.

*HL:* For what reason? Why Pauline Johnson?

*GYI:* Because she was the earliest Indian poet to be recognized in Canada. Because even to this day she is probably the most widely recognized Indian poet that there has ever been in Canada.

And I think we can learn a lot from her dichotomy of world views, the confusion that she was going through. That is what our people were going through at that time, and still are to a lesser degree.

*HL:* Is there something like a network among Native writers in Canada? Or are there just a few that know each other well?

*GYI:* Well, I guess I would call it an informal network. Definitely I think most of the prominent Native writers are people who know of each other, and I think most of them actually know each other. And a lot of them are friends, either from meeting each other at conferences, doing presentations together, or collaborating on books. There is definite networking going on.

*HL:* Is there something that you would like to say to a specific audience or the general reading audience as a writer and someone who has been engaged in Native affairs and Native issues?

*GYI:* I would say that there have been centuries of misinformation about Aboriginal people. First Nations have been misrepresented by anthropologists, politicians, archeologists, sociologists, and people from other so-called established disciplines. And the only way that the misinformation is going to be turned around and corrected in people's minds is to start listening to the voices of the First Nations people. That can be done through listening to speeches, going to conferences, or just talking to people on an individual basis. But the medium that is going to reach most people is the written word.

119

There are a lot of Native writers. So I would say: "Read them!"
**HL:**  How do you feel when someone like me, from a different culture, different country, is nosing around, interviewing people, and says that I would like to put this into a book? Is that appropriation, does it make you feel uncomfortable?
**GYI:** Well, there are always people coming around to First Nations communities, and approaching individuals. And a lot of them are non-Native people.

In terms of the non-Native people, I think that we don't want to shut anybody out, just because of the colour of their skin. But at the same time, we are just going to have to rely on our certain feelings and trust that we feel for the people who are approaching us, and just approach it that way. I can't think of any other way of doing it. I do believe, however, that outsiders should make sure they are welcome and be very humble and respectful.

I have seen your work before and heard a bit about you. I had no problem in talking to you.

# ANNE ACCO

▼

*Anne Acco (Cree) grew up in Cumberland House, an Indian and Métis community in northeastern Saskatchewan. Listening to the stories told to her in Swampy Cree by her elders awakened an early interest in words and reading, and she decided to become a writer herself. A more than 20-year "interlude," during which she raised six children and spent three years in Trinidad, interrupted her "literary career," which she resumed in the eighties in Ottawa, her present home. Her first book of poetry and prose vignettes,* Eko-si, *was self-published in 1989 and sold out within a year. Some of her poetry also appeared in* Canadian Woman/les cahiers de la femme *(1989), and in other periodicals. Anne Acco's impressive reading performances demonstrate the importance of sound in her literary works, which centre on the psychological and social effects of the history of colonization in Canada.*

*The interview was recorded on 14 October 1990 (a day before Anne Acco's first grandchild was born) in Ottawa, following the CINSA Annual Conference* (copyright Anne Acco/Hartmut Lutz).

---

**HL:** How did you start writing?
**AA:** I started writing simply because I like what words do. I am a linguistics student as well as being an English literature major, University of Ottawa.

In my little community, Cumberland House, in the northeast part of Saskatchewan, people spoke up to four languages. They definitely spoke in the Cree language, they spoke three dialects. I grew up hearing French, and Cree, and some English. Because of where we were situated, the radio came through in English. I was interested in sounds. How people made sounds, what they stressed, and what their emotions showed as they were speaking the language, as opposed to the language showing what they were feeling because of what they said. I wanted to hear what it is. Were they speaking loudly? What happened to the tonality of their presentation?— be it a speech, be it a straight exhortation saying, "get out of here" or "stop that!" I began to really listen. When I was 19 I was going through university, my very first and only year. I wanted to become a health care worker, either a nurse, or a doctor. It quickly became very evident to me that I had no money, but I had enough education to go on to be a laboratory technologist, and I did three years in histology. So from that background you can see that I was well on my way to becoming a "terrific" writer. But when my children were born and I realized that I had to stay home with the six of them, I found that I was becoming less and less able to write in the English language and express myself properly. So, what I started to do was to write essays, letters to the editor, gather any books I could.

I just loved to read as a child. I was very lucky—a man by the name of Jim Brady[1] had left us with some of the classics. We had a very dry warehouse, and he was able to leave his books in my father's care. And he also told us that we could read the books. So by the time I was 10 I certainly had read Somerset Maugham and the poems of Robert Frost and Carl Sandburg. I realized the power of words. In realizing that to learn this, and in later life to be able to keep up with this kind of thing, I just wrote. It got to the point where I had about five boxes of different kinds of writing—everything from poems to short stories, just trying to teach myself how to keep up with the writing. And then we were going to move from Montreal to Winnipeg, and I threw everything out, all the writings.

*HL:* You said you were up at Cumberland House at that time? So, from the standpoint of urban Canada you were quite "isolated."

*AA:* Yes! I left home when I was 15 years old, and I only spoke Cree.

*HL:* I see. There are other authors I talked to, like Ruby Slipperjack. She also grew up in a very isolated community, and she started writing as a child, really urgently. Maria Campbell relates how they read Shakespeare and enacted scenes. Peter Deranger, the storyteller, who is up from the Northwest Territories, only had the Farmer's Almanac and comic books, but he too was a reader and a writer. Tomson Highway also comes from an isolated northern community. So there seem to be several Native authors who are really isolated and have this urge to write. I asked Peter, "What made you do that—was it a jump from the oral tradition?" He said no. Maybe you can say something about that?

*AA:* Well, I can say that it was another means of communication, and you were always looking for ways of communicating. And if that book can communicate something to you, then you want to read it.

When we were in the encampments, and this is spring trapping, my cousins and I all had a cache of comic books, and little books to read. So, towards the end of the winter, I had gotten to the end of my powers of observation to read these things again and again and again. I was fed up. So on the very first, fine, spring day, we started to walk with our comic books to exchange them with the next campsite, which was 20 miles away. Halfway there we met them with their comic books coming to do the exchange with us. That kind of drive is a tool, a way to communicate.

You have to go back to the history of the Cree people. The Cree people had their own syllabics. They had their own way of communicating. I think from the time it was introduced among the Crees, within 10 years, anthropologists say, every man, woman, and child with the ability was able to read. And in that exchange there was always somebody. The scribe was always prized. He was the person you could take something to, to read, to decipher. So the person who could read became a figure not of accomplishment but of usefulness.

Within the oral tradition the way to tell a story is very strict, and you were taught. If you were able to tell stories, the people came to visit you. Your aunts, your uncles, would tell you stories from the time you were a toddler, and somehow you become attuned to storytelling in such a way that it becomes a part of your unconscious reality, and you are able to pick up. The process was already ongoing so that the step to writing was very natural. It is this kind of thing I want to stress.

I saw a picture taken by a famous American photographer, and this particular picture said: these are people from the Apache nation sitting down for some storytelling. To me that said an awful lot, because any time Native people gathered, they would go into their storytelling mode. And now we are just experimenting with some of the ways we speak.

My mother is a wonderful poet. She does not write but some of her phrasing is so poetic that it just literally blows me away. I can give one example: she was just simply watching the rain come down. This is in Montreal, and we had four scotch pines in the front yard. She said, "Look at that, the rain has come to wash the faces of the trees." She said this in Cree, and I cannot retranslate it and catch the essence of the beauty because you would have to hear her voice. This to me is very fascinating that somebody could embody a thought, transcribe it into her own communicative process, and come up with something that touches the human heart so profoundly.

**HL:** I realized the other night when you were on stage with Willie Dunn, reading your poetry, how important sound is to you. There is a lot of melody in your reciting. You raise your voice, and then it goes down, you speed up, etc. So, you use voice a lot. You said your first language was Cree, and it has all these possibilities that you probably don't have in the English language. Could you say something about that, about mastering a different language and trying to get across something that you could express more easily in Cree?

*AA:* I will try to read Angelique: Just before her death. (READS IN CREE) Can you hear the rhythm?

*HL:* Oh yes, and you have a lot of what I would describe as "clearer," vowels, much clearer than in English, where in a multisyllabic word you generally have only one clearly pronounced, stressed vowel, and the rest is "aw," "aw."

There is one word that I understood. That was "Batoche," which has a wonderful sound to it. You hear it in so many different pronunciations.

*AA:* Again it is Angelique, my great-grandmother.

ANGELIQUE
Just before her death, I was taken to see my Great-Grandmother Angelique. It was my fourth birthday. I went to share a piece of cake with her. She rose from her wooden bed, dignified, alert but weak. Her words, directed to a destiny I was to have, meant nothing to me at the time. I never forgot Angelique, the occasion and the words.

Years later, I came to know this was the woman whose husband was killed at the battle of Batoche, 1885, officially listed as a suicide. In this country of long silences, it took three generations to write the truth burned into her heart.[2]

*HL:* That is a powerful story. "Three generations of silence." I guess that is one thing that Native writing, I think any writing, should be about: to *break* the silence. I feel that a lot of Native writers in Canada, maybe all of them, are doing that very consciously.

*AA:* Oh, we have to do it!

*HL:* So it is not the kind of literature that you have in the mainstream, where a lot of it is literature for literature's sake.

*AA:* Absolutely different.

*HL:* The message is very important.

*AA:* The message! The people themselves are dying out! We have to obey the tradition because we come from such oral people fascinated with words. People have to trade with different people. You had what were called "illiterate people" who knew six languages. If you think about my line, my grandfather Lionel, who I write about in this book, spoke about prayer and its place in our lives in the natural way that is typical of a truly religious people. He was himself a trader. He travelled a thousand miles up and down. I used to see him in his trading. Well, he could count. That is one thing he could do, and he could write down numbers, but to say he was a literate person in the sense that he could come and sit down and start writing a story for you — no. But he could tell you a story, and he could quote from the Bible like no one I have met in my life. Whenever he spoke we had to be very quiet. In this particular story I say a very small snippet of what I wanted to say:

LIONEL
My grandfather Lionel, spoke about prayer and its place in our lives in the natural way that is typical of a truly religious people. He never doubted his God. He paid homage whenever possible. I can still see him sitting on his wooden bed, his grub box under it. His grey woollen blankets and his feather robe were folded away in a corner. His room and the stove that kept him warm helped him think of his Manitou. As our grandfather he let us know that we had to be good to one another and to think the best of each other. He told us that as a group of people we were distrusted and afflicted from without. He felt the practice of prejudice was a sickness of the heart and mind. He asked God to forgive all of his enemies. This is but a glimpse of the kind of man my grandfather, Lionel Carriére, the son of Dumas and Angelique, was to his children and grandchildren, in spite of tremendous hardship. (22)

This person could speak so many dialects of the Cree, he could speak Dene and its different variations, he spoke French, and he also spoke English. But, as I say, he was illiterate — but in numeracy you could not beat him.

**HL:** So he learned everything that he needed for his life.

In the beginning I asked you how you started writing, and you went into the tradition that you come from through your childhood. What made you start to write this book? How did you get down to doing that?

**AA:** How I got down to doing this was simple. I felt that there was a lot of writing about Native people, yet writing in a manner that seemed to be all right but wasn't quite all right. In other words, not obeying the tradition. I said, "What is the responsibility of myself, as a Native person, as a storyteller? What I have to do is: I have to master the language. That is all I have to do!"

I already had the stories! If I have the stories, and I can master the language, I just go ahead. And now I write. If I am published or not published, that is not my problem. My problem is to get it down on paper, to type it out, and that is exactly what I did! I started to read in public. I started to do that three years ago when I came to Ottawa. I had to do it that way. I was separated at the time, and felt more motivated to write to fill the hours. But at the same time, because of the tremendous upheaval that was going on in my life, I was able to write and pour out an awful lot. Before I had been writing, but I had not placed any kind of importance on what I was writing. By that time, my brother Ken told me that what I was writing was very important because it came out of my experience. And because it came out of my experience and because I was able to use the kinds of phrases I was able to use, he felt that I really should try to write down as much as I can. In doing so, I could see the value of my own work because no one knows Abel Kanada. No one else knows this man [but because of my poem] young men have come up to me and said, "Thank you for writing this, I feel I know an elder and that he is my friend!" So that ancestry is there, and other people can tap into it. It is very, very important. Phillip, who is an artist, people like this, I just describe something, an incident in their lives, and they become very, very much part of the tradition. In the same way, I suppose, when you say "Rumpelstilzchen," I immediately come alive! (LAUGHS)

And how I got interested in poetry, I learned, "Abu Ben Adem put up his tent one night ... ," and I forgot the name of the author, but I will always remember: "Abu Ben Adem put up his tent one night ..." And I really found that, with the stress on the "night," I said, "That is something I can do!"

*HL:* That is powerful.

*AA:* Very, very powerful.

*HL:* It makes you expect something. You know something is going to happen. Sometimes you have openings like that.

*AA:* And I also saw that this was a man out in the desert, and his name is "Abu," and if somebody had not sat and written about Abu, I wouldn't know anything about him.

*HL:* Okay. But I have to challenge you on this. I have heard some people, although not very many, who say, "Well, the oral tradition is just the oral tradition. It is in the traditional languages, and if the people who have this language and who belong to that culture are not able to carry on the tradition, and the language, then the stories will go, because they are tied to that language and to the *oral* storytelling. If you write them down, you kill them!" What do you say to that?

*AA:* The challenge is to reach into your creativity and to bring as much as you can out of that translation! I will show you a story that I wrote called "Elizabeth."[3] It did not work as a short story, but it worked beautifully as a poem. And again, this shows you that if one form doesn't work, you reach into another form, which implies that you have to study.

*HL:* Some of these stories or poems are monuments to people who passed away, so they wouldn't be forgotten. They are something from your immediate experience, or from your family tradition. Other stories are parts of the oral tradition, are sacred, are not personal—could anything be written down?

*AA:* I would say, if you are reaching into the metaphysical, and if you are reaching into the spiritual, those are always hard subjects in any language, and you have specialists for that.

*HL:* So you would say that you limit yourself ...

*AA:* To what I know, to what I *can* do. I am not a philosopher, but somebody else might be. And I know these people. They are wonderful philosophers, and they will write. But they might write allegorical things, or they will write essays. They are just beautiful writers. But I am more historically orientated. But, again, I was extremely lucky. Not everybody has this capacity and also has the memory and that kind of memory training. Again, this is done very early, and you are not aware of it as a child that your memory is being trained, deliberately trained. This again is something that is passed on.

I would like to think that as Native people begin to appreciate what is in their culture, and to learn to see it for what it is, they will not try to put too much into one particular aspect of, let's say storytelling, passing things on in an allegorical manner, of myth—they have to be able to extract it and to approach it with a great deal of respect, and to completely analyze what they are doing.

There are some stories that would approach almost a sacred tradition, in the same way that very few people can tell the story of Louis Riel. The story has yet to be written. A lot of people make comments. You can read his diaries, but as I see it, you have to almost be a linguist to start to read what it is he was doing in his diaries. Because he is doing something. I don't know what it is, but maybe at some point the key will come. There are key words that he uses which say he is going into a different world or different way of expressing himself. And it is for us to begin to understand what it was he was doing. That has not been done yet.

So there are people we do not touch in a manner of saying, "Okay, I am going to write a history of this person." And you know, it will just be another book. There is just "no other book" about certain people! And certainly, the different myths that we have, as they come up from the different traditions, and from the different languages, they have to be treated as, say, "This is a myth! This is how it works as a teaching tool!" People will choose the people they will want to write about. You could see that tradition very strongly in Willie Dunn, and he does it very well.

*HL:* Absolutely.

*AA:* You can sing his songs in 1970. You will sing them in 1980, and they will be singing them probably a hundred years from now. And they will just hold completely. This is the kind of writing that we are doing in this country right now.

*HL:* You mentioned earlier the classics you read because they were there in that storehouse. You also said that you write from your own personal experiences, and stories that you know through your family. Are there any Native writers, any other literary sources, especially Native writers in Canada, who influenced you?

*AA:* The West Indian writer V.S. Naipaul. His approach is: "Do your

127

homework! If you are going to write a historical novel, if you are going to write anything about your people, make sure that you are historically correct! Do not invent! If it is 1885, put it in perspective!" The West Indian writers deal with colonialism. We have to deal with colonialism.

*HL:* Absolutely.

*AA:* We cannot ignore any aspect of our life! If we have family breakdown, violence, that comes out of being poor, being marginalized. That is what we have to write about.

*HL:* So it is also very much political writing?

*AA:* It becomes automatically political writing.

*HL:* I totally agree with you on that.

*AA:* Yes!

RAILWAY STOP
Reaching the railway stop,
Catching the rail-liner,

Seeing them riding high,
Doffing toque, knowing my place,

My place somewhere inconspicuous,
My tribe is supposed to be dead.

I come to this railway stop,
To remind you and the governments,

I didn't die from all those diseases,
Nor do I despair, shoot myself or
                    drink river water.

Then again, another is born to take
                    my number;
I heard you don't die and you don't
                    want to be replaced.

I don't worry my head under the toque,
It's your turn to die while I replace.

            Good day to all of you!

This is about a displacement.

*HL:* Yes, and appropriation.

*AA:* Appropriation. The railway stop that existed between Cranberry Portage and The Pas, Manitoba. Again, straight out of my experience.

*HL:* I like this, "Nor do I despair, shoot myself or drink river water." It is a good line because you counteract the stereotype. "I don't commit suicide or drink" refutes the stereotype of the drinker, but here the *river* is polluted, and who polluted it? That is beautiful.

*AA:* Bound to pay attention. "I heard that you don't die," because you

want to be forever young, "and you don't want to be replaced": you don't want to have children. That's white society! You don't want to die, but you don't want to be replaced either. It's a dichotomy, I can't picture it.
*HL:* I think it's despair. If we continue in our ways, the ways we have followed for hundreds of years, that road is leading us to death. Some people anticipate that. That is why they stop reproducing. I think so.
*AA:* Hm, hm, and they don't look at the environment ...
*HL:* You feel bad for the children because you, as an adult, although you are struggling, have not managed to clean it up for them and make it safe. So people despair.
*AA:* Yes, I suppose that is exactly where I see ...
*HL:* They may not articulate it.
*AA:* Yes. That is a good point. But I also have other messages. I get my inspiration from many sources, right through life, and I don't reject whatever it is that can influence me.
*HL:* I told you about this project that I am hoping to get done. How do you feel about an outsider like myself putting together an anthology? Is that appropriation?
*AA:* Putting together an anthology is not an appropriation, because you are using the words of the people. You are not saying that this is something that I learned, and this is the way "I" see it. An anthology is not an appropriation.
*HL:* Well, that was an issue that was contended by some people very strongly.
*AA:* We are saying that the challenge is that we have to be more careful who does the anthology. That they do a damn good job. That they are good editors, that they pay attention to even the way they put things together, and I think that is their responsibility.

What you have to say to yourself is, well, who is this person, why does he want to put an anthology together? I mean there are people in this country who might say, "Oh, okay, I'll get 3,000 poets, and I will get a dollar from each of them, (Laughs) and I will produce an anthology." And they know nothing about poetry but hire an editor of short stories, and put this kind of person in charge. I am very wary of the person who becomes an expert after a couple of years of reading this kind of material. So for me, we are learning too.
*HL:* Everybody is learning.
*AA:* We are learning. This is a whole new field.
*HL:* This looks good to me.
*AA:* But it is exciting. There is no doubt, for me, this is very exciting.
*HL:* I have used tape recordings like this in classrooms in Germany. Would you have objections if I used this there?
*AA:* Oh, absolutely not.

**HL:** And if I use it like that, is there something you would like to say to young people in Germany, students?

**AA:** I think, whatever your approach, the Nobel Prize is given to all kinds of people writing in all kinds of languages. So there are bodies of literature that you are never going to come across except in translation. You can only hope you have a good translator. You can only hope to have a good transcriber. But when people are writing from their tradition, and they are now transcribing, we have the responsibility to be faithful. Even as we are writing fiction, to write as close to the truth as possible. That we don't put things in there that are foolish, that make the people appear stupid. In this country we have humour that is totally untapped. We haven't gone into that section as yet. There is so much of it among the Native people, and I am just literally bursting, wanting to write in that way. I realize that to be funny is a very hard task because you are transcribing. So that is something that I am going to have to look at.

When students hear somebody like myself speak: listen to how I start my sentence and how I stop it! You will hear something. Just pay close attention. From there you might have an idea of what kind of a person I am. Once you have an idea of what kind of person I may be, you begin to understand what kind of people I come from. I hope that I am a good representative of my people, because their investment in me was one of time, in very difficult situations. They brought me through sickness, they brought me through water, literally, ice water. They brought me through times when it was horribly cold. My mother sewed my moccasins, my shoes. She sewed everything for us. My father hunted in the dead of winter. So, I am a commodity that is hard-won, and I am a very important person in my family. Often this has been a tragedy among Native people, that they were not important enough to their families. Something vital was lost. People like myself were so privileged that I had grandfathers, that I had aunts, uncles, in the family circle, to give me that sense of place.

Consequently, if I bring anything to literature it would be that sense of place, and I hope it comes through in my voice and in the writing. One of my daughters has learned German at Concordia University in Montreal, and because of this interest of hers she has gone to Belgium, France, Europe. She also is looking to understand peoples. She comes from six different nations, from four races. When I think of my daughter who is taking a liberal arts education — she will have been in school now for five years before she gets her degree — what I see is a young woman striving to understand herself. So when students listen to me, they are not only trying to understand me, they are trying to understand their reaction to me. They should analyze that and should something be amiss, should they feel something is not right, they should analyze that. Maybe it is them, or maybe it is me. I think that is the purpose for going for higher education. I think that is all I should say now.

*    *    *

If you ever have a chance, go up to Nistowiak Falls. There you will hear something in the night, and feel something in the night, because as early as 1820 George Nelson travelled through there, and my own family travelled there. In the log books of the Hudson Bay it says that some of my people passed through there. That is in Lac La Ronge, northern Saskatchewan. There are trails through the bush along the Nistowiak Falls that you realize are really ancient. As you spend time in this place, you begin to enter a different realm of reasoning. Your life just slows right down. You become another person.

It is that kind of a place, it is like magic. It is like the magical kingdom, and even the trees are like magic. We took photographs of them, and you could see where the stories come from, because the trees overlap, and they are full of moss. They have different colours during the different times of the day, and you could begin to see shadows almost like "little people" close to the ground, and sometimes you see a great, big tree which just comes out at you like a big giant. You could see that these are the stories that manifest themselves. It is a wonderful place but you could see why these stories were told because they are so much a part of our subconscious.

I think to be a storyteller is to be a privileged person. At the same time, if we are going to see it as an art form, you have to be a person who obeys that muse. You have to obey it. At the same time you have to look at the language, and to see that it obeys you, because it has to say what you want to say. If there is a better word, use it. And if there is a simple word, use it. So it is very tricky. I am finding that I have to work.

One of my uncles, his name is Uncle Bill McKenzie, was a consummate storyteller. He was the one who used to come and tell me stories. So one day, I was three years old, during the war, I had eaten an orange and I was so sick that I decided that I was going to die. So I told my mother, please put me in my wicker rocking chair and give me my blanket and give me my doll because if I am going to die, this is where I want to die. So I am sitting there in front of the stove dying and my uncle came in and I told him, "I am dying." And I am sitting in front of the stove to make sure I am warm while I am dying. Being warm while I am dying! He said, "Okay, I have a story to tell you." And in telling me this story, I forgot that I was going to die! (LAUGHS)

**HL:** (LAUGHS) I like the idea of sitting by a stove to be warm when you are dying.

**AA:** That was the idea. (LAUGHS)

131

*HL:* So there was some hope to be warm when you were dying.

*AA:* Yes, there was hope that somebody was going to rescue me, and it was my uncle because he was able to tell me this story and I forgot my illness. So that is the power of storytelling. It made me forget how ill I was and it had to do with an orange. It started with me eating an orange at a time when we had no fruit, fruit was very scarce.

Many times I used to sit by the stove early in the morning, and he used to pass by our house, I would say by eight-thirty. He would already be coming from where he had been, and passing by our house for his second cup of tea, and my mother would have it there for him. He was on his way home, and he was still 20 minutes from home, so he would come to visit his sister, have tea with her, and then he would say, "What's the matter?" And I would say, "I am too sleepy, and I don't want to go to school." He said, "No, no, don't worry about that. Your sleepiness will pass but in the meantime while you are sleeping and you don't want to move, I will tell you a story." And he would tell me this story and he would suck me in completely. I forgot how sleepy I was, I forgot how grumpy I was, I forgot I didn't want to go to school, and next thing I would say, "I am late, I am late! Where are my clothes? I have to go to school!" So this again is the magic of words.

The other thing that I have to say is that my father decided that we were going to have films in our village. So from the time I was seven years old, we had to pay five cents once a week to go to the movies. We had the projector, and the generator was run by the Canadian Legion. And my father said, "I am going to bring in quality movies!" And everybody wanted cowboy stuff! But once a month I would get to choose a good movie. Consequently, I saw *Casablanca*, all these wonderful stories. Again appreciating another medium, another well-told story, realizing all this time that this is what it is all about. And the commentary that used to come from the people during the story would be really funny! At times they would say, "I saw that rock in last week's movie!" (LAUGHS) They began to recognize the scenery, and my aunt would say, "You damn fool, can't you see what she is doing to you? She is telling you lies!" She would make these comments in the same way that people get so involved. Or they would have a running commentary during a very important scene, and then you knew it was a lousy movie.

*HL:* When I was between nine and eleven, my best friend in school was a farmer's son. They were really very hardworking people, it was just a family farm. I would go there very often, and later on take my bike out there. They were about the first people that I knew who had television. They had this, and in the evening we would all sit in front of it. There would be the grandmother, his father, sister, his mother, he, and myself. And once they showed *Hamlet*. I remember I was so spell-bound! I remember it was the scene with the skull. Neither I nor these people had ever read Shakespeare, or anything of that kind. They were not very well educated in terms of schooling, and the play was even in German. Here was this guy talking, and we were so spell-bound, and all of a sudden, I don't know what made it happen, I "woke up" and I realized that I had tears running down my cheeks, and I turned around. Normally his father, as soon as the news was gone, would be sitting on the couch snoring because he was so tired. He was working all day. Everybody was awake, and the grandmother, and the mother, they were all crying!

I always use that now when I teach classes and I get all these "Oh Shakespeare!" comments. So there must be something there if he can make that happen.

*AA:* So, here you are! And aren't you glad somebody sat down and wrote the *Canterbury Tales*? I am just studying them.

What fascinates me in that tradition, again, is the ability to tell a good story. So in each tradition there is an ability to tell a really good story in whichever form you want to take. I grew up listening to Hemingway, rather hearing about Hemingway, because media really started to pay attention to Hemingway because he was a rather flamboyant character. But then I read *The Old Man and the Sea*, and I began to see the power of this man and the power of the understatement. And I began to see an undertow, that it is possible to have an underlying theme. That too is very, very powerful.

I am a student of literature, and because of the kind of analysis I am doing at the university right now, at the undergraduate level, I am beginning to see. I am already writing. I have already done all of the oral, and because I still like to hear a good story, I am beginning to appreciate the kind of critical analysis I am forced to do in order to get my grades. I am not always successful. Sometimes I am totally wrong but even that I appreciate, because at least I have attempted to understand the story. And if I am mistaken I am told, "No, you look at it from this point of view," and that to me is enhancing to my understanding of the story.

Again going back to the way they hand out the literature prizes or Nobel Prizes, you never know who really is going to get it, and what language, and from whom. So you begin to realize this whole power out in the world. I am thinking of the other writers too. I am thinking of Carl Gustav Jung who is a very popular interpreter of dreams.

*HL:* I read a lot of Jung. I am biased against Jung.

*AA:* The only thing we are interested in as Native people is Jung's attention to dreams, and the passing on of the ancestral.[4] You don't know what it is that gets passed on to us, in terms of memory in the cells, and what is released. I think some of us are born with memory. This is my honest feeling that the template is there. I don't know how it works, but somehow it is there. Because something will be evoked in my memory, and I will think, "Gee, I recognize that as *déja vu*," and it happens to me a heck of a lot. Less and less as I get older. But when I was young, I would be transfixed by a moment and I would not know where it came from.

I think the other writer who pays attention to that is Thomas Merton. He does pay attention to it in his writings, where at different times he has felt that he has been here before. He would analyze it, and then he would work through it, and he'd say, "Well, I have never been here under any other circumstance." There are many occasions like that in my life.

**HL:** Yes, I have had that too.

**AA:** I have been very lucky to have had wonderful storytellers! I lived three years in Trinidad, and right next door to us, the tradition in that family was to tell stories in the evening. Grandmother would lie down in the hammock, and we would all sit on boxes that they have, they were very poor, and they would just start telling stories. Sometimes they would bring the harmonium over, and they would play their East Indian music. There I was able to see again the power of the story, and you had to have very good practitioners. People would come from all over the little village, and they would come and tell their stories. They would talk about their memories, etc. It was just very moving. I cannot forget how that worked.

I always appreciate it when somebody tells me a story. That is the other thing—appreciation. You really have to pay homage to the storyteller. That is something I have always done. I can remember this, I think in *Casablanca*. I said to myself, I appreciate the actress Ingrid Bergman and her ability to say in her tone, "Play it again." I said to myself, "What is it in her voice that says something to me in my heart when she says, "Play it again"? What is she saying to them? I would start to imagine all kinds of things in this very short sentence, the way she says it. All of a sudden I have begun to appreciate something from another aspect of storytelling, and I guess I use that in the performance, I bring it out in a phrase or bring it out in a totally different way.

---

## NOTES

1. For a biography of the Métis socialist teacher and community organizer James Brady and his comrade Malcolm Norris, see: Murray Dobbin, *The One-And-A-Half Men: The Story of Jim Brady and Malcolm Norris, Métis Patriots of the 20th Century* (Regina: Gabriel Dumont Institute, 1981, 1987).

2. Anne Acco, *Eko-si: That is it* (Ottawa: Anne Acco, 1989), 22. (All subsequent references to this text are indicated by page numbers in brackets.)

3. Anne Acco, "Elizabeth," *Canadian Woman Studies/les cahiers de la femme*, 10.2,3 (Summer/Fall 1989): 74.

4. Carl Gustav Jung. *Memories, Dreams, Reflections*, ed. Aniela Jaffé (New York: Random House, 1955).

# HOWARD ADAMS

▼

*Howard Adams was born during the Depression, in St. Louis, a small Métis community on the South Saskatchewan River, south of Prince Albert. He first attended the local public school and then transferred to the only high school available in the vicinity. In his last year he attended the convent in St. Louis, run by Catholic nuns. After moving to the west coast and working at various jobs he attended the University of British Columbia, completed his B.A., and then taught high school in Vancouver for a few years, before entering the graduate program at the University of California in Berkeley. He did his doctoral dissertation on the history of education in Canada, becoming the first Métis Ph.D. During the 1960s and 1970s Howard became one of the most prominent Halfbreed nationalists, whose speeches and actions inspired many Natives in Canada. His book,* Prison of Grass, *a history of the Rebellion of 1885, has become a classic study of (de)colonization. After having taught at the University of Saskatoon and the University of California at Davis, Howard Adams is now "retired" in Vancouver, but returns to Saskatchewan each summer to teach at the University of Saskatchewan and the Gabriel Dumont Institute. He is presently writing a book on Native slavery in Quebec and related issues, and is "busy working on the overthrow of the Mulroney government."*

*The conversation was recorded at his home in Vancouver on 10 October 1990 (copyright Howard Adams/Hartmut Lutz).*

---

**HA:** Cultural nationalism is one of the things we really have to be careful about! That is what the government promotes for us. It funds us for cultural and nationalist activities like "Back to Batoche."

Back to Batoche is a cultural nationalist thing because it has no ideology that goes beyond itself. During the whole ceremonies, for the entire two or three days, nothing is discussed in terms of politics. There is no ideology that promotes a sense of growing, just a superficial nationalism that doesn't go very deep, and doesn't really have any serious meaning. Except, perhaps, that it tells you you can just be an Indian, and be a very traditional Indian, and believe in a lot of myths, and believe in a lot of spirituality, and religion—those things that can become more oppressive and finally drive you back into becoming more conservative.

**HL:** Yes, but people have been colonized, and alienated from who they are, being made to feel ashamed of themselves through school, and church, and all these factors! If they then go back and learn about their own history and traditions, this can strengthen their identity, too, and be a first step towards decolonization.

**HA:** Well, for sure! That is the thing about nationalism! I think nationalism is a great thing for colonized people! In the 1960s and 1970s I was, and I still am, a Métis nationalist. By all means. I was a real promoter of Métis nationalism.

**HL:** Where is the borderline between Métis nationalism—I understand this to be still based on historical knowledge—and cultural nationalism?

**HA:** Well, I don't know whether it has borders. It is so closely interwoven and hangs together in such an integrated way that it is very difficult to separate them. It is really very slippery.

That is the problem that we had in the 1960s and 1970s. We promoted Métis nationalism. You were proud to be a Halfbreed! That was the first thing that had to happen, and that did happen. We were proud to be Halfbreeds. In a sense it was purely psychological and cultural. There was nothing else that we could then base our sense of heritage on. For the first time we realized that we were no longer ashamed of ourselves, but we couldn't define it, or explain why we were proud. But we really were proud. We were proud because we were now able to get out of our ghetto and get out of our ghetto-mentality, and get away from the deep subordination of ourselves.

But that was also filled with a lot of hate. The first expression of it came out as hate for the white man. I have been in meetings where there would be only one or two white men, and a Métis person would stand up and say, "Mr. Chairman, there is a white person here!" That's how nationalistic we were.

**HL:** You know, I have thought about this a lot, being a white person myself. I have been in situations where being white was very uncomfortable. Sometimes, you get a lot of the hatred from people, because of hundreds of years of very negative experiences with white people, and since you have the white face it is directed against you. But the ironic thing about that is, those people who really are convinced racists, against whom the hatred would rightfully be directed, would never even go to those meetings, or even meet with Métis or Indian people on a you-and-I, person-to-person basis. The "liberals," the people who sometimes get all this "racist crap," are the ones who often are actually politically supportive of Native issues. In a way, that is an irony. You experience as a white person a lot of anger shown against you, for very understandable reasons. Sometimes, it can also turn you off.

*HA:* Well, sure it can! It can damn well turn you off.

*HL:* I was interested in the Native struggle originally because I saw and still see it in the larger political perspective of Third World issues, and ecological issues, and class issues. That's largely why I got involved in this, and of course there is also the very German romanticism about Indians.

Then, as I met Native people, I found a lot of friends and people I could talk to about issues that are close to my heart, perhaps even more so than in Europe. But since I am together with Native people, I get some of that hatred, too. More so, I think, when we were in Davis, California, and less here in Canada.

I want to ask you something else, I was asked to contribute to a book on Canadian literature in the 1960s, put together by somebody here at UBC. She asked me to contribute on something that I have done at a conference in Oslo, where I looked into Native literature, and how Native poets address the issue of Canadian nationalism, "O Canada" (the Canadian anthem), and so on. And she said, "Couldn't you do that in the context of this anthology that I am publishing, but the focus is on the 1960s?" And I looked at my sources, and I said, "I can't, because in the 1960s there was no, or hardly any, Native fiction or poetry or drama."

This set my mind thinking. You have been around in the struggle for so long. I thought I would take this opportunity and ask you about the 1960s.

*HA:* No, there was no literature!

Native people were not at all at that level of concern. We were still in the ghettos, and we were still concerned with issues of bread and butter on the table. You cannot talk about culture or literature when you are hungry. So, there was no way! I had tried it, and I would only get insulted from my own people. So, there was no way that we would talk about literature at all. We were just not there!

*HL:* Howard, I like your approach. In the old Marxist way, you always put issues on their feet again. Like saying, "bread and butter come first!"

*HA:* That's right!

*HL:* Sure, I agree with that.

*HA:* (LAUGHS) And that makes sense, you see. But that was 20 years ago, or more. Since that time we have moved along in many different ways.

*HL:* In the 1960s you were starting to think politically, and if you look at the development from then until now, where are the changes?

*HA:* The changes are rather considerable. I teach at the university in Saskatchewan now, and I find a lot of Indian and Métis students at the

137

university. They are there! They are very ambitious in terms of getting an education so that they can get a job, teaching, or into the law profession.

They have a lot of the values of mainstream, whereas in those earlier days we didn't have that. We were at the real level of the ghetto, and we were people with rough, rugged, and violent ways. I don't blame some of us for being very anti-white, as they would put it, because we were living a very oppressive life, and we were very deeply colonized.

Today there are a lot who are decolonized. They have decolonized themselves, and they are able to get along fairly well in the mainstream system. They are fairly sophisticated, they are articulate, they know how to work the mechanisms of the bureaucracy to move ahead. They are now much more confident people. The main thing is that they have developed a sense of pride within themselves. That's the big thing! They have a sense of confidence about themselves. Those are the things that have really changed psychologically.

To a large extent, also, they are in the mainstream of the workforce. They have developed certain skills, and they are into carpentry, and plumbing, and those kinds of things. That's what I see them doing now, and they are moving into academia to some extent.

What I am still unhappy about, and dissatisfied with, is that they are strictly into the professions where they do not do any sort of analytical thinking. They are not into conceptual thinking yet. They are into what is still the narrative kind of thinking, the descriptive way of thinking, chronological and so on. Their mind is not really into conceptualizing, analyzing in an abstract way. They can't really do that. I had my class this summer, and I worked them over.

*HL:* The moment you talk theory ...

*HA:* ... you have lost them!

*HL:* I think that is understandable, and I don't see that necessarily as a deficiency. Maybe it is, though, when you are thinking in political terms, and especially when you come from a Marxist political or theoretical approach, then it is a deficiency. But it is also a reaction, I think, against the Western philosophical tradition, and everything that it entails, i.e., the results of Western ideologies Native people have been subjected to for centuries. Don't you think so? If they say to you, "Okay, you have all those theories! Come down, let the air out! Let's talk about basic issues!," I can understand that!

But I think you are right, there is a deep suspicion against theories!

*HA:* Very.

*HL:* I think that is also something learned from the past, wouldn't you think so?

*HA:* Yes, I would think so. There is a certain suspicion about it. But one thing I wish they would say to me is: "Now listen, Howard, you're presenting theories to us, but they really are Western world theories! They are the white man's theories! We have theories that are Indigenous. They don't correspond, we think differently!" I wish that they would come up with that kind of thinking.

I think there is a possibility that our mind can think differently. I think, over the years, since I've been educated and have become involved in academia, that I do think differently from a white middle-class professor with a Eurocentric perspective. I have a different perspective. I have a different way of analyzing things. That is what I am working on right now. I think it is possible, and I think that should happen for us, because we do grow up as children in different ways.

Earlier, in my day, we grew up with different kinds of institutions around us. The schools we went to were schools where they were all Indigenous kids. So, we all had to think, and talk, as Indigenous kids. The teacher may have been white. He could teach the curriculum, but we could converse, and read, and think in other ways.

For instance, when I left my ghetto I thought that I spoke English well. I was middle-class and thought like English men, and I looked like one, and I thought I had passed. Well, now I find out much later that I didn't pass! Friends, who met me when I came into the mainstream, I have now met again, 30 or so years later, and they said, "Howard, we had a great deal of difficulty understanding you, because your speech was very different. We couldn't figure out whether you were Spanish, or Mexican, or Italian, but you had a different speech that we couldn't understand." But they never told me in those days! They apparently did their best to understand me, and would respond to me without insulting me, because white middle-class people want to be polite! (LAUGHS) And I was probably aggressive and loud. But my speech patterns were different, and obviously my thinking patterns were different too!

I do think there is such a thing as what I just explained.

*HL:* I think so too!

Something that I have thought about a lot, and I wrote something on that, is: Europe has appropriated so much from Native cultures, from other Indigenous cultures, all over the world. Usually they appropriated material goods, but it was not only that, ideas too! One example that I "harp" on and on about is the Great Law of Peace, the Constitution of the Six Nations. If you think that Engels learned from them via Morgan's study, if you think the US Americans have adapted their Constitution after that, and today feminists discuss this! In the Great Law of Peace, there are so many thoughts, it is such an intricate kind of democracy, that people from all over the world, in different centuries, from different countries, from different perspectives, go to it and find,

139

"Well, this is something that can help us in our thinking, and our way of living together in this world!"

I am sure that one would find other examples! I think it is only now that some Europeans, and European intellectuals perhaps foremost, try to decolonize our own minds. We realize how much we have appropriated and displaced over centuries.

Now, Marxism, in the perhaps limited way I see it, hasn't really accommodated some of these issues adequately, for historical reasons I guess. The ecological dimension, I think, is the paramount question really. And if our Mother, the Earth, or whatever we call her, doesn't survive, we can forget about the class struggle, and a lot of other struggles, too!

Those issues have changed some of the Western perspectives! Some have assured us, "Okay, here is Marxist theory, and Leninist theory, and that will answer everything, and help us about solving the problems of the world, the problems of colonization and all that!" But now, there are other issues on top, and I think this is where Native theories, philosophies, and experiences are incredibly important! Not only those of Native people here, but also those of other Indigenous people.

**HA:** Other Indigenous people around the world.

**HL:** Yes, around the world, Fourth World people! And when I say "Native theories," I mean also the whole culture, the way of life, the practices — and that includes the spiritual aspect of all things as well.

So, I think there is a big "rethinking" going on. A lot of the borderlines that have been established artificially, even the borderlines of race and gender, are becoming obsolete, or should be becoming obsolete, in the quest for a coherent ideology, a way of action that will help us all to survive on this planet! So, discussions like the one we had earlier, the "issue" whether somebody is white or non-white, is really immaterial, reactionary really. Although, unfortunately, skin colour is still reflective of a very real inequality of power. I am *not* denying that, because there *is* racism!

The reaction against white people on the side of non-white people, I don't see that as the same kind of racism, as structural racism, which is white racism. Structural racism is white racism throughout the world. What we may experience now, occasionally, as white people, is personal racism. It is not backed up by a whole system of economic, social, cultural power, and oppression. But structural, systemic racism, is white racism.

You know, the Norwegian peace researcher Johan Galtung defined "violence" as a state in which individuals are barred from developing to their full physical and mental potential, and there are various forms, from subtle intimidations to outright killing.[1] And he made a distinction between structural violence, which is inherent in the overall social system, and personal violence, which is individual and not backed by the system. If you apply his categories, racism, sexism, and capitalism are forms of systemic violence, structural violence.

*HA:* Yes, unfortunately racism is among the oppressed people, the Native people, the Indigenous people throughout the world. I somehow know, by having the experience, that racism is the most prominent issue with oppressed people.

With me it was too! Racism was the issue that I reacted to most violently, and with the most spontaneous, instant, violent reaction because racism is, of course, very vivid. That is the thing you can see, the colour of the skin, or the physical features, right away! That is what happens, and why people react to racism.

I didn't look like one, but that didn't mean anything, because where I lived all Adamses were Halfbreeds. Because it is so vivid we would react to it. There is so much hate, and there is so much emotion tied into racism because of that kind of visual experience.

Like in Tyman's book,[2] he would look in the mirror and see that he was part Indian. And then he would react to it violently! White people react to a person who is not white like them, and it is the surface thing. It is what they see most immediately, and they will react to in the most violent way.

Yet I think that racism is an issue that really has to be taken out of the whole struggle, the whole movement. As Native people, I think that we need to play down racism as much as possible, because it doesn't have any real basis of any kind.

*HL:* No, it is tied with other "isms," or it is tied in with colonialism—period! If you think of South Africa, there you have the ultimate of structural racism, which is also structural violence. Or if you think of Nazi Germany, fascism utilizes racism, paradoxically arguing on grounds of biology, although the "visibility" between "German Germans"—whatever mix we are!—and "Jewish Germans" was practically nil in the vast majority of cases. It was the ultimate of biologizing human descent, and the most direct and devastating form of racism in this century, I would still think. So those forms have to be attacked! But usually the ideological side of racism is hooked onto, or is overdetermined with, imperialism or with class in capitalism. This weaving together of oppression via race, sex, or gender, and class makes it so difficult to say, "Where is the root?" Is it in the minds, because racism is something that is in the minds, and so is sexism, whereas class exploitation is something very concrete, man-made, and tangible, and can be altered. You can't alter my skin or my sex, but you can alter attitudes towards these.

*HA:* At one time, in my earlier thinking, I felt that the overthrow of capitalism would get rid of racism. That was my real idea. Anyway, I always wanted to overthrow capitalism ever since I can remember.

(LAUGHS) Because it is the cause of all evils! I used to think that would really do it, because my argument was that racism began when Columbus landed here. But now that I understand the situation much better, I feel that even if we overthrew capitalism and buried it, we would not necessarily be rid of racism.

*HL:* No, I think so too, and that is a big issue. Comrades and colleagues have been discussing that for a long time.

There are examples even from classical Greece where they were calling other people "barbarians," looking down on them, just as racist as you can get! Then there are other theories. Some describe it as a contagious disease. I don't see it like that at all, but if you look at it on a phenomenological level, you could say that it spread like a contagious disease that started in Europe. I don't think it is physically contagious, but it was certainly spread over the world from Europe and became part of a ruler ideology of conquest and imperial subjugation at the beginning of merchant capitalism and colonialization. It was incorporated into a ruler ideology.

*HA:* Then you see the imperialists, the European imperialists! They came over and conquered and subjugated the Native people, and to "legitimize" that they used racism.

*HL:* Sure! And in Africa, the same situation.

*HA:* Everywhere.

*HL:* Everywhere we went, we did the same thing.

*HA:* So, you see, they brought that racist ideology. It permeated the whole society, wherever they went, and wherever they are. And that is here right now! So, racism is bound to be very much a component of society. It is now up to us to get rid of it. It is not easy to get rid of it. It is not easy to get rid of it among ourselves. We have racism in class. I have racism among my own students.

*HL:* I have racism myself, of course! Every day almost, I learn things, and I think, "Oh, you reacted in such and such a way because that person was black, or brown, or something!" I mean I catch myself continually, because I was raised with it.

*HA:* My students, some of them will say, "Well, of course there is racism among the Status, and Non-Status, and the Métis!" There is racism in that area.

*HL:* And that is a good example of racism incorporated in a ruler ideology, incorporated in the "divide and rule" of colonialism.

*HA:* Yes, because Indians live on reserves, under the Indian Act, and have treaties. Therefore they consider that they are better, that they are more "pure" Indian, and things like that. They will condemn the Non-Status, and the Métis.

But there is even racism among the Métis, among ourselves. Some feel that they are better than others and will condemn them, in a sense on the basis of racism. I have heard them say that in my class. So, I would bring up the issue of racism, and they didn't realize that they were talking in racist tones—saying these things against each other is really racist. Sometimes they really condemn white people, and now here they are condemning their own brothers and sisters in the same sort of terms. But they don't catch that, unless you stop them, and make them think about it.

It is understandable with them growing up the way they did, in that kind of a ghetto. Ghettos are really terrible things for developing a mentality that is very unique, or peculiar to a ghetto. Sometimes it is more "ghetto mentality" than it is "Native mentality." That is what one has to think of! "Is this really because I am ghettoized? Is it because I am colonialized?" They go hand-in-glove. But you should be able to sort that out.

Those are the problems we have among ourselves, and, I guess, some of the things that I have too! It is a real problem. I think we will be a long time in resolving it. The Oka affair really brought it out a lot, to show how divided we really are.

*HL:* Yes, I think that really put racism on the agenda, the Châteauguay riots, the stoning of elderly women and men and children, the burning of effigies! We have had it all in Germany, burning books, burning effigies, and then burning people.

*HA:* It didn't surprise me.

*HL:* It didn't surprise me either. I am sorry to say this, but I have always thought that Canada's wonderful reputation, internationally, of being very civilized with regard to Native rights, was a complacent myth. At Oka reality was slapped right into the public's face.

If you listened to some of the politicians, I mean the non-Native politicians, on TV—how little they actually knew about the people they are supposed to be dealing with, and didn't deal with! Nothing about Mohawk sovereignty, nothing about the Six Nations being still an independent, sovereign people, travelling with their own passports in Europe. No indication of knowing that! Reversal to a pattern of behaviour like over a hundred years ago at Batoche, exactly the same pattern!

*HA:* But I had always felt that Canada is definitely a very racist, white supremacist society. After Oka, I'm quite convinced that one could draw parallels to an apartheid system. I don't know how you would describe apartheidism, but I think that is Canada! When you look at it historically, the British Empire went out and colonized Canada, New Zealand, Australia, and Africa. And some of those places became very apartheid, like South Africa, or like Rhodesia, and other places. I don't think that the British system was any different in any of these colonies in which they operated, and the structures and the institutions, the ideologies, the governments they developed were the same structures everywhere.

143

So the Indigenous people in all these countries now suffer under the same kind of apartheidism. It is less severe in some places, but in Canada it may be more severe than elsewhere because it has been hidden so well.

*HL:* Just an example. I talked to somebody at a reception in Regina. He is a lawyer. He asked me where I was working, and so we got talking about the Indian Federated College, and that I was working with Native people, and he said, "Of course we are racist here, nobody can fool me! I have a lot to do with real estate people, and there are certain areas in Regina where real estate people would never show an Indian person a home, because it is a white neighbourhood. There is a very clear colour line, and everybody in the business knows it."

*HA:* Absolutely.

*HL:* And that is "apart-heid." Literally, "apartheid" means something like "the state of keeping apart." That is exactly what it is.

*HA:* So that is apartheidism. Certainly it became obvious in the Oka situation, and it spilled over into the open eyes of Canadian people. I think Canadians were a little bit shocked themselves, to find out that they really support apartheid.

*HL:* I don't know how long this will last, but a lot of non-Native people grew very concerned and very upset.

*HA:* Oh yes.

*HL:* And really also shamed.

*HA:* Yes, ashamed because this went around the world, this was on the news!

*HL:* Yes, and also ashamed of their own society.

*HA:* Oh yes. Part of it was really the fact that they were being revealed around the world as being very racist in their behaviour. They were truly ashamed of it, to feel that the world knows, "We are really racist people. I'm a racist person and I have to accept that because I am part of the Canadian scene." They were disturbed about it. I think it was the first time that they had to deal with the situation personally, in a sense of their own racism, and it bothered them, it disturbed them.

People I would talk to, white people that I would talk to, were really very uptight and very concerned, very disturbed about it. They wanted to talk about it and I felt, "Well, so what, look at yourself! For Christ's sake, you've been like this since the country came into existence, and now you're being concerned! Maybe because you feel that you are being seen for what you really are! The world sees you, and you don't like the picture that the world is seeing of you. So psychologically you are really disturbed about it."

The white friends that we have here in Vancouver, as far as I am concerned they are very typical, white racist, very middle-class people. They are really disturbed about the situation. They wouldn't have any

Indians close to them, or wouldn't have them as their friends or anything like that, unless they behaved exactly like I do—like middle class!

Yes, that's a world problem. Oka really shook up Canada and it will never go back again either! It will not return to the same situation, because the Native people have moved to a different level of understanding, to a political awareness of the situation. Although there are still many Native people who will oppose what the Mohawks did and say that they were wrong in showing such acts of violence and behaving in such negative and disruptive ways.

*HL:* Yes, but that also comes from a very uninformed way of thinking about the monopoly on violence the state reserves for itself.

*HA:* Oh yes.

*HL:* In terms of structural violence and personal violence, the stuff I talked about before. You take the Oka situation, okay? There were some people who picked up guns. But then you see the reaction! See all the APCs, all this massive equipment, hundreds of people! I mean, who has the violence? Who has the monopoly on violence? It is not those Mohawk guys!

Personally, I think picking up guns, being ready to shoot people, I don't like that at all. But I am not blinded by that into saying that the Mohawks are the people who are the most violent. I certainly wouldn't say that.

I think a government that for years and years turns a deaf ear to grievances about land, and then lets one place like Oka go ahead using that land for the expansion of a golf course—who is misusing violence there?

You know what I heard from Mohawk women? When the Sureté du Quebec moved in the warriors were not even at the barricades! They were somewhere else! There were women and children, and when those armed policemen moved in the warriors were alarmed and they had to run all the way back to a certain centre to pick up their guns. Whereas in the news it was reported as if the barricades had been bristling with armed people. All this is going to come out gradually. I think there was much less of the image that was given the public, of everybody with big automatic rifles.

*HA:* I have such a hard time understanding when people talk about violence, and who is behind the violence, and who is ready with the violence? You see the situation as we saw it in Oka, when the government brought out those huge tanks.

*HL:* Yes, instead of addressing the issue politically, they sent somebody to criminalize those people.

*HA:* Tanks and machine guns.

*HL:* Same as Batoche.

*HA:* Same as Batoche! And they killed in Batoche! They came up there to kill! So what the hell reason did we have to think that they may not kill again?

*HL:* Step by step, this is the point that I am making, step by step the same thing. First there are land grievances, and not addressing the issue, until some people finally get so desperate that they decide, "We'll do something about it!," and pick up arms. They send in the police. First, at Duck Lake it was Crozier with his RCMP, who got their licking and had to go back. That didn't work, but Ottawa was still not addressing the issue politically. Same with Oka. After the Sureté du Quebec got their licking and lost one police officer they sent in the army, as at Batoche in 1885. And when the army had finally surrounded them, and they were forced to stop fighting, then those the authorities could get their hands on were handed over to the judicial system for processing, and they were criminalized. This time there will be no hanging in Regina or elsewhere, but some people will go to jail and will be criminalized. And yet, the government can sit back and say, "We solved the problem in a very civilized way, a very clean, legal and 'non-violent,' traditionally Canadian manner, very lawfully!"

But still they will not have addressed the basic issue of who owns the land, which is a political one.

*HA:* Yes, you see, they call it "lawful" and "legal" because that is their way of doing it. As far as I am concerned, as an Indigenous person, I say those are the power structures. They have the institutions, they have the judicial system to make those kinds of laws, and they also have the power to send the police with their guns, the cannons, and the helicopters, to kill if they have to. They have all that kind of power.

As far as I am concerned, as an Indigenous person, if we are really going to have to liberate ourselves, probably it is going to have to be with violence! Because they don't seem to understand anything else, other than violence. They say, "Look, we will not negotiate until you put down your guns!" Well of course, any person who is fighting for his liberation damn well understands better than that! Any person in the world, if he puts down his gun, is totally powerless. He is dead. If I was in a struggle like that I would say, "I will never put down my gun and then decide to negotiate. We are going to negotiate and I am keeping my gun right with me until those negotiations are completed." I am a violent type! I believe in violence. I would have no hesitation to fight, to use a gun, to kill if I have to. I have always believed that. I have no hesitation about violence, not at all. And I think that may be not necessarily because I am an Indigenous person, but because I grew up in the ghetto, a violent place to grow up. That is my belief.

*HL:* There are situations, I think, where violence would probably be the only way to move anything.

146

But I wanted to get back to literature!

*HA:* Yes, okay.

*HL:* See, Howard, I am a white liberal, (LAUGHS) so, of course, I am not comfortable talking about violence!

*HA:* (LAUGHS) You don't have to go into the scenes, or the neighbourhoods, or the ghettos, where there is violence! You can stay out of that if you want to. Mulroney can do the same thing.

*HL:* Yes, he can go fishing. In the news it was reported that his fish hook caught Bush's nose, or something, and he caught two fish and Bush caught three, or whatever. Nice! At the same time the army was marching up on Oka. I think that was sick!

*HA:* That was really sick!

But the thing is true, there are so many other dimensions, or so many other parts of the world, and I am thinking of the Native world that has to grow, and develop, and maneuver in some way, or has to change as we move along, whatever it is. Hopefully it is towards liberation! But in all these dimensions, educationally, literally, or technologically—whatever it is—it has to grow in all dimensions.

I guess, as an academic, I am always concerned that we should grow intellectually and academically. I am always dissatisfied that we are not growing fast enough. That is the problem. We have too damn many people who are sellouts! They are leaders, and they are the collaborators, and they are bought off. They are our oppressors, and that is so typical of the colonial situation.

*HL:* That reminds me of when I asked you earlier, "Where is the progress?," and you said, "Well, there is a new awareness, and a new pride. People are not ashamed any more about who they are, and they are moving into mainstream jobs," and so on. Of course there is a lot of hope attached to that, and it's certainly an improvement in economic terms.

I mentioned to you earlier, José Montoya. He is a Chicano activist, and he said, "Yeah, things have changed! Now, the people who arrest me have got brown faces!" That was how he felt! Affirmative action or similar programs are getting persons of colour into the same oppressive mechanisms. Again there is the "divide and rule" by corrupting people and recruiting them into the police force that holds down other persons of colour, and also by buying them off into nice administrative positions. What do you do against that?

*HA:* That kind of thing is assimilation. To me that is genocide.

*HL:* Yes.

*HA:* And I tell my students, "For sure, you are going to be teachers, you are going into middle-class schools, and you are going to work for middle-class people, and teach middle-class curricula to Native children! In the end that is genocide, because the thing is that those kids and you will

147

have to fit into the system. You will have no other alternative! You cannot go into another uniquely different society that will protect you, where you will be able to function as an individual and make a success out of it. You are going to go into a mainstream system that's going to really continue to oppress you because that is the nature of that society!"

Those are the institutions and the structures we are talking about. They oppress Native people, and they will continue to oppress them even though they have become middle-class people! They are not going to lay off just because they are middle class. I know it. I've been in middle-class society for a hell of a long time, and I would not say that I have been oppressed that much, but I have experienced the same kinds of discrimination to some extent.

But on the other hand, as long as I live in a community where I participate as a white, middle-class person, I am respectable. I follow their rules and their laws, and do everything that is in accordance with that system, but if I started to behave according to an Indian type of way, or according to my ghetto culture, I would become oppressed and dealt with by the oppressive forces, and the institutions, and everything else that exists out there. I couldn't be an Indian.

*HL:* In a way, I think, there are two options, and both are really deadly.

*HA:* Oh yes.

*HL:* On the one hand there is total assimilation, and that is ethnocide, because the people as a people belonging to a distinct ethnic group, and culture, and history, cease to exist as ethnically distinct if they all get absorbed into the mainstream.

If they consciously stay out of that, it is in resistance. It is in poverty. It is in political powerlessness. It is in marginalization, and very often in becoming criminalized, being addicted, being shunted aside into poverty, misery, and destruction of those people as an ethnic group, as well. I think even cultural nationalism can turn into just a new form of ghettoization, in terms of the dominant society.

*HA:* Yes.

*HL:* If people refuse to become absorbed into the mainstream and manage to stay clear of the powerlessness, the abuse, the criminalization, stay proud of their heritage, their identity and say, "Okay, we practice our Indian way now and stay out of politics, stay out of assimilation," then, again, they become totally disempowered in terms of larger society because they are socially and politically marginalized and ineffective.

*HA:* Oh yes.

*HL:* I mean that is a new form of ghettoization, this cultural nationalism.

*HA:* I see what you mean by the idea of cultural nationalism, in the sense that it does move you into a kind of unique group of people that has no base. That kind of cultural nationalism is just a sort of religion, a

148

belief based on a lot of traditional myths that may not even be authentic, that have been contorted and reinforced by white men purposely! That is the real danger of cultural nationalism. All you create is a cultural ghetto, saying that you are Indian, and Indian strictly by culture, by the fact that you dress in a way that is Indian, and you perform in different kinds of dances and ceremonies and rituals that are strictly Indian. You *write* what you think is strictly Indian, the traditional kinds of things that the elders have told you. But what they have exposed, or talked about, handed down, may not have any authenticity. But it really gets you into believing and identifying as "Indian"—through a kind of cultural heritage that may not even be authentic! It may not even be true, and yet you believe it.

On the other hand, what is there to support you in that kind of framework? What you end up having is a cultural ghetto. We are going to have our own schools, we are going to have our own literature, we are going to have our own curriculum, and our own religion, our churches, our sweat lodges, or what the hell ever! All of those kinds of things.

But where is our economic base to support ourselves? Where are our political institutions or forms that are going to be able to create some sort of a sub-state, or a sub-nation of some kind that can get boundaries and definitely has an economic base to it?

*HL:* And a future.

*HA:* And a future, and that you can build into a total society. The whole total society I am thinking of.

*HL:* Yes, I think that's often true.

*HA:* But, you see, how are you going to build a total society that is going to have the kind of economic base where we can be independent? Where we can be sovereign, and we don't have to go with cap in hand to Mulroney and ask him for a handout? Where we are able to manage our own society with its own economic resources and the political system that we have autonomy over, that we are the decision-makers about?

*HL:* I can't see that possibility at all, right now. I guess you are right, and I have always believed this since I woke up politically in the late 1960s. And in a way I'm glad you force me to acknowledge again the somewhat frustrating truth: it can't be solved without the big turnover in society at large, when economic resources and everything will be redistributed. It can't be done in any other way.

Unless you want to say, "Okay, this is my 'homeland,' and this is where I am economically 'independent'"! I mean "homeland" in terms of the homelands of South Africa, or by creating new islands, new ghettos! And that is not the solution!

*HA:* That is not the solution! I guess the thing is, in the 1960s I thought of things differently. But what I think today is that: if as Indigenous people we could not develop our own total society in the ways that I have talked about, in Canada—and that means all of the Indigenous people in Canada would have to come together—then we would have to come together in a common territory, or something like that. There has to be some way, and I haven't figured it out, but I think about it. It means that we must be able to have a common ground somewhere, or we may even have to link up with the Indigenous people of other parts of the world, and only as a compound community or a total government of Indigenous people throughout the world can we form our own international government, and have this kind of exchange.

Unless I could see something like that happening, I don't think I would bother struggling or making attempts, because I just do not see the situation of working in a kind of strictly cultural situation, spending time going over a lot of myths and traditional behaviour and going to ceremonies and sweat lodges. Not that I think they are wrong! I am for them, and I have worked with them, and I believe in them, but I think they are not good enough alone. We cannot stop there.

We have to think beyond, and that's where I think a lot of Native people are at fault. They are not doing that kind of analysis. They are doing a certain kind of, I think, creative work, and advancing some ideas, and enhancing the state of our culture, and our history, and our heritage, which is good. How else are we ever going to start tying together as people, which did happen in the 1960s! But now we have to go beyond that, and I think that is not happening.

Well, maybe it is a good move in the sense that we are now bringing our own literature together. We are trying to define our literature that is Native, so we can understand who we are as a people.

**HL:** I see your book *Prison of Grass* as historiography, and political analysis, and part autobiography. Do you see it as related to Native literature in Canada, as it is being written now? I mean fiction and poetry and all that? Do you see it as part of that, or would you like to see it as a separate, academic approach, which is not the same as the creative approach?

**HA:** I would not want to see it as academic. In fact, I deliberately made an effort not to be! And I tried also doing away with certain things like footnotes. I did it deliberately, because I want Native people to think in other ways than that, and not to see *Prison of Grass* as being a follower of that kind of academic tradition.

The book that I am doing now, on Indian slavery in Quebec, will be a much more Native approach. For instance, I want to see that Natives are centre stage. The history of white man and interpreting about the Indians, that is not what I want to see. I want to see Indians interpreting their own Indian history. They are to be the movers and the shapers of the society that is developed here! I don't want to talk about Sir John A.

Macdonald, and Middleton, and La Vérendrye, and all those people at all. They are not in my book. I want it to show that the Native people were the ones who contributed extensively. I want to show that there were Indigenous structures that were actually functioning at that time. They had institutions that they used that were Indigenous. There were Indigenous ways of teaching each other, a system that functioned that way. I want to get it across that we have an Indigenous way of thinking that is different from that of Eurocentric historians. I want to get away totally from the whole idea of civilization versus savagery.

*HL:* When you say the thinking is different, do you also think so in terms of European, Eurocentric linear thinking as opposed to—this seems to me to come out of Native thinking—opposed to thinking in circles?

*HA:* Absolutely.

*HL:* Which is a much more sophisticated and multidimensional way of thinking, as opposed to the linear, materialist, one-dimensional, "forget about the past, don't think of the future, only think in the now," the Western tradition. I think that is exactly the kind of thinking that has brought the world, with European people as the forerunners, into the dilemma we are in now.

*HA:* Yes, exactly! That is what I want to try and develop! There has got to be some sort of philosophical discussion in it, for sure, because in a holistic kind of thinking, or the thinking that went on ...

*HL:* I don't even mean "holistic" in the way it is used by the New Agers, but I mean "holistic" just as a process where you don't say here's point A, and there's point B, etc., but everything as intricately related, as in system theory, where, when you take just one part out the whole system is changing and restructuring. So, you have to think of the whole thing, and not just the one part you are concerned with. That is the kind of thinking that is much more elaborate.

And this "holistic," multifaceted but at the same time interrelated thinking, in the case of Native traditions, would not only include other people but truly "All My Relations," meaning the whole environment.

*HA:* I think there is a lot of truth in that! I never really paid too much attention because Indians used to always say, "Well, that was our culture," when I think of "in harmony with nature." I have now come to understand there is a lot to that "in harmony with nature."

*HL:* If there is something that I learned in the years of meeting and learning from Native people, it's to think about the circle. To me the circle seems to be the most important concept there is in philosophy, and if we don't come to that structure, we are on the road to death.

*HA:* Well sure, yes.

*HL:* And it is a straight road, a very straight road.

*HA:* That is what I really want to develop in this book! That's why I've

151

taken quite a long time to get it off the ground, because I am having to do a lot of reading, and then a lot of thinking, analyzing and restructuring.

*HL:* Perhaps you can't even adequately put it in the structure of a book, because in that structure there are words going from here to there, and you've got one sentence and *then* the next sentence, and so forth, in a linear process.

But perhaps, what you really have to have is not a book, page by page, but say, a ball, where you have one part and it is related to this, and this, and that, and you can read as many dimensions. And there are some people writing literature along those lines.

*HA:* See, well I am handicapped. I want to talk about Aboriginal things from an Aboriginal perspective and terminology, but I am handicapped by the fact that I grew up after, in the mainstream. I became educated, and very educated, of course—I got my Ph.D. I've been educated into the European system, and the language, and the concepts, and so I am hobbled by that! I find myself that I don't have the vocabulary to express the things that I want to really express in an Aboriginal way because I am really using those European terms, and the kind of philosophy that I got into. So, that really is a very big obstacle for me.

*HL:* In this book, *Minority Literatures in North America*, that Wolfgang Karrer and I did together, we wrote a big introduction, and we started out by saying that "for too long we have learned to dissect in a linear fashion what really is whole." [3] In our discipline, in academia, and in that conference, we had so many discussions about this. It is a learning process that a lot of people in Europe are going through, seeing, "Hey this is not going anywhere!" And in a way we are getting frantic, and that is why some people try to take a shortcut, fly in some Indian gurus, and some "gurus" from here, and take off again in an individualistic New Age cult for the privileged and forget about society! That is not what I am concerned about. But to analyze the process of Western thought, and our social and economic historical development, how it has alienated us from our own surroundings, from other people in our own groups, and has alienated us mainly from nature.

*HA:* Yes, well I guess that was what Marx was saying, wasn't he?

*HL:* Yes, absolutely. Did you ever read this by Russell Means, where he describes Western thought as a continuous process of secularization? [4] In a way he is only addressing one aspect of it, but it is part of this process of alienation. I am not saying, "Try, now, to put in this ritual, by all means, put in the spiritual again, because we have been secularized!" But rather, "Try to understand what has happened in this process! What has happened to our thinking, and what has happened to our attitude towards all forms of life?"

*HA:* You know one thing that really got me involved, and I think it is part of the alienation, is existentialism! That really seemed to speak to me. That really seemed to tell me something about being alienated from myself. And it goes, partly I guess, with the loneliness and everything that I was experiencing in life. Loneliness, because I was away from my own people, my own community.

*HL:* When did you read existentialism? Now, you mean, or when?

*HA:* It would probably be 10 years after I left my community.

*HL:* And it appealed to you?

*HA:* Oh yes.

*HL:* Well, that's the ultimate, in a way, of Western thought, and it makes a lot of sense. Because if you think along the lines of the individual, the final questions are: how do you face death? How do you face loneliness? All these so-called existential questions. But the existentialist insistence on the individual as alone and isolated is also the product of bourgeois individualist thinking, isn't it?

By contrast, think of Vine Deloria's words, which I can't quote by heart, but they are something like this: "To think of an individual as alone would, in a Native tribal way, mean a terrible loss of identity!" [5] Maybe it would mean psychological illness, if the individual is just by her- or himself and not part of a larger web, the extended family, or the tribe. And what we have developed in Europe is this ultimate isolation and loneliness. Maybe I am idealizing, and I don't want to, but I think there still is, in many Native communities, a much greater spirit of sharing, and respect for everybody, and being together. And for people who leave that surrounding and go into the city, that circle is broken, and there is total alienation and isolation.

Well, who am I telling? You went through that!

*HA:* I think that is one quality that still exists with the Native people.

*HL:* Yes, not only Native people here! A lot of other Third and Fourth World people, poor people, working-class people, and even white working-class people. If you read Richard Hoggart's *The Uses of Literacy*, or even if you experience it. Years ago, having been invited to a small mining community in northern England, I was exposed to a totally different atmosphere from the low middle-class background that I come from. The sharing and looking out for the elderly, for the kids, and always sharing, not just in the nuclear immediate family but the whole street, the whole village. It's a totally different culture.

*HA:* Oh yes, that is one thing that still exists.

*HL:* But it is not the kind of culture or value system that gets you ahead.

*HA:* No, no. You see it isn't, and that's the thing when we are going into things like being teachers, and lawyers. I am telling my students, "Now you are into a world where it is highly competitive, let me tell you! You don't share," I said, " and when you write the exam tomorrow, don't share!"

153

# NOTES

1. Johan Galtung, *Strukturelle Gewalt: Beiträge zur Friedens-und Konfliktforschung* (Reinbek: Rowohlt, 1975). [translation of title: *Structural Violence: Contributions to Peace—and Conflict Research*]
2. James Tyman, *Inside Out: An Autobiography of a Native Canadian* (Saskatoon: Fifth House Publishers, 1989).
3. "Too long we have learned to fragment what is really whole, and to dissect complex problems into component parts, thus presenting in linear, written chronology what would really demand a more complex, multi-dimensional and simultaneous capacity for abstraction." *Minority Literatures in North America: Contemporary Perspectives*, eds. Wolfgang Karrer and Hartmut Lutz. (Frankfurt: Peter Lang, 1990), 11.
4. Russell Means, "The Same Ad Song," *Marxism and Native Americans,* ed. Ward Churchill (Boston: South End Press, s.a. [1984?]), 19–33.
5. "The possibility of conceiving of an individual alone in a tribal religious sense is ridiculous. The very complexity of tribal life and the interdependence of people on one another makes this conception improbable at best, a terrifying loss of identity at worst." Vine Deloria, jr., *God Is Red* (New York: Dell Publications, 1973), 203.

# DANIEL DAVID MOSES

▼

*Daniel David Moses (Delaware) grew up on the Six Nations Reserve near Brantford, Ontario. He holds an M.F.A. in Creative Writing from the University of British Columbia, and he is one of the few full-time professional Native writers in Canada. He has published two books of poetry,* Delicate Bodies *(1980) and* The White Line *(1990), and a play in two acts,* Coyote City *(1990). As past president of the Association for Native Development in the Performing and Visual Arts, and as a former director of Native Earth Performing Arts, Inc., Daniel David Moses has been untiring in his support for Native artists and writers in Canada. His poems have won him international recognition, having been anthologized in numerous publications, including the prestigious* Harper's Anthology of 20th Century Native American Poetry *(1987). He lives in Toronto.*

*The conversation was recorded on 25 October 1990 at the "Vancouver International Writers' Festival" at the Festival Center on Granville Island, Vancouver, British Columbia (copyright: Daniel David Moses/Hartmut Lutz).*

---

**HL:** How did you start writing? What made you write, what makes you write?

**DDM:** I guess "pleasure" is the simplest answer. I know that at a certain point in high school I had decided that I needed to be an artist. I was concerned about all those things that were talked about when I went to church, but the church wasn't doing it.

**HL:** Which church was that?

**DDM:** It was an Anglican mission on our reserve. I think that I was being very practical. Having listened to people say that an artist's was a difficult and impoverished life, I was just thinking about pencil and paper not being expensive!

At that point, I had already had a number of experiences in doing work for school, where, in the composition of a piece, I had entered that state of mind where you are totally involved in what you are doing, and there is just a real excitement that a story is coming out.

*HL:*    So you said that by the middle of high school?

*DDM:* That would be about grade 11. I think at that point I had decided that somehow or other I would focus on writing. I had become aware that language itself is a centre to many things in the way society operates, and it would be useful to pay attention to it.

*HL:*    Do you speak any other languages besides English?

*DDM:* I can get by with a patient person in French. In high school I also studied Latin as long as I could, and I feel like that was of real value.

*HL:*    In what terms?

*DDM:* Just because it gave me a sense of the deeper meanings of words. I would compare it to the things I have heard of the nature of Cree, or Ojibway. They sound like very image-based languages; the roots of the meanings are right on the surface, and I feel that by having some knowledge of the roots of our modern languages, we can have a similar experience.

I use the example that my friend Lenore (Keeshig-Tobias) talks about. When someone first brought a kettle into their community, there was no Ojibway word for "kettle." But they did have a word for "pail," and they did have a word for "duck," so the word for kettle is now "duck-pail."

It reminded me of Tomson (Highway) talking about when you are speaking Cree, you always feel that you want to break out in laughter. It struck me that if your entire language was made up of images like that, of course you would want to laugh when speaking the language!

*HL:*    That is true, even though English is in many ways very abstract. If you think of Latin, that is pretty abstract too, I think. The other influence of course in English is from Germanic languages, and in the region where I come from, they still speak "Plattdütsch" (Low German), which is very close to English, or rather, English is still very close to that. In our "official" language, "Hochdeutsch" (High German), one example is the word for hippopotamus. We call it "Flußpferd," which means river-horse; or, rhinoceros which is "Nashorn" which means nose-horn.

I think I know what you are talking about.

*DDM:* I have this feeling that it really connects to a part of the imagination which has to do with metamorphosis, with transformation, with possibility, that I think is also—just because I am talking in those terms— connected to our physical beings, a part of the imagination that in contemporary culture we don't see much of. I think it has to do with that denial of our physical realities that goes on.

The only place we seem to run into that sort of imagining is in horror films, for example. I saw a show of Inuit sculpture recently by a friend

156

of mine, where he was using the conventions of Inuit sculpture that have to do with shamanism, as well as, say, our daily dilemmas. But because he works in a city, he is aware of the usefulness of naturalistic details. Suddenly, they jump out at you like that part of the imagination. Because there are these details from our everyday life in the middle of fantastic things. I was quite excited by it.

*HL:* I think that is something that struck me in your poetry! Very often you take very ordinary little everyday things, and write about them. But through the way you write about them, and the way you portray them, they acquire a totally new dimension, and we see them in a way that we would never have seen them before! For example, the one where you write about the fingers,[1] things like that. So the visual aspects seem to be very important. You see something, and describe it in terms I think most other people have never imagined or seen before, I guess. And thus you help us to see things anew.

*DDM:* I think I am really interested in visualizing, and I think it is part of the conventions of modern literature; I mean we talk about images, and the first thing that comes to mind is visual imagery, even though images also mean other sorts of sensation.

For me, it is also very deeply rooted in my own body, in my own poor eyesight. I had the "good fortune" to have somewhat of a "quack" for an optometrist when I was a child, a man who believed that if you force the eyes to work they would cure themselves. So I went for a year with inadequate prescription lenses, during which time, of course, my eyes deteriorated. But he also believed that television is no good for you, and it was during that year that I first really got hooked on reading. So through that bad luck of having this quack for an optometrist—after that my parents took me away from him, and took me to someone who gave me glasses that would do the job, and would not cause me headaches, and would not give me problems!—my going through that piece of bad luck, I mean, has probably given me this direction to my life where not only am I someone who is interested in words but who is also interested very much in seeing things clearly.

And that results in the visual imagery, and also results in being a movie addict. Where I live in Toronto is right on the subway line, which gives me direct access to three repertory cinemas, and when I first moved into Toronto, for the first couple of years, I would see four or five, up to eight or ten movies a week. And that was just evenings!

*HL:* When you think about yourself as a writer, or poet, or dramatist, how would you like to see yourself best? As a poet, or dramatist, or as a writer, as a Native writer? Do you think in those terms at all when you think about yourself as an author?

*DDM:* I guess, if I had to use any terms, I think I would hope to become a storyteller. I'm actually gradually moving towards the idea of gathering a repertoire to actually be a real storyteller in the traditional sense. I find that what I value in the use of language comes from that idea of an oral presentation. As much as I can appreciate the beauty of poems on the page, and can appreciate the concepts behind things like concrete poetry, I find that they don't move me as deeply as something I can hear from someone else's mouth.

**HL:** Were you exposed to that kind of storytelling a lot as a child?

**DDM:** No. My family was Christianized with my great-great-grandfather's generation. To that point our family name was "Cornelius." His first name at the time was Moses, and when he converted to Christianity, he just flipped his name around and became Cornelius Moses.

But I think that my sense of the beauty of the English language probably is rooted in going to that Anglican mission on our reserve, and reading the prayer book, and hearing hymns.

**HL:** Did you go to an all Indian school on the reserve, or was it a mixed school?

**DDM:** Well, it was basically all Indian. There were always a few white kids living on the reserve, whether their parents were working there, or whether they just married into our families.

Ours is such a big community, and such an old established one, that I was really never aware that there was a problem of racism anywhere else. It was only once I got off the reserve that I ...

**HL:** When was that?

**DDM:** When I finally went away to university, then I spent a large amount of time off the reserve. I mean, certainly, prior to that I would go off for vacations and things, and to visit relatives and friends, but before university I just hadn't experienced the ...

I guess I'd always assumed that the way people treated each other on our reserve was Christian, and when I was off the reserve and saw how Christianity was functioning out there I had to question my assumptions about the way we were behaving. And I think we were really behaving like Indians! But we were calling ourselves Christians, not to upset anybody.

**HL:** Are you a Christian these days?

**DDM:** No.

**HL:** I didn't expect that.

So when you now use Native traditions like the Coyote story that you said came from the Nez Percé, if you use Native materials, mythology or oral tradition, historiography, are those contents that you have learned in later life through reading, through hearing, observing?

**DDM:** Yes! I had a bit of luck when I was going to university. At that time the education branch of the Department of Indian Affairs was putting together a bibliography of books by or about Indians, and they hired Native students in the summers to come to Ottawa and compile this annotated bibliography.

So, basically, for I guess three summers, I would read on average a book a day about a Native subject. So even though I don't have a mind that holds on to detail, I have this big reservoir of almost an intuitive sense of how different Native cultures operate, just because I've done enough reading to get me two or three degrees.

**HL:** Sure, it accumulates!

When you said that you would like to eventually become a storyteller and accumulate enough stories for a repertoire, could you see yourself then as a storyteller who travels around and addresses audiences, works with schools, or communities? Who would you tell the stories to? Who would you want to tell the stories to?

**DDM:** I guess, basically, I would like to talk to adult audiences. I have not been able to quite understand the separation of children from adults in mainstream culture, and as a child I always resented being treated like a child. And I do my best not to do that to any young person. It's really dispiriting. It's a form of cruelty, I think.

**HL:** When you write, or tell stories, or start bringing something together, do you have specific audiences in mind, and do you write for, say, a Native audience, or a mixed audience?

**DDM:** I don't usually think about an audience to begin with. I usually have a story that excites me, or a way of telling a story that excites me, and I believe that if I can write it and instill the piece with my own excitement, that I shouldn't have to worry about a particular audience. I mean, once again, I think it's a similar thing to seeing children as a separate audience. I really believe just from, well, my own experience of having grown up and seeing a lot of things that are not necessarily meant for children.

I can remember when I was in public school, in grade four, finding a copy of *Gulliver's Travels* in the school library, and knowing about it from children's versions or movies, and deciding that I would read this big book, and finding it a real challenge. I'm sure I didn't understand all of it, but I read it, and I got out of it what I needed. Yes, I've gone back to it since.

Basically, I believe that to say, "This is for children, and this is for adults," I mean, that seems to me a form of censorship.

**HL:** It is! And it is intriguing, if you think of the Western literary tradition, European literary tradition, that so many of the historically very important books later on were termed "Children's Literature."

You think of *Robinson Crusoe* as the expression of modern man, entrepreneur, colonialist, slave owner, and whatever he is, but he incarnates some ideals of that time, which I would say, now, are the wrong ideals. But still, it is a very important book, and it certainly was not written for children. *Gulliver's Travels*, being a satire with very direct political comments, all of a sudden has all the edges taken out, and it's turned into children's literature! That's an amazing process!

It also shows that children are not really taken seriously, because a lot of the good stuff is taken out.

**DDM:** Yes, I believe you can come to a piece of work, and you find what you need in that piece of work.

**HL:** So, when people read your poetry—I guess when you read it, you have certain images that you associate with that, and you interpret it your way, the way you wrote it. Now, I usually tell my students, "Listen, your reading may be totally different from what the author intended, but I still think it's an important reading because the text is a link in a chain of communication. Even though you don't know the author, you bring something to it, you find it, and it's like a mirror, and you have an experience. Somebody else has a different one. There's no gospel truth!" That's what I feel.

I don't know, but do you feel like that as an author too? Or do you feel that people read something into a poem that's not in there?

**DDM:** No, I mean, I have on occasion run across some pretty wild interpretations of things I've written, and I mean, certainly, I cannot make those connections, and I don't understand where what these people are talking about has come from.

But I believe that once I've completed a piece of work, and put it out into the public, that it is separate from me, and that what people can give to or take from it is part of the process of the way art articulates and embodies the values of our society. I do not believe that I have control over that. I have control over my writing, over that technique.

**HL:** In the moment that you write it, right?

**DDM:** Yes.

**HL:** And when it's finished and out there, it's out there. It's on its own. Yes, I think so too. I know that a lot of writers are very uncomfortable with that, and I guess some Native writers perhaps too. If they put something out, and non-Natives read it and see something quite different in it, that must be very painful at times, I guess.

Do you see yourself at all, very prominently, as a Native writer or just as a contemporary poet? Or is that a racist question?

**DDM:** I guess just for practical concerns I'd like to call myself a Native writer. I use this example all the time, but I heard an interview on national radio with a 19-year-old Cree man, who at that point was an ex-alcoholic, -drug addict, -street prostitute, and he told the interviewer, "Well, as I was growing up, it was the only choice we had, to be on the streets!" And

I think it's really important for people to know that I'm a Native person, and that there are other choices in life, that being a writer is not something only mainstream people do.

When I go into the centre of myself, the labels of "Native," or "writer," or "male," are not there!

I was told by parts of my family that, even though as I said, we've been Christianized for a while now, I'm a member of the Bear clan. Now, because I don't have the connections to know what that means, I'm making my own connections, and it's become important to me. Every once in a while a bear poem pops out of me, and I'm not sure where it's coming from, but I think it's some sort of psychic relic, or psychic creation, that's just indicative of my own maturing, my own spiritual journey.

**HL:**   Do you think there is something like the collective unconscious that you tap into, that is inherited?

**DDM:** The inheritance idea bugs me. But I really do think that there is something that functions in culture. I mean, just in language itself, and even if we are not consciously aware of all those under-meanings that I was talking about earlier, I think that they function.

**HL:**   Oh yes, okay. So it would be not in the Jungian sense, something you inherit, but something that is part of the culture, and that people can tap into. And that is acquired through each person's individual socialization. That's the way I also see it.

I'm not very happy about Jung's concept at all, I mean because of the inheritance idea. I heard that he even went as far at one stage, although he was safely in Switzerland, to talk about a "Semitic" and an "Arian" collective unconscious, and that's exactly where I throw up.

Here in Canadian literature, for years and years, there was a lot of myth criticism, and still is, I guess. Some of it, I think, comes from Jung in the long run, although Northrop Frye and other people are part of the linkages in there. But those ideas about inherited psychic or even mental characteristics for me are politically or ideologically suspect, exactly because of this inheritance idea. The next step is, "It's in the blood!," and I don't go for that at all.

**DDM:** I really am troubled by people who use the word "race," because scientifically we are all one race. We have different physical characteristics, and we've gotten into the bad habit of thinking that makes us different. But I mean, I try always to use the word "culture," because I think that forces people to apprehend that it is the differences in the way we live our lives that are at the real root of our conflict.

**HL:**   I absolutely agree with you! I mean, most people in Germany wouldn't at this stage, but I certainly do! One of my colleagues is a black German. She's doing my job right now, while I'm away. Being German

161

is a cultural thing. That's what she is, that's the language, that's how she lives. It has nothing to do with skin colour. I agree with you absolutely!

That's why I was worried whether you feel that it may be a racist question, or uncomfortable question, the categorization "Is this a Native author or a non-Native author?" But the way you explained this from the culture makes a lot of sense to me.

If you take that concept, the culture concept, what do you think? Are there some common structures that distinguish Native writing, Native literature, from mainstream literature? Where would you see that?

**DDM:** We seem to be developing some sort of dialogue on aesthetic concerns. This may be simply because these are my own concerns. The oralness, or orality, storytelling—it seems to me that in the other Native writers I met those are common concerns, aesthetically.

But I also think that we have come to the point where we are consciously aware of the traditional values of our society: of respect for the other person as an individual spirit—that particular value is a much clearer way of positing for democracy than the Western democracies have—and of our parallel value of respect for the Earth, of the environment as a living entity that's connected to us in the sense of being our Mother. That is certainly a more viable way of living our lives on this planet, and making sure that those of us who have children will have a way to live, and a place to be.

We were talking about our names earlier, and I have always resisted becoming the prophet that "Moses" implied. (LAUGHS)

**HL:** I thought, when I saw your name, Daniel David Moses, "God, that guy is carrying quite a load!" That was my reaction.

**DDM:** In my own thinking, and in the thinking of my friends, and in the way the world is going, with the collapse of what was happening on the other side of the curtain, and the smugness that is going on here, even though we have problems here that are as great and as threatening to the human spirit as any that were happening there, I mean, they seem to me to be parts of just one system with two sides. I'm getting so that I feel like I have to explain that this is where the writing is coming from, this concern for larger things.

**HL:** That's what you have in common with a lot of other Native people!

**DDM:** My first book of poetry was lyrical, was personal, about my family.[2] And the reception that I did get, although it was limited, was: people liked it. I could have easily gone on writing those sorts of poems, and I can still write those sorts of poems, but I thought that I had to find other ways of writing, things that would allow me to address larger issues. Because, at root for me writing is a spiritual thing. Spiritual, just in the sense of what it all means, what are our values.

**HL:** Talking about Native literature: you said it has to do with a place,

162

a sort of spiritual place it comes from. This is what I heard from other writers too, and I think it comes through in a lot of Native writing. Maria Campbell said it comes from the Mother. The language comes from the Mother, and the way of seeing things!

If you think of the Native oral tradition and contemporary Native writing, the whole range, would you sort of apply categories like "drama" and "poetry"? Those genre categories, are they meaningful, or how would you treat the whole body of texts?

*DDM:* I find that I am dissatisfied with those genres. I'm not sure whether it's simply sort of a natural resistance to codifying something that seems to be in the process of developing. You don't want to give something a wrong name before it's really been born. Or whether it would be just simply a mistake to accept those genre forms when, perhaps—I think I'm repeating myself here. (LAUGHS)

I think we have an opportunity here with the influence of an oral aesthetic, to develop things that go beyond those genres, which are categories that are very much a result of a book culture.

*HL:* You know, when I look at Native writing in Canada, what I know about it, and then I read Native writing coming from the US, there are quite a few differences! I was always wondering, "Why is there so much more drama in Canada as compared to the US?" (Now I've used one of those categories!) And I think, I thought, okay, partly it's the government policy, and Tomson Highway indicated that as one of the influences too, because there *are* subsidized theatre companies and so on, which don't exist in the US. But that couldn't be all, and then I think the most meaningful answer I got to it, and I hadn't thought about it in those terms, was Tomson Highway explaining how drama is the kind of artistic expression that is closest to the oral tradition.

And if you look at most of Native writing in Canada, that distinguishes it very much from a lot of very good, very famous writing out of the US. It seems to me much closer, in general, to the oral tradition, to the storytelling traditions, whereas the most prominent authors writing in the US are people who are often English professors, who work within that Western literate and even academic tradition, and blend it with Native cultural elements they also have access to.

Would you say that this makes sense to you?

*DDM:* That seems true to me. I actually haven't read all that much of the American writers. The ones I've come across, most of them, seem to have beautiful writing, but it's writing that for me is often too beautiful. It has lost its impulse, or whatever is telling the story. There's a certain point where, I guess, it becomes art for art's sake rather than for the story's sake, or for communication's sake. And, I mean, I distrust some of my own work that has become that beautiful. I think it's somehow smug and self-satisfied, and I try not to do that.

*HL:* When you say that, which text do you think of?

*DDM:* There are a few poems in the new book that are. I think of my editor saying, "God, I wish I'd written that," and I was thinking, "I'm not as satisfied with having done it!"

Let's see, which one did she say? "Passing Above the Black River," for instance. I mean it's a sequence of lovely images. I think it gets the experience across, but somehow, I think it's too pretty. And the actual drama gets lost. There is a story, too, in there. It ends up being perhaps over-refined.

*H.L:* That turns it also into an academic literary tradition, almost, if you say it's too refined. Or am I off the track?

*DDM:* Yes, that's a good description of it.

*HL:* That somebody who knows a lot about writing would say that's beautiful writing.

*DDM:* I think it has to do with my moving into the ideas of writing as performance, where you come to realize that every performance is unique, and has its own beauties, and that the obsessiveness one gets when one's writing poetry—one wants to get everything right—at a certain point, it's just wasting one's time.

I've learned in writing plays that you can get your message across without having every word the way you want it, and that there are times when your actors can just not handle some of the things you are doing.

*HL:* So you worked with actors when *Coyote City*³ was produced, right? Did you work with a cast?

*DDM:* Yes, and it's very important in the process, just to make sure it's all working.

*HL:* Do you find that when you are working with actors who are putting it on stage, you revise the play?

*DDM:* I did certainly. I removed one long sequence from the play.

*HL:* What made you do that? Did you realize it didn't work on the stage, or it was not dramatic, or theatrical?

*DDM:* It wasn't working on the stage, and the necessary information I was able to integrate into other scenes. It was just slowing down the play. It wasn't as alive as the rest of the piece.

*HL:* I asked you this earlier when we were eating lunch: I realized in reading *Coyote City*, that there is the "Orpheus and Eurydice" myth in there, or at least that's what I "recognized" in it. Also, it is a story, or a play, that happens while the story, the Native story it is based on, is being told. So, it is also a play about telling a story, or a story fulfilling itself, or whatever you call it. What I wondered was, if you consciously blended the Greek tradition and the Native tradition?

*DDM:* Well, actually, it was the Native traditional story that got me going!

I mean, I sort of vaguely remember that there was a Greek one that ...
**HL:**    Oh I see, so that didn't influence you at all then?
**DDM:** Well, very peripherálly. But it's really "Coyote and the Shadow People." Lenore Keeshig-Tobias showed me that story one day. And it really went to my heart, and I knew that something would grow from it.

Attempting to tell the story while the play was happening was my first experiment of trying to deal with the different ways of presenting. Actually, I think we've come to term that sort of element in a play as "presentational" as opposed to "lyrical" or "poetic" elements.
**HL:**    Is it also a play about a story, where, while you tell the story, what you tell in the story begins to happen? The reason I'm saying this is that two of Leslie Silko's writings, the short story "Storyteller" and her novel *Ceremony* as well, both are, in a way, about words having effect beyond words, or about a story having to be told, so it can fulfil itself. I saw a parallel in *Coyote City*.

But maybe, I'm off the track there, or did you let the story be told as sort of background information, say, this is what it's based on?
**DDM:** Certainly, that, I think, is the way it functions when you watch.

But as I was making it, I was really dealing with the individual character's psychology. So it was for the character of Boo, this is what she has to hold onto through the play. And equally for Johnny, this is part of Johnny's problem. And that it worked out, that I managed to tell most of that story in the play through those character's dilemmas, is both luck and art.

That, in the final analysis, it plays for the audience as something ceremonial, something that has to do with story as guide or representation of life, that is the broader thing that one hopes will happen!
**HL:**    I think that is at the root of a lot of beliefs, and stories, and myths, or whatever. Even if you think in Christian terms: "In the beginning there was the word." There is a conviction that words have a power beyond what I see on the written page.

I thought one could see that play also as a documentation that there are some stories which fulfil themselves. If you then take a European audience, seeing that and not being aware, only learning about that Coyote story through the play, but "recognizing" some of the stuff that is going on in the play because they know the Greek myth—I think that would seem to document that there are certain stories which people are familiar with, or relate to, from various cultures. And I find that very intriguing, maybe because I'm a non-Native person.
**DDM:** It is one of those great human dilemmas that love and death come together like that. Those simple human situations, I mean, are common to all cultures, and I think there are arguments for there being certain stories that you will find again and again. But I have to caution people that there

165

are only a certain number of those stories, and not all stories are the same.

I can remember hearing one of the more popular children's entertainers and storytellers in the city of Toronto talking about how he really believed that stories were for everybody and everybody could share stories, which is a very nice, liberal thing to say. And then he went on to talk about how he had gone up into an Inuit community, and how they told stories back and forth. And, just by the way, he mentioned the fact that in about 75 percent of the stories he didn't understand what they were talking about! He didn't get it, and they didn't get what he was talking about. I mean, most of our stories are based on our separate cultures.

And this goes into the appropriation thing. It's when people from the opposite culture try and tell those stories, they don't know what's going on. They are just going to screw them up. I mean that's what's getting us upset. You say you want the freedom to tell our stories, and then you just screw it up. Freedom of the imagination shouldn't be the freedom to destroy.

**HL:**    I think it's also the clash between an oral way of transmitting stories, and a written, recorded way.

For example, there is a written story, and maybe there's an alternative version somewhere, then I can compare them, and find out which version may be the "truer" one. But if it's an oral story that is handed down, again and again, verbatim, then the word-by-word accuracy becomes much more essential than for a story that is written down. And if you come with a frame of mind that a story is written down anyway, or is somewhere preserved in a book which anybody can read, then I can tell it to somebody else, and if it is not accurate, the "true" version is still intact in the written form. In that case, you don't see how important it is that everything is really given verbatim.

But in the oral tradition, the particular story only happens at that moment when the story is told, and if you change something, you change it altogether. If there's an error in something written, you can often do a collage, or pastiche, and look at other versions of that story and say, "okay, there's something wrong here," and you can trace it back. But if it's told, you can't.

And if you take something out of the oral tradition, and write it down, and there's a mistake in it, that mistake stays. This is just part of the technical side. I think the underlying question is the colonial appropriation and the displacement of origin.

**DDM:** Yes. And finally, I mean after all the arguments about the philosophy and the aesthetics that well up in the appropriation debate, we just keep seeing people making money off our stuff! I mean it seems as if that's the only reason they're suddenly interested in our stuff, because we've been working hard to get attention, and now that we're getting attention, they just want a share of our rewards.

**HL:**    It's true. So how do you feel about *this* project?

**DDM:** I think it's useful.

I think this has been, certainly for me, an opportunity to articulate some things. I mean, normally, I just sort of go my way doing my work. It's an opportunity for me to hear what I think. I'm one of those people who sort of doesn't know what I think until someone asks me.

**HL:**    Yes, well, I think a lot of people feel that, I mean, about themselves.

Are there certain writers, Native or non-Native, that have influenced you in your writing? In your thinking?

**DDM:** Well, certainly Lenore Keeshig-Tobias has. For this last decade, we have shared our thoughts, and our work, and our concerns. I guess beyond that I feel that I just hooked onto anyone whose writing has been sufficiently oral to excite or intrigue me.

**HL:**    You mentioned *Gulliver's Travels* earlier. Could you mention some other texts that intrigued you for a long time?

**DDM:** I go back to the plays of Joe Orton. I go back to the plays of Chekhov. I go back to the darker plays of Shakespeare, the tragedies. I discovered Sylvia Plath long before she got martyrized. Emily Dickinson, Gerald Manley Hopkins, e.e. cummings. I mean, I really am up with the pleasure of language. So it's those people who do interesting things with the language, who make things out of it.

I've made two words so far. (LAUGHS) I've stuck them in poems and they've gotten by.

**HL:**    Which words?

**DDM:** "Shrinkling." And what was the other one? It was sort of a back formation, I think, "conflagrate" as a verb, because "conflagration" in English is a noun. I couldn't find a verb, but I needed it.

**HL:**    You know English is limited in some ways. It's very difficult to create new words. It's easier in some other languages, where, in German for example, you can create new nouns all the time by just hooking several together until you get the exact meaning. And sometimes you can turn that into a verb too, although it's not done all the time. But I think that's very difficult in English, and I can see why you are happy about having done those verbs, because that's a difficult achievement.

If you had to teach a course on Native literature in Canada, which texts would you include?

**DDM:** *Halfbreed*! *The Rez Sisters*—it's the better of the plays so far.

I don't really want to go on. I just feel like I'm naming my friends.

**HL:**    Okay, you might get into dire straits and conflicts with other contributors here, "why did he leave me out?" Maybe I shouldn't have asked that.

Do you find there is a good anthology in poetry, of Canadian Native writers? Actually I can answer that myself, I don't think there's a representative one.

**DDM:** I don't think so.

**HL:**   Not yet. There are various regional collections. Similarly with short stories. Well, *All My Relations* is doing it now, I guess, in the way of short stories.

**DDM:** It's just such a big job! I mean, a lot of the people who are doing the writing are not doing it professionally yet. So it really is just difficult to get that work done, but it is coming. People are beginning to see that it is important work, that it's not just something that they do in their spare time, that it is something that can be—I say this a lot, but it is not a cliché—an honourable way to live your life.

**HL:**   Is there anything that you would like to add?

**DDM:** I guess, I hesitate to sound millennial, but I really do feel that some of the things that I'm saying, some things the other Native people are saying, are essential things for our life here on the planet, and I hope people can hear them.

---

## NOTES

1. Daniel David Moses, "The Hands," *The White Line* (Saskatoon: Fifth House, 1990).
2. Daniel David Moses, *Delicate Bodies* (Vancouver, B.C.: blewointmentpress, 1980).
3. Daniel David Moses, *Coyote City: A Play in Two Acts* (Stratford, Ont.: Williams-Wallace Publishers, 1990).

# LEE MARACLE

▼

*Lee Maracle (Métis) grew up in a poor working-class neighbourhood in North Vancouver. During her adolescence and young adult life, she drifted between Chicano communities in California, skid row in Toronto, and her Vancouver urban environment. These years are depicted in* Bobbi Lee: Indian Rebel *(1975) her as-told-to autobiography, which was republished in an expanded version in 1990. Throughout her life, Lee Maracle and her family have been involved in the struggle of oppressed people for the humanity that every person has the right to experience and express. Her second monograph,* I Am Woman *(1988), is the literary expression of that struggle.*

*Besides being a dedicated mother and an untiring community worker, Lee has spoken and written on many occasions about Native culture and politics, and has edited the works of other Native authors. Her essays and poetry have appeared in journals, magazines, and anthologies. In 1990 she co-edited and contributed substantially to* Telling It: Women and Language Across Cultures.

*The conversation with Lee Maracle was recorded on 27 October 1990, at the Vancouver Hotel during the "Vancouver International Writers' Workshop," the morning after she and her daughters had performed, together with many other Native cultural workers, writers, and activists, at the "First Nations Cabaret," organized by her husband, Dennis* (copyright: Lee Maracle/Hartmut Lutz).

---

**HL:** I have one question about your first book, *Indian Rebel*. In the English language introduction it says that it's based on tape recordings, and at another time when we talked, you said, "No," you wrote it. So how was that put together?

**LM:** It was part of a course I was taking on how to do life histories. We each did each other's. I did my partner's, he did mine, and I helped transcribe them. Because the oral presentation was quite good they decided to publish it.

**HL:** Is most of it verbatim?

**LM:** Well, not really. They had to shrink it down, gravely. There were 80 hours of tapes to that story. It was quite long, there's about three inches of manuscript. In the taping I had the same problems with hearing my voice as you had when you first interviewed me. So, some of it is pretty mixed up. Some of the events didn't happen the way they are presented in the book. But I left it the way it was. I wanted to redo the whole thing, more in the voice that I actually spoke in. There were moments of almost poetry in the spoken version, in the transcription. But it would have made what they call "uneven narrative" in English. So the editors made the decision to make it all even throughout.

I wouldn't have done it that way. I'm planning to write a novel and it's not going to be an even voice, because here the speakers try not to use their own voice. They try to let the voice reflect the subject. Just a different way of speaking.

**HL:** Well it comes across as something that is, as you said, "even," that's round in itself. And if you say it was always the same chronology as events happened—but it's like flashbacks. So I reread it ...

**LM:** It's not chronology! The chronology is there, but sometimes it's doing what I'm doing, and I'm doing what it's doing.

**HL:** No, but I reread it, and it's really a very straight and very readable narrative!

**LM:** Yes, so I decided to leave it that way.

**HL:** About *I Am Woman*. When we were on the phone the other day, you said it comes from the oral tradition. I thought I'd like to tell you how I saw that book, and maybe get your reaction to that. If you look at the book as a whole, it has poetry, it has history, it has personal narrative, it has various sorts of aspects. If I use Western categories it "transcends genre," and I think a lot of minority writing, and women's writing, does that. The one that I had in mind when I read your book, and the parallel I thought of immediately—I remember reading it in Penticton—is Gloria Anzaldúa's *Borderlands*,[1] where she consistently and deliberately transcends the borders and moves from one mode of narrative, from one genre, to the other. It reflects her own form of what Hartwig Isernhagen has called "liminality." Liminality is what a lot of minority people, especially of mixed ancestry, possess: they share in various traditions, and refuse to be marginalized, or put in "their place." They invert the common notion of ethnicity as belonging here or belonging there. She says she "straddles" the border, and from that position has access to various cultures. I thought that *I Am Woman* reflects that process. I didn't see it, then, as coming from the oral tradition at all. But then, when I heard you perform last night and witnessed that, I realized how important performance is for you.[2]

*LM:* Well, in the Big House, you are standing in the middle of the road, and if you are going to talk for a long time, which usually happens, you better be interesting. That's one.

Second, for us, words and meaning are more important than structure.

And third, the voice you use should reflect the subject. Certain things can't be said outside of humour. Certain things aren't funny. In English they have a word called "syntax" for the way things are framed, but for us "syntax" is even bigger than in a sentence. It's in our life, in our conduct of being. There is a syntax in the book that's very, very different from English.

The other thing is that the beauty of the language has to come out. I don't know if you read any of Pauline Johnson's translations of old stories? I saw my first copy the other day, actually. I never did read her work until just recently, at least not the stories, but the voice of Capilano is what I remember most distinctly.[3] She was true to his voice, the beautiful language that he used in English. I also wanted to do it that way, to show that our great-grandmothers and great-grandfathers really did speak English very well in the beginning. The residential school robbed us of both languages. Those who didn't go to residential school had no problem learning English or speaking English, but we do speak it differently, and I try to capture that essence throughout the book.

The last thing it is, is a presentation of theory and philosophy, and that is best done through story and poetry. So it moves in and out of story and poetry.

I think in English the so-called theoreticians and philosophers kid themselves if they think that they don't have story in their presentations. They do try to take the passion, and the spirit, and the life out of the story, and then they call it an example. To me it's all just story, and the more interesting and entertaining it is, the better. So I did a whole bunch of things with *I Am Woman*. I tried to, but I wasn't concerned with English "genre." I didn't even know what that word meant.

*HL:* It's just a category that I had in my mind and that I operate on. It's the etiquette, label ...

*LM:* Please let me explain. There's a point I'm making here. Before I did *I Am Woman*, I hadn't taken any English literary courses. I have since, because I want to do a novel, so I have studied some English literature. I had no idea beyond meanings of words, and thinking, and being, about how a book is structured. Actually, it does create some problems with the book because some people think it's a novel, or an attempt at a novel. Some people think it's a collection or some sort of anthropological presentation. Some people don't know what to think about it. Some people think it's an uneven voice, or faltering narrative, or just a number of things,

171

but in fact it isn't any of those things. It's theory coming through story. That is what it is! Colonization, decolonization, very, very simply.

**HL:** Well, you talked about where the various thoughts, the theories, the experiences that you have and that you express come from. You mentioned as one source the Big House, and of course, your background, and Pauline Johnson. So, there's a regional aspect, if you think of those stories. In *Indian Rebel* there's quite a bit of Western or European theory too, political theory. I'm coming from theoretically a similar background, Marx, Engels, and so on. For years since I worked with Native people and learned from Native people, I have had problems with my Marxist convictions because that Marxist perception of material reality very often is just too one-dimensional.

At least, that's what I experienced. How important is Western political theory in your thinking and in your expression? I mean theories of decolonization are written mostly by people who are decolonizing themselves. However, some of them still also refer to European thinking. How do you see that connection?

**LM:** Well, I'm really glad that you asked that, actually, because I had spent such a long time trying to come to grips with the essential disagreement between myself and all of the European philosophers I read, including Marx. There's something about all of them that they all hold in common, that I don't care for. I think it's in the relationship between thinking and being, the concept of thinking that Europeans have, and the objectification of thought.

For us, thinking is a complete and total process. In a sweat, or the Big House or wherever, around the pipe, you harness all your energy, physical, spiritual, emotional, and intellectual, and you retreat into solitude to work out the nature of your particular solidarity with creation. And you retreat into lineage, as well, because the farther backward in time you travel, the more grandmothers you have, the farther forward, the more grandchildren! You actually represent an infinite number of people, and the only physical manifestation is yourself. Also, you own your own "house" and that's all you own. It's this "house" that I live in. The "I" that lives in here is the thinking "I," the being "I," the "I" that understands creation, understands that the object of life is solidarity, understands that there are consequences for every action.

In European thought, beginning with such men as John Stewart Mill—there were others that came before him, but he's probably the most famous—thinking, depending on the humour, is to become dispassionate, to drown the passions. Why is that? Maybe because they are wine drinkers instead of rum drinkers? I don't know! And they calculate. That's what it is—adding, subtracting, multiplying, and dividing! It's all done very mathematically. And I'm not sure which came first, the calculating intellect or the industrial revolution, but they work well together. Everything is debit and credit, balance and reconciliation, of that sort.

That's not how things are for us! I think Seattle says it best, and he's one of our ancestral intellectuals: we don't spin the web of life, we're responsible for its continuation. That's the basis of thinking for us. We also have a story, an origin story, here on the west coast. Everything was thought, at one time, and then, because we kept tripping over each other, or whatever the case is, we were transformed into physical being, along with stone, and flora, and fauna, and all the rest. And then consequences came into being and thought took on some significance.

Marx agrees with John Stewart Mill on that. All the current sociologists and theorists agree that thought is a mental activity, a head activity. We don't feel that way!

*HL:* Maybe I use the term "European" differently from you. I don't know. Sometimes when you say "European," I, as a European, object to it, because you are talking about European-derived Canadians. But when I say "European," now, I really mean people over in Europe.

*LM:* Is a cat in Egypt a cat?

*HL:* Sure!

*LM:* A European here is a European!

*HL:* Well, it has to do with a lot of feelings and reactions that change over time and separation. I didn't really want to get into that. What I wanted to say is that in Europe, I think more and more people, and also many people in Germany, although we are still a minority, try to think in different ways and act in different ways that are less linear, maybe less secular and "realist." We realize that linear thinking is on the road towards death. Right? We have to come to think in a "holistic" way—I don't really like that term very much—but in a much more complex way. A way that takes into consideration all our actions and all our thinking, all the generations, the coming and the past, and all the beings around us. I don't know much about system theory, but apparently there are theories where you say if you take one part out of the whole system, the whole thing is affected. It sort of reshuffles and changes. You can't just change one thing without affecting so many other things. I think more and more people in Europe and in other countries are realizing this. We are very grateful for a lot of help that we've got in the last years from Native people. Helping us to rethink and also to decolonize *our* minds.

*LM:* Yes, there are a lot of people that are trying to think differently here too. I don't think that is where the problem lies. I think it's in the feeling.

And I believe this. I am familiar with European writers and thinkers. What European influence I have in my life is from meeting Europeans. I prefer to read your Europeans over North Americans. I think there's an inherent lie in everything that comes out of North America that doesn't exist in Europe. The lie of the colonization process.

*HL:* The denial of colonization, the displacement?

*LM:* Yes, exactly. So when I say "Europeans," I also mean those in Europe, and I think it does centre on feeling, and spirit, and coming to grips with that. I had noticed that the struggle to come out of linear thinking is still taking place in the head. I think it's triggered from historical change, and that's seeing the writing on the wall. There's nothing wrong with that. I'm not putting that down, but I don't think yet that Europeans feel truth. I don't think they feel it in their bones. I think it's still a matter of calculating, figuring out. Yes, they're going into lineage memory, but I will tell you about that. Wolf has tremendous backward and forward vision, and I think that some Europeans are coming to their "wolf sense." Wolf has a high sense of cooperation, but is willing to travel alone. Wolf has the capacity to travel alone. However, there's a problem with that, in that Wolf is a great thinker. Raven has the heart. So there's no Raven on Wolf's shoulder yet. In our culture, the backward and forward vision is well respected, and I think that's where I was when I did *Bobby Lee*. I had no Raven on my shoulder, and my whole community took me to task for not having Raven on my shoulder, which is why I went back to voice and oratory and heart. Too much work.

*HL:* I really like what you say there! It reminds me of Odin. The supreme north European god, Odin, has two ravens on his shoulders. He was always accompanied by two wolves. He also gave one eye because once he wanted to see in the future, to save the life of Baldur. When you said, there is no Raven on their shoulder, I immediately had that image. Thank you!

*LM:* Yes, and I think that many North Americans are coming to that, but they are coming to it by Raven rather than by the Wolf. So, when I speak of Europeans, here, I really go back to the origins of Europeans, to 1600, to 1750. That's not as important for Europeans in Europe, because they don't have the same recent history. It's not so crucial for them to remember how the hell they got here. They didn't get here on a Boeing, (LAUGHS) illegitimately. You were called here by some Indians, and that is different! But the Europeans that are here need to have their lineage memory. I think that a good many of them have Raven, but no lineage memory.

*HL:* We're amazed about the amount of research that non-Native people in the US, mainly European-descended people, and in Canada, are doing into lineage, into genealogical research. I wonder why they're so fascinated with it. A lot of people in Europe won't know much about the ancestors — maybe two or three generations — but they know this is the region, this is the valley, or this is the town, that they come from. And, in a way, you learn about this hill, and you learn about that spring, and somehow

I think you relate ancestry, not necessarily through lineage or names of human beings like "this was my great-great-grandmother or grandfather," but also to a *place*. That is a dimension that Europeans in North America don't have! At least not out west because they've been here so recently that there's very little to relate them to the land, I think, to specific parts of where they grew up, the stories that are attached to ...

**LM:** The most important thing they remember is how they got here, and what happened when they got here, and what's happened since then, and the nature of the monstrosity that's been built here, in most cases, apart from themselves. But some of their contributions have been pretty outrageous, pretty anti-human, and I think it's because of their origins, who they were before they came here, and how they got here. The tiers that they travelled in and in the boats that were ex-slave ships, really, with just a couple of tiers knocked out to crowd them in; and the death and destruction that happened before then.

The origins of capitalism. I think Europeans have that as an assumption in Europe. It's an unconscious kind of knowledge that guides their thinking. You can see it in the writings and the literature they produce. Zola and Dickens and Chekhov, all of the big ones. We don't bother with them over here much! (LAUGHS)

Here, history for the ordinary citizen in this country begins with the First World War, really the big tragedy of their times, and with unionism, especially the intense unionism of the 1930s. That's their point of consciousness, really. Before that they were busy burying their past, and the great shame of having been dumped here by their own, and the shame of having conducted themselves in the way they did. And I think it's because they don't understand at all how the factory life of a child distorts humanity. And they haven't gotten beyond that. Europeans have gotten beyond a lot of their beginnings in capitalism, and they have done a lot in Europe to reclaim their sense of self. But here it isn't the case because they can't begin without the beginning. It's right now quite painful for them. We have the highest rate of schizophrenia in the world, in this continent. We have murder, violence, almost industrial revolution violence. You know, it's almost that kind of intense violence.

**HL:** I saw some statistics recently, and the homicide rates in the US were way, way, way above any other country. Also, way above Canada. My family and I lived in the US for one year. We were just astounded! I don't want to go into that now, but I'd like to come back to literature. I'd just like to ask, to learn. I said earlier that in my mind I've got all these Eurocentric categories. One of them being genre, and as I witness the development of Native writing in Canada, especially in the last year, it is so vital, there's so much coming out! It's almost exploding. It's so powerful and it's so multidimensional. That thing last night, the First

Nations Cabaret, was a visual and auditory manifestation of this vitality. It was just wonderful.

Of course, coming from the background that I come from, I always think: here I am drawing charts, or in my mind trying to determine how this connects with that. This is more like this, so I categorize them together. How do you feel about that? Do you refrain from any kind of categorization?

*LM:* I don't think of categories, no. I don't think *in* categories.

*HL:* Or descriptions? I don't mean categories in the sense of saying, "Okay, here's the whole thing and now I cut it up like that," but ...

*LM:* There's none of that, really, simply! Tom E. Hawk is so outrageous! Tom E. Hawk is so powerful! Jeannette is so intense! So-and-so is so! We compare the person to the person, and how they are, what we think their essence is, what we think their essential spirit most reflects.

When we write, I believe that what we are doing is reclaiming our house, our lineage house, our selves, because I think we already have a spirit of cooperation that just underlines everything we do, and when you reclaim the self, there's no category. It's significant with the person. It's wonderment. Absolute wonderment. That's how we see each other's work, and we want to read each other, and to see each other, and to experience each other, because the more pathways we trace to get to the centre of the circle, the more rich our circle is going to be, the fuller, the rounder, the more magnificent. There just aren't words, I think, in English. "Siem," is like "all one." It's equivalent, I guess. But "Siem" is personal and achieved through the hearing of all the voices, both in lineage, and through all the people that you know. I think that's what we feel when we see other writers, and when you feel things you can't categorize. It's just not a possibility.

The standard for us is if this person is being true to himself, he's a good writer for us. When they're really putting out what they honestly feel, and their essential thread of lineage is woven in there, then he's a really good writer, or she's a really good writer, or she's a really good performer! It's just powerful. It's just so wonderful, and it's so inspiring, that you want to move on to recover yourself some more and you want to wake up to every cell of your body and feel life. That's what we're going through, recovering our cells' movement.

*HL:* The writing is that process where every person is sort of on the journey towards her- or himself. I guess that is one way. At the same time it's also a sharing, right? Sharing that process with others.

Now, is it sharing that process with other Native people, or sharing that process with anybody who would like to share it? Are there certain exclusions? Maybe I should make this more specific. If where I come from is not what you learn or think about writing, and if my literary, scholarly criteria are just alien and inadequate according to your standards, would it be better if academia, or literary journals, don't write reviews, don't discuss Native literature, because the categories that are established in most academic and literary theories are just not good enough, or the wrong categories, to do justice to Native writing? So would it be better if we Euro-critics would just be silent?

*LM:* Be silent? Oh boy!

*HL:* No, for the critics! Because, if it's that journey, that inward journey, and the main thing is the feeling? You see, that's what I'm trying to get at! So, if those words are inadequate, maybe it's better not to say anything?

*LM:* Let's do a critique. Let's deal with critique for a minute, and then go back to *I Am Woman* and how it's not a critique of the colonial process, or a criticism of anything, but it's more a search for meaning to us, to me, personally, and to the people in my life, and a search for what happened in my life that is universal to us.

Careful selection of stories reflects first of all my personal thinking, and being, and feelings, and my search, but also embraces the experience of Native people in general. I really stuck with that. Critics don't search for meaning, and no, I don't think it's a good idea to be silent at any time. I think at some point, though, there's going to have to be a literary revolution in the approach to literature. When I read *Germinal* now, and I see this woman, this young girl, her moment of ecstasy and her death at the same moment, the becoming and going out of being at the instant of her becoming, and all of the wonderment that goes with that, I kind of see our own lives. I understand something about Zola, and where his heart is, and that's enough. Beyond that, the story has not got much meaning to me. (LAUGHS) I understand also that he has a great deal of meaning to others, Pip in *Great Expectations*. *Great Expectations*, great expectations we have not! But I love that *Great Expections*. I think of all the books that I read to my kids—I was a bit crazy, I read literature to my children because we're supposed to read books, right? But I didn't read any kids' stories. I read them Shakespeare and Zola. They loved *Great Expectations* and they have great expectations! Nothing to do with Pip's great expectations! He was kind of like a trickster to them, a bumbling Pip, you know. (LAUGHS) He was a pip. But they have great expectations of life. Of living, being, love, passion, and they are very passionate and wonderful children. Well, they are adults now, they are not children any more, but they grew up with that, and I use that *Great Expectations* as a conceptual desire quite a lot in my writing, recently, especially because I want us to have great expectations, but I put it in a slightly different context.

*HL:* Slightly, yes! What do you hope for in the future in regard to Native writing and cultural expressions? I think, maybe, I should explain that aspect. After the end last night, when Howard (Adams) and I were going back to the car and talking, he said, "Gee, I wish I'd been born 20 years later," and I said, "But you should be proud and happy of this coming about, because it didn't exist 20 years ago!" He said, "That's true!," and I said, "Yeah, you are one of the people who started a process." "Exactly." And I said, "You should be happy that you are a part of this!," and he said, "Yeah, that's true! That is a development. There is something we fought for, and it is happening!" If you spin on into the future, what would you see in the future development?

*LM:* First, I want to say something about Howard. Inadvertently, Howard inspired a good many of us to pick up a pen. There was a doctor that was a Métis. My mother's a Métis. She had virtually very little education until she was in her 40s. Not that she stopped learning, but there's a traditional European style of education, institutional. So, education was very, very important to her, because like I said: 50% one way, and 50% another way, 100% straight down the middle! That was my mother!

When Howard came out and talked, he sounded like any old Indian I've ever heard, or young Indian I've ever heard, on the west coast. He is a tremendously powerful orator. And then, the distinction between writing, and speaking, and being a doctor, and being an orator was gone. But anybody can talk, anybody can write, as long as you can grab a dictionary and learn to spell and come to grips with some of the words, the meaning of words. And I still remember his speech, word for word his speech, and particularly his definition of "red." (LAUGHS) "Red light" district, always go "right." I mean, it's a wonderful little anecdote! And his understanding of colonization! Howard was a Marxist who was going against the tide! And that was so wonderful because we all felt that there was something wrong with the Marxism in this country, and Howard defined it as the lie, the great deception, the displacement of Native people, as you call the "Verdrängung." [4] Sorry, I shouldn't say "displacement."

*HL:* "Verdrängung," "displacement" is fine.

*LM:* I mean the German "displacement," your "pushing down and out."

*HL:* It's good like this. A lot of effort goes into it.

*LM:* It's a process, yes! That was all made clear by Howard's one little speech that I heard in 1968, to a number of us. That was tremendously inspiring. So, in an indirect way, Howard kicked it off.

At the time I met Howard, I was verbally silent, paralysed they call it. Up till I was 18 I was paralysed, but his voice cut me loose. It's not that I was not clear about much of this world. It was that I had no way of measuring my clarity. No way of seeing my clarity and testing it, until after Howard's little presentation on our reserve over in North Van there. The priests and nuns had told people on the reserve they'd be excommunicated if they came to the meeting.

*HL:* Did this really go on at that time?

*LM:* Oh yes! We were still back in the 18th century. (LAUGHS) 1968. It was just incredible, but it was wonderful. All of the wickedry that went with it, we loved the wickedry, it cut my tongue loose, I think. I was able to talk.

*HL:* Did you ever tell him? He'll read this.

*LM:* No. Oh yes, he'll read it! We never talk to each other about such things. We're talking behind his back now.

*HL:* Coming back to the future, what do you see as future development, or what do you hope for?

*LM:* Well, I've always believed that leadership and power are ideological questions, if you like, or questions of influence. I think that Native writers are going to be the most powerful influence in the next 10 years on the global front, not just our front. I think we have an understanding of the revolution process. It's very significant. That's what I think. From the outrageous Tom E. Hawk, right down to my young daughters, who just have a tremendous grip on themselves.

*HL:* If I use this interview in a European context, is there something that you would like to say to whoever may be listening to this over there?

*LM:* Sure! Just one thing, really, and it's got to do with particularization and categorization, and all that sort of thing, is that the Christian God ostensibly does not discriminate: "he so loved the world that he gave his only begotten son." It is not negative if people start to feel the world around them, and look upon the world with their heart, primarily, and love the world, and their selves, and as a human being embrace this Earth in solidarity with creation.

Look upon your heart and desire for a better world as the real significance of your self. It's most sacred.

*HL:* Thank you.

---

## NOTES

1. Gloria Anzaldúa. *Borderlands/La Frontera: The New Mestiza.* San Francisco: Spinster/Aunt Lute, 1987. See also Hartwig Isernhagen. "Literature—Language—Country: The Preservation of Difference and the Possibility of Relation. *Zeitschrift der Gesellschaft für Kanada—Studien* 6:1 (1986):81–94.
2. At the "First Nations Cabaret," featuring a great variety of Native writers, actors, and musicians at the Vancouver International Writers' Festival, 24 October 1990.
3. Emily Pauline Johnson, *Legends of Vancouver*, 1911. (Toronto: McClelland and Stewart, 1961.)
4. Here Lee Maracle is referring to a manuscript on "Cultural Appropriation and the Displacement of History and Peoples," in which I used the original (German) Freudian term "Verdrängung" instead of "displacement." [To be published, hopefully, in the *Canadian Journal of Native Studies*, Fall 1991.]

# EMMA LaROCQUE

▼

*Emma LaRocque was born in northeastern Alberta and grew up in a small Cree-speaking Métis community. She received her B.A. in English/Communications from Goshen College, Indiana, and holds two master's degrees, one in Religion (Indiana, 1976) and one in Canadian History (University of Manitoba, 1980). She has been a professor at the Native Studies Department of the University of Manitoba for 14 years, teaching and publishing on literature, human rights, (de)colonization, and women's issues. She is also a well-sought-after lecturer, who has spoken to audiences throughout Canada and the United States. She is presently finishing her Ph.D. dissertation with a major in Aboriginal History and a minor in Women's Studies.*

*Emma LaRocque's best-known publication is her book* Defeathering the Indian *(1975), which has become a standard text on Indian stereotyping and (de-)education in Canada. Besides, she has published critical articles in periodicals and anthologies. Recently, she has come out with her poetry, in addition to her scholarly writing.*

*The conversation was conducted in two parts. Begun on 7 December 1990 in Regina, it was continued two weeks later at Winnipeg airport on 20 December 1990* (copyright Emma LaRocque/Hartmut Lutz).

---

### 7 December 1990, Regina

**HL:** What made you become a writer?

**EL:** Well, it is hard to tell. As soon as I knew what writing was in grade eight, I wanted to do it. And mostly I think it came from a profound need to self-express because there was so much about our history and about our lives that, I quickly learned, has been disregarded, infantilized, and falsified. I think I had this missionary zeal to tell about our humanity because Indian-ness was so dehumanized and Métis-ness didn't even exist.

I guess partly it was that and partly I come from a background of beautiful oral literature. Both my grandmother and my mother were fantastic storytellers, and I think that influenced me. The ability to tell

181

a story, and the energy, the art, and the creation that goes with that. And since I couldn't be an actor, though I contemplate being a playwright somewhere along the way, writing just came.

How I got to be a critical writer? I guess, in a way, it comes from a place of protest about our conditions, about the need for our liberation. Part of protesting is that you have to become a critic. But I also became interested in literary criticism proper, and though I got derailed into history, and I haven't had as much time as I would like to further study literary criticism proper, I just kind of do it. It isn't a field in which I have been specifically trained, though I am trained in historiography which makes me a critic.

Concerning poetry, I am still not sure I consider myself a poet. I just put down words, stretch them out into a vertebrae form, as I say, and then it looks like a poem. (LAUGHS) But seriously, I consider poetry to be one of the most challenging forms of writing. Poetry is not a personal journal with sentences arranged into a poetic format. I think many people have reduced "poetry" to this level. Nor is it just craft without emotion, like so much of contemporary prairie poetry. Poetry is the art and discipline of expressing the inexpressible in as choice words as possible. Poetry demands honesty, perception, passion, and skill out of a poet. I do not think many Canadian writers, including myself, have achieved what I envision the best of poetry to be. My excuse is academic training. (LAUGHS) Academia teaches caution—one must forever qualify one's words with miles of footnotes. With poetry it is different—poetry must have exuberance, a poet must stand on one's own feet.

*HL:* I realize that in some of the poems there is lots of alliteration and sometimes there is even rhyme. There is one "rhyme" that I thought was so beautiful—that of "lover" and "mother." The words sound similar, and the warmth, the love comes through very much in that. And so, I hope there will be more poetry by Emma LaRocque in the future!

*EL:* Well, I am sure there will be! In *Writing The Circle*[1] I refer to doing my Ama poems in one volume. "Ama" and "Bapa" were/are our family terms for my mother and father. But hardly had I finished saying that, when my dad died, just recently. And as I said to somebody, "Well, I guess now I have to write Bapa poems."

*HL:* Your poems seem to come out of a lot of pain or sadness.

*EL:* My family is very close in the oddest sort of way. No matter the distance that I went in terms of miles and in terms of culture, maybe just because of that distance, there was always this deepening of emotional connection to my family, to my parents especially. The sadness/pain in my poetry is not only because both of my parents have now died, but also because they represent a way of life that we will never see again. The pain also comes from my having to leave my family at such an early age to pursue "education." Sadly, by the time I was ready to come home, both in terms of consciousness and resources, cancer felled my mom, and now my dad. I will always be haunted by the fact that colonial forces, such as schooling, stole me away from my parents, and then death stole my parents away from me. You may be interested in my autobiographical essay included in *Living The Changes*,² which goes into analytical detail about my journey away from home in northeastern Alberta and into the jaws of white Canadian society.

*HL:* Is *Living the Changes* your book?

*EL:* No, it is edited by Joan Turner. I just contributed an essay.

*HL:* And that came out where?

*EL:* It is just coming out this week from U of M Press. I start my autobiographical essay with a poem that is called "Where Did She Go?," which is about the significance of my mother's death, not only that I lost a mother, but also that she represented my language, my original culture. In a sense, part of my life too is gone forever. The meaning of losing older people grows sharper with time. First you go through so much cultural bombardment and disturbance. Then, you are just growing up, and you are just beginning to pick up the pieces to understand this and understand that. You are just beginning to come home, then, the damn death comes and swipes you one more time in a very final way! So that is where a lot of the pain comes from. But as human beings there is no way we can escape pain, and especially as Natives in this country.

That is why I must write. Being a historian, working with footnotes and all that is one thing, and sometimes I enjoy it. But there is a part of me that also needs to go into something like creativity, such as writing poetry, just to keep me sane and remind me of who I am.

*HL:* Your Ama and your Nokum, I guess, spoke in Cree?

*EL:* Yes.

*HL:* Do you, when you meet people from your family or other relatives, speak Cree?

*EL:* I speak Cree. I don't speak it as well as I used to. Words don't come like that (SNAPS HER FINGERS) any more. I sometimes have to think many minutes. That is the other loss I felt when my mom died. My mom always anticipated what word I was needing when I was conversing with her. She was my teacher as we went along. Both my parents taught us a way of life that was more, much much more, than words. So, there is that loss too. Yes, all my family except my nieces and nephews speak Cree. A few weeks ago we were at a wake for my father. Goodness, I never knew I had so many relatives! I left when I was 14 and I didn't recognize half of my relatives but I had heard their names in Cree. If one could say this during one's father's funeral, it was a healing wake because it was a very traditional Métis wake, the kind I had experienced as a child. One of the beauties of it was that I heard Cree all night from every corner of the house. And I thought, "Wow, it is still alive!" And that part was wonderful. My mom's three sisters were there, and they are just as animated storytellers as my mom used to be. It was just so healing to hear them tell stories, and of course, they reminded me of my mom. They were also filling me in on details I never knew about my parents, all in Cree. We just mixed it with a few English words here and there.

*HL:* What about French?

*EL:* Well, our Cree is inherently peppered with French of sorts, i.e., "le" and "la." My dad used to say a lot of words in French but I didn't know that they were French until I took French in high school. After that when I heard my dad saying his French things, I said, "Bapa, that is French," and he looked at me like, "yes, and so it is. It has always been!" (LAUGHS) "Well, why didn't you tell me?" "You never asked!"

Emotionally, we were very Métis but you have to understand that western, and particularly northern Métis-ness, does not identify ethnically with the French. We are at once very Cree and very Métis. The French part assimilated into the Cree part in the northwestward movement from the 1870s to the 1900s, that exile from the Red River.

But when I went back to Winnipeg—and I say "back" because in a way for me, it was going back but I didn't even know it until I was there—anyways, when I met French-Métis, they were very different from "my" Métis, ethnically speaking. It took me a while to accept them as Métis and I think it took them a while to accept me as Métis. So there are definitely differences also among the Métis.

*HL:* Oh sure! You talk about your grandmother and your mother talking in Cree, and being such wonderful storytellers. Now, when you write poetry, you write in English. If you compare that to Cree, is there a disruption? How does that relate?

*EL:* Well, it isn't difficult for me, but what I wish is that other people understood Cree so that I could use it more freely in all my writings without having to put it in brackets and explain what it means. As I said in *Writing The Circle*, it is quite distracting, yet you want to, especially in poetry. You want to do what is popularly known as "soul language." But for myself I have never felt that there was a hopeless disruption. My whole life was Cree. It is very animated, very passionate, but when you know English, it is possible to move easily between the two languages. It does mean getting to know English intimately. And it does require inventiveness. For example, when I am teaching original oral literatures, say in my Canadian Native Literature classes at U of M, I do not literally translate Cree. What I do is retell Cree myths and legends so that they will be meaningful and appealing to a modern, English-speaking audience. This way, I can retain much of the spirit and energy of the original telling.

I have seen how literal translation infantilizes Native oral literature.
*HL:* How does it infantilize?
*EL:* Literal translations lose all the nuances of style and cultural context. The net effect is anachronism, stagnation, and distortion. Literal translations reduce Indian legends into a grade one, grade two level. You know how stories are told at these levels: see Spot sleep; see Sally run; see Puff play. See Wisakehcha wink; see Wisakehcha fool a fox; see Wisakehcha dance with ducks. It doesn't work. Now, listen to a Wisakehcha story in Cree (TELLS IT IN CREE)—see, how in Cree, you can just take off, get all the nuances and see what is going on, and you can hear how animated and alive it is! Nothing like: (SAYS IT AS IF IN GRADE ONE) see Wisakehcha run.
*HL:* It is a very musical language, eh?
*EL:* I don't know. I have never heard it (LAUGHS) from the other side. It certainly sounds lovely to me!
*HL:* I was thinking of some other Métis authors who use both languages—English, and maybe some Cree, some French. I also think of Chicanas and Chicanos writing in "Spanglish," combining Spanish, Mexican, and Nahuatl, and English, and whatever. It could almost become a distinctive trait of Métis literature, that authors would be able to move freely between languages and incorporate Cree as "soul language." Have you ever thought about that or been experimenting with that?
*EL:* It is a good concept and of course you are familiar with some linguistic work on the Mitchif language, and the controversy whether it is a language or the pidginization of two languages. That would be difficult to do in written form for me but I am not sure why.
*HL:* But if you use your "Nokum" and "Ama"?
*EL:* Oh I use Cree but I don't mix the Cree. I wouldn't do "Spanglish." Spanish and English are related languages, Cree and English are not. It is, I would think, much easier to do Spanglish then Creenglish.
*HL:* No, but that is what Chicanas and Chicanos do too. When something is close to your heart and experience, you use the appropriate term, i.e., if you say "Ama," it is something different from saying "Mother," and that is why you use it. That also marks for an outsider, "okay, this is very private. This loving warmth experienced from childhood and love can only be expressed in that language because that is part of that culture."
*EL:* Oh yes! I hope there will be enough of us writers, soon, using Cree or whatever other Aboriginal language, so that non-Native critics can even begin to develop a vocabulary that they can become familiar with. There is also another difficulty, and that is that there is no standard form for writing Cree in English.
*HL:* Yes, except for the syllabics, I think.

*EL:* Right, but even I don't know syllabics. My mom did, my mom was literate in syllabics.

*HL:* Oh yes. I think Cree, of the Indian languages, is probably the one that has the greatest chance of being a literate language, seeing more literature in Cree. I know that some things are coming out in Cree. I know even Tomson Highway's book is supposed to come out in Cree.

*EL:* I just hope that there are enough people that know the syllabics system so they can read it!

*HL:* I don't think it will be in the syllabics, or maybe they will be doing it in both, I am not sure about that. The only parallel that I could think of is Inuktitut, right? There are things that come out in Inuktitut with an English translation, with the syllabic, and with the roman orthography. I think that would be an interesting project for Cree also, because it marks that there are these different forms.

*EL:* Well, I hope more of it comes to pass. I think this has been done in certain parts of the country. But it is unwieldy. It is perhaps more symbolic than practical.

*HL:* You said something, I think it was in the "preface" in *Writing the Circle*, about the dilemma that Native writers can be caught in. On the one hand, you need all the energy and all the support to put Native literature out there, so it is visible, because it exists and it is very beautiful and rich. On the other hand, it is tagged "Native literature"! So there is also the danger of ghettoization, of saying, "okay this is Native literature!—something that is 'kept in its place.'" How do you resolve that dilemma? Historically?

*EL:* I think the Native writers themselves cannot resolve this dilemma on their own. The mainstream intellectuals and critics—assuming the two are not mutually exclusive (LAUGHS)—they are going to have to start taking our writing seriously.

*HL:* Oh yes.

*EL:* When they do, we can begin to dialogue and not stay marginalized, and yet we can still retain pride in the fact that this is Native literature—then, we may resolve it that way. Because the dilemma now is in the loneliness of not being taken seriously, and the loneliness of not being understood simply because white Canadians are dismally ignorant of Aboriginal peoples. I don't mean this as an insult, I mean it as a historical fact.

And so, you are forever forced to explain before you can even begin to dialogue. A lot of energy is being derailed and drained that way. So you are lonely from that aspect of it. It is also an isolating experience, which is further deepened by the fact that Native writers do not have a large Native intellectual community to draw from, thanks to 500 years of colonization. Who will nourish our hungry minds? Who will nurture our weary hearts? Who will sustain us through our doubts? Who will

186

challenge us to move past our obstacles? Who will inspire us to reach for the best in us? We can grow only if we can dialogue with both the white and the Native intellectual communities, but as I have pointed out many times, dialogue is a two-way street.

*HL:* I like what you said, the dilemma is not just a Native dilemma. It is the dilemma of the mainstream. I absolutely agree with you. But I tell you we are working on it. I said "we," I say "I."

*EL:* (LAUGHS) I know, you certainly have done some work on this. You have to come from Germany and teach. The irony!

*   *   *

### 20 December 1990, Winnipeg Airport

*HL:* I liked your book *Defeathering the Indian*. In your article on "The Métis in Canadian English Literature," I felt you are too hard on the case of Margaret Laurence. I always thought that she is very perceptive.

*EL:* No, I thought I was very generous with Margaret Laurence.

*HL:* Yes, you said, it was a nice try but still it was the old Noble Savage theme.

*EL:* Yes, to some extent. I mean, I absolutely agree with you. I think she is probably the most perceptive writer Canada has.

*HL:* That is how I see it, exactly.

*EL:* And she perceived a lot about the place of Métis people in Canadian society. I especially like how, with each novel, the marginalized Tonnerre family moved in closer and closer to white society. Literally and metaphorically, they moved in from the outskirts of town *to* town, finally, even, *into* Morag, sexually speaking. But even Margaret Laurence, for all her perceptiveness, plays into some big stereotypes. The Métis are presented as noble, even if a little wild. Jules Tonnerre doesn't like fences and is lusty, mysterious, and of course, dies with nobility. But the larger point I was making in that article was that we have yet to be treated to a great novel by a Native writer, one that would catch the ethos of being Métis.

*HL:* Yes, that is true, I agree on that. In *Bird in the House* there is this one short story, "Cry of the Loons," where Vanessa, who is Margaret Laurence I guess, is up at the cottage. And they have Piquette Tonnerre with them. She has a limp and it is not healing very well. Vanessa's father is a doctor and they take her along so she can recuperate. All of a sudden this non-Native girl, Vanessa, realizes she is being fed on stereotypes, on Longfellow and all those authors. All of a sudden she realizes, "hey, this is a Native person!" Vanessa was raised on lofty notions about Hiawatha and so on, and she realizes, "this is probably as close as I might ever get to a Native person." She is intrigued to know more from Piquette about the law of the woods and all this. First Piquette cannot respond to that. She responds that she is not interested in the stereotype.

187

I found that the most perceptive passage I have ever found in non-Native literature—about somebody realizing how the stereotypes sort of superimpose themselves before you can actually meet *people*. And I always gave her credit for that.

*EL:* Oh. My lifetime experience!

*HL:* I know you teach Native Literature. You said that there is still no novel yet that treats Native people from their own perspective. Can you think of any novels that you think come close to that? Or maybe are on the way?

*EL:* I believe I said: there is yet no definitive "great" novel on Native peoples. There are, of course, fine novels that carry a "Native perspective." Also some plays now.

*HL:* Which ones, for example?

*EL:* Well, mostly I am thinking of Tomson Highway. A couple of his plays, *The Rez Sisters* and *Dry Lips Oughta Move to Kapuskasing*. But I am still waiting for that "great" novel. I had a student a number of years ago in my Canadian Native Literature class. I think he is going to write that novel. I have been after him to get to writing. He is potentially a brilliant writer.

*HL:* What about you writing that novel? Have you ever tried that?

*EL:* No, I am not sure that I could. If I was younger with energy, time, and vision ... I like plays more. I have puttered around more with plays, short stories, and poetry. I don't know if I would ever write a novel. I think that I would have to be well rested. I taught full time for 13 years non-stop, which exhausted me. Teaching and research make you feel like you are never done. You feel like you are running around all the time with all these things you have to finish—reviews, projects, refereeing manuscripts, this book. I can't write when I am feeling like there are so many loose ends. I keep thinking, "well, one of these days, I will organize my files, clean up my desk, have all my lecture notes prepared well ahead of time. I'll stop going on lecture tours, and then I will write my great piece of literature!" (LAUGHS) I don't think that will ever come to pass but maybe I will get disgusted with academia yet, and just go into writing. Some people have asked me "what would you really like to do with your life?" I would really like to write.

*HL:* Just write full time?

*EL:* Yes, I would really like to just write full time.

*HL:* Write what?

*EL:* Oh, I think I would write novels. I definitely would write more poetry.

*HL:* Literature—fiction or poetry.

*EL:* Yes, fiction and poetry. Also non-fiction. I do like criticism, critical writing.

*HL:* But just go into literature full time?

*EL:* Right. You know after I wrote *Defeathering the Indian* I learned that you would starve yourself if you stayed a writer in this country. So most writers write because they love it but they can't live on it, and so they don't do it full time.

*HL:* I think Tomson Highway may be the only fully professional writer in Canada.

*EL:* Native or non-Native?

*HL:* I mean Native professional writers. But even then he is director of this agency, Native Earth Performing Arts. So I am sure his income doesn't really come from publications. I don't think there is any professional Native writer yet in Canada.

*EL:* How about Maria Campbell?

*HL:* From the times that I have met her, I understand that she is always on hand-to-mouth projects and sometimes she is very, very poor and in very dire straits, and then she may have an offer writing and I guess doing project works or scripts and stuff—which keeps her going. I don't know whether that is the bulk of her income. I just don't know. Maybe she is close to that, yes.

*EL:* Well, that is a very Canadian way of life too, isn't it? There are so many people who have to go contract to contract and they really do live hand-to-mouth. I used to live like that 20 years ago and I decided that it was too difficult. That is why I have stayed with teaching. I do for the most part enjoy teaching but writers compromise a lot because we have to make a living. I think chasing after contracts is very draining. Mind you, teaching is quite draining too but at least it is a bit stable.

*HL:* Yes, exactly. The job gives you security to a certain amount.

*EL:* As soon as I had my leave, I did more creative and critical writing than I have done for some time. I find that I am drawn to this type of work and writing. But my work has been slowed down because of family illness and my own exhaustion. Among other things, my eyes get so tired.

*HL:* Are you still working on academic research?

*EL:* Oh yes.

*HL:* I guess you have to, eh?

*EL:* You have to, yes, in order to survive in the university, you have to.

Ah, well, perhaps I have made history that is worth mentioning—I got what I wanted for my Ph.D. program but it took a while to negotiate. I am majoring in Aboriginal History at U of M and it is not in the calendar. So I felt very good about that because, my goodness, I am 41 years old and I have worked the last 20 years on this history. I also have two masters degrees. Why should I now go into something totally new and be 60 years old by the time I get to know that area! Aboriginal History should be one of the fields one can major in in graduate studies. It is as much a field of study as, say, Canadian, European, or American History. [Editor's note: Since this conversation was recorded, it was decided not to add Aboriginal History to the graduate studies level.]

*HL:* Did you have a lot of obstacles to remove?

*EL:* Well, I guess other people have had more but I had my share.

*HL:* Mainly in which way? That it didn't fit the established academic structure?

*EL:* First, that it did not fit the structure so I had to convince persons and committees all along the way but I expected that, and my supervisor and my advisory committee have been wonderfully supportive. It just took extra time to muck through the system, you know.

There were obstacles, such as lack of money, energy, and time, all those things that have prevented me from finishing my Ph.D. years ago. You know, those of us who have supposedly "made it" into a middle-class income status. We continue to pay the price of poverty and prejudice, financially and sociologically.

There are also slippery "obstacles"—the invisible but insidious kinds. For example, a colleague from a university did a reference for me for my Ph.D. application. I had assumed we were equals, but much to my amazement he wrote this patronizing reference in the manner of a white social worker discussing his Native "charge," as missionary journals put it! His opinions had no basis in fact and revealed, among other things, a very outdated understanding of current scholarly works and debates going on in Native Studies and in Women's Studies, even in historiography! The arrogance of such a reference is nothing less than intellectual colonialism. I have to say that a number of colleagues from Native Studies Departments across the country have reported experiencing similar things. It is something we are beginning to expose. The only way I know how to combat any kind of oppressive behaviour or attitude is to open it up for discussion. On this note, the Aboriginal Women's Symposium from the University of Lethbridge is publishing a collection, and will include my article, "The Colonization of a Native Woman Scholar." How else can one put these things? I am a writer, a poet, a historian, I must tell about these things, about all the abnormal "obstacles" we, the Natives, face in our land. Intellectual colonization cannot be spared. So you asked me about obstacles in my Ph.D. pursuits—that puzzling reference was way beyond the standard parameters of an academic reference and certainly was aggravating. I had to have it removed!

*HL:* Yes, also at a personal level.

*EL:* Oh yes, it was very personal—I thought he was a friend, you know.

*HL:* Yes, yes.

*EL:* But who knows these things! (LAUGHS) I live and learn. I am minoring in Women's Studies for my Ph.D. To me, the most exciting and the most refreshing kind of thinking and creativity and therefore excellent scholarship coming out right now is from Women's Studies and from Native Studies, because we are bringing questions and ideas and substance that conventional scholarship has not even begun to think of. Partly because we are multidisciplinary in approach, so we have to have a broad theoretical and empirical base.

*HL:* Did you read this introductory piece that I sent you?

*EL:* You mean *Minority Literatures in North America*? I perused the whole thing. That reminds me, I had a bone to pick about something in there. And that was, I forget the details now as to who the author was, but the title was something about scholarship and "squaws," and it was in reference to Native American writers, Native women American writers.

*HL:* But it was probably put in quotation marks, not as a serious term? I wouldn't use it as a serious term.

*EL:* You? It wasn't you! It was someone else. No, I know that you wouldn't.

*HL:* It was in a quote, eh?

*EL:* It was a title in a quote and it was in reference to Paula Gunn Allen, I think.

*HL:* Oh, I think I know what that is. It is the title of an article by Elisabeth Hermann, "Academic Squaws." [3]

*EL:* Right! That's it!

*HL:* I recall having a long conversation with her, and I said I would take that out. Even if it is a quote from Paula Gunn Allen—no, I think from Wendy Rose. She has a poem, I think, "Academic Squaw." So it is a quote from a title of a poem by a Native woman.

But still, personally, I wouldn't have used it for a title but she said it is okay! And she knows, I think, both the people she is writing about, and she thought it was okay. But I have the same feelings about that.

*EL:* As I said, I was just perusing it and I am going to look it up again but I am uncomfortable with the perpetuation of racist/sexist terms such as "squaw."

*HL:* Yes, so am I. That is what I foresaw. That is why I talked to Elisabeth about it.

*EL:* It would be interesting to chat with either Wendy Rose or Paula Gunn Allen on the usage of certain terms.

*HL:* I think Wendy Rose is sort of turning it around the way Howard Adams uses "Halfbreed," he turns it around.

*EL:* Well, you get into the question of language. How much is reclaimable? To me, there are some words that are not reclaimable and "squaw" is one of them. I happen to agree with Howard Adams about "Halfbreed." In fact, I prefer "Halfbreed" to "Métis" because I feel that "Métis" is so aristocratic and I, happily, do not come from an aristocratic Halfbreed background. We never used the word "Métis" until I came to Manitoba, and some very colonized Métis were highly offended by the term "Halfbreed." Well, it is all in the way you use it. So I certainly understand. It is like "black is beautiful." I have problems with the term

191

"squaw" because of its origin, because of the way it continues to be used, and because I think it reflects an internalization problem, depending on how it is used. I mean I can use it in a certain way, in a sarcastic way or in a cynical way to make a point. But to use it to refer to myself, no! For example, I would not join a march that would say "squaw is beautiful." Nor would I perpetuate Hollywood by referring to myself as an "academic squaw."

*HL:* Well, we would have to have the text here to really look at it. I wouldn't either. In that case, if it is referring to that poem, I think it is an ironic inversion using that term that has always been used to slander, to throw it back. But I still would agree with you. First, personally, I wouldn't use the term. And second, it also makes a difference whether Paula Gunn Allen or Wendy Rose decided to use it for a specific reason. Maybe as a political term to throw back. And it is a different thing for a non-Native to use it.

*EL:* Yes, I think there are all those levels but it is true it all depends. Perhaps this discussion reflects the differences between Canadian and American Native intellectuals, a difference that has not been appreciated.

*HL:* It is a very objectionable term, I think.

*EL:* I guess part of me wants to get away from Hollywood jargon, and even I myself now have second thoughts about having titled my book "defeathering" because I meant it as ...

*HL:* Because of the assumption that the feathers are there!

*EL:* But of course I was referring to school curriculum which assumed that. But still it has been misused and misunderstood. And it is still in response to the stereotypes which in 1975 were a huge problem. Today some things have changed, I think! Still I do get tired of titles that are a throwback to Hollywood and comic books. Beth Brant's "Mohawk Trails" comes to mind, so does "Academic Squaws." There are many tacky titles and they are so kitsch.

*HL:* That is a good discussion. Let's check out some other terms like "voice." "Native Voice," "Northern Voices," "First People, First Voices," are these okay?

*EL:* (LAUGHS) Well, it depends on who wrote it!

*HL:* I don't mean the contents, I just mean the term, for example, "tales." There were *Tales From the Smokehouse, From the Longhouse, From the Igloo*. All these tales. Are we saying it is oral? And now "voice." Sometimes I think the terms create maybe a new stereotype, because they are used over and over again.

*EL:* Yes, well, in my preface to *Writing the Circle*, I address the reference to Native people as "voiceless." That was a cliché about five years ago or so in Canadian literature: "Native people are voiceless!" When I first heard it, I had quite a reaction to it. In my preface I systematically raise questions as to the overt and subtle meaning(s) found in presenting Native people as voiceless. The opposite of voiceless, I guess is voice. The title of my preface—"Here Are Our Voices—Who Will Hear?"—is in response to the inferences. I really should have titled my preface: "The Place of Contemporary Native Literature in Canadian Intellectual Life"! Less poetic, isn't it? (LAUGHS)

*HL:* So you see it as a reaction to the stereotype of voicelessness? Okay, I understand. Well that is why I was asking.

Did I tell you, I would like to call this collection of interviews "Contemporary Challenges," and as to the subtitle, I haven't made up my mind yet. Either "Conversations With Canadian Native Authors" or "Canadian Native Authors Speak."

*EL:* I would go for "Conversations," I like that word myself.

*HL:* I like it too.

*EL:* It is one that I use in some works.

*HL:* What about "Contemporary Challenges"?

*EL:* Well, I should tell you, and I am sure you know, that there is a book by J.S. Frideres, a sociologist, called "Contemporary Conflicts."

*HL:* Well, this will be "Contemporary Challenges"—that is not the same. I think I can stick to the "Challenges." The reason I wanted that title is because originally I had in mind "Native Literatures in Canada." But a book by that title has appeared recently, as you know. Actually it is called *Native Literature*, not literatures. Native literature is growing so fast that it is really a challenge to academia, to the established English Departments, to actually see what there is and not exclude it. And it is certainly very much contemporary. That is why I didn't want to look in the past again. I am glad that you go for the "Conversations" but you see, if I use "Conversations," I come into it more than if it just says "Native authors talk." Do you understand?

*EL:* I do, but you are part of it.

*HL:* Yes, that is true.

*EL:* You are very much a part of this discussion, and I think there is more integrity if the title of your book reflects it. If I am going to speak myself, I will myself write a book.

*HL:* Sure.

*EL:* Whereas I see this as a conversation, as a two-way thing. You create it as much as I do. In fact, you are kind of letting it happen. You are very much influencing it.

*HL:* I think I might stick with that. I have asked a few people and they said that it is okay, go ahead. I don't think in this book there should be that much editing, and it is not because I am lazy but I don't want to hone it down into something that *I* think is important. People should have an input.

*EL:* I was thinking there was something that I wanted to add or revise. You said my poetry had a lot of pain.

*HL:* I realized the way you reacted that you weren't happy with that. What I meant is that there is a lot of pain or sadness in the background, and I had the feeling that that part has stimulated the poetry. I am not saying that you are whining about something. I don't mean that at all. But there is pain and suffering in the background.

*EL:* Oh, I didn't take it in the way that I was whining. But sometimes, one of the thousand other images associated with Native people is suffering.

*HL:* That is true.

*EL:* To be sure there is suffering for Native people, but it does not have to be presented in a stereotypical way. It is all in the way that you deal with it. You can see the same thing but one person may deal with it in a very racist and stereotypical way, while another person will deal with it in an intelligent and, hopefully, compassionate way. But I also wanted to say, I have always wanted to show the multifaceted aspect of myself, of my family, of my community, of Aboriginal people in Canada. And so, I just wanted to say that some of my poetry is whimsical and playful.

*HL:* Oh yes.

*EL:* But interestingly, I have had problems getting that kind of poetry published because it doesn't fit. Well, like I said in *Writing The Circle*, some of my poetry has been returned because it wasn't "Indian" enough. I have submitted say, poems about hoarfrost, or about trying to fit into my dad's boots and squeaking around in the snow in the moonlight. To me, both poems had lots of nuances, lots of meaning, but those poems have been rejected. Now they could be bad poems, I don't know. Maybe I need to revise them, but I think it is because white publishers and editors want something that fits into their stereotype of an "Indian poet"! Throw in a Cree word or pepper it with tragedy or spirituality, then, maybe they will take it. I am, as a personality, a very animated person who laughs very easily and loves life for the most part. Believe me, I have had my share of suffering, but I wouldn't be here if I hadn't been able to laugh, dance, and enjoy! I have an urgency to get across the fact that we are multidimensional. That is partly why I want to be a poet as well as a scholar. Incidentally, the other obstacle is that some people think if I write poetry or literature proper, then I really must not be a proper scholar.

*HL:* That is weird—that people in Canada should say that because it is often the case that people writing literature are affiliated with some English Department. Maybe the problem is that you are with history. (LAUGHS)

*EL:* (LAUGHS) Exactly!

*HL:* If you were in the English Department, it would be no problem?

*EL:* Perhaps. We live with many anomalies as Native scholars. Yes, it is partly the problem with disciplines, but that is what I wanted to add about pain in my writing.

*HL:* I think quite a few Native writers are reacting exactly to the expectation that texts "must" be sad, because there is so much sadness. And they refuse. I don't know if you have read Ruby Slipperjack's *Honour the Sun*?

*EL:* Oh yes. I discuss it in my preface.

*HL:* I regard that as a really wonderful, wonderful book.

*EL:* You too, eh!

*HL:* And behind that, I know there is an immense amount of suffering. So much suffering.

*EL:* I know, I could tell that.

*HL:* In reading it twice, you come across how it is also a statement about the violence against women and children despite all the exuberance and joy of life. And if you interview the author, she is adamant in not writing about the dark side of that. And yesterday, talking to Rita Joe, was exactly the same. She wants to do something on residential schools and she says that she is not going to write about those dark areas because she refuses to write about these negative things. And I think there are quite a few Native authors who say so much has been written about "the lament of the Indian, I am so sick of it and there are so many other things." Tom King for example. Maybe you find that more in the east than in the west, or here in the middle, perhaps too. But I found that interesting.

*EL:* My reaction to that is, yes, I absolutely understand these writers, why they are saying this. I, for example, have refused to write my autobiography in book form because my lifestory is quite dramatic and could easily be sensationalized. But only my closest friends know, if even they do, the extent of the suffering that is also a part of my life. I have refused to write it because I saw what Canadian society did with Maria Campbell's book and with Beatrice Culleton's book. And I have seen those white-Canadian social-worker types who disguise themselves as readers and critics. They just drool over people's pain. This is not saying anything negative about the books. I think they are exceptional books.

*HL:* Yes, I think so too.

*EL:* And I think these two women are excellent writers and they shared so much. I have just been made impatient by the social-worker types who receive Native writers by their "pain" or "anger," rather than by their intelligence or analysis. I have a bone to pick regarding white critics and, equally, white audience response. Those of us who have written more analytical than political or personal material have suffered lack of acknowledgement. But really, you can't win. In my case, if I refer to "facts of biography," my scholarship is suspect! Also, the white audience likes a "sad" story but it can be indifferent or hostile to Native intellectual analysis of white society. Even when it is done with some sense of "wit and velvet gloves." For example, *Defeathering the Indian*. It was one of the first Native-authored books to analyze the Canadian *mainstream* school system. In my opinion, it was an important assessment, yet it received way less attention than autobiographies or "angry" books. It is very frustrating because what I really would like is to be taken seriously as a Canadian thinker/writer. Whether I am an academic writer or a popular writer or a critical writer or a poet, I want to be taken seriously. I am tired of being marginalized or ghettoized, and I want to be engaging in a discussion about what this country is about. What Canadian culture is about, that we are as much a part of this Canadian culture. At least "we" the Métis.

**HL:** Absolutely!

**EL:** And it is about time whites — and some Natives — see this rather than always seeing us as something in the fringes, you know, like the Tonnerre family that hasn't come in yet. We have been in for a hell of a long time, even if our presence exposes the hypocrisy in "multiculturalism."

**HL:** Historically there is no group that is as genuinely Canadian as the Métis!

**EL:** That is how it has been said, yes! (LAUGHS)

**HL:** I mean "Canadian," when you think of present day Canada as a state. Manitoba of all places first, right? This is not to discredit the Indian population or the white contributions, but it is the Métis who got about Canada first.

**EL:** Well, I will stay away from that as a historian ...

**HL:** (LAUGHS) Okay.

**EL:** But I wanted to finish this thought on pain in Native writing.

**HL:** I am very glad about what you just said.

**EL:** As much as I myself have consciously chosen, as yet, not to divulge my autobiography, which has both joy and pain, I still cannot agree totally with refusing to deal with pain in our writings, or with the assumption that doing so is just being negative. I was having this discussion with my childhood best friend. She said that she didn't like *Writing The Circle* because it was full of pain. And I said, well, there are definitely some pieces that I did not want included, but I wasn't the editor, so I didn't have the final decision. But I said to my friend, "you cannot escape pain." You have to deal with it in some fashion or other.

Now there again, I go right back to how you deal with things. We don't have to divulge personal information or reduce discussions of injustice and oppression to "personal pain." We can deal with pain — like you can deal with every aspect of life — from a place of integrity, from a place of authenticity and particularly from a political place, from a politically conscious place. We as writers cannot escape the discussion of suffering. Violence against women, for example — my god, Native girls and women have suffered so much from male violence in Native communities. So, we have to deal with it. We don't have to deal with it personally, as such, but we have to deal with it politically. And for me that is where a lot of my passion comes from—my strong belief that we must confront oppression wherever it exists, be it in our homes or in white society. I am not much of an activist or anything but I know that, in terms of consciousness, you cannot be liberated unless you have articulated what that pain is about.

*HL:* I am not going to edit this out!

*EL:* (LAUGHS) And you know, I really believe very much in articulation. Articulation does not mean that we just open our mouths. It means we take the time to understand the places of invasion in our lives, be they historical, cultural, emotional, psychological, or physical invasions. We must understand what colonization or abuse has done to us before we can be truly decolonized or healed. By articulation, I mean an intellectual and emotional comprehension of our oppression. All forms and sources of oppression.

*HL:* I agree with you.

*EL:* But I have to say that my position on this has been misunderstood a lot. I want to make a comment on Rita Joe's poetry, which I like, especially the earlier stuff. There are hardly subtle nuances to her suffering.

*HL:* She said, in the first one, she still articulated anger and she decided not to do it any more. In talking to Ruby she told me she once went to the Pen Conference, I think, and there was an extra group of young writers from Third World nations. She said, "I listened to that and we all had the same problems, and why is it? I think I know why it is," she said, "it is colonization." There it was! So it is coming—the understanding.

*EL:* I have to comment on Ruby Slipperjack's novel. I love that novel. I have never met her. I talked to her on the phone, but I feel like she is one of the least acknowledged writers. And that book is very good. It is one of the first novels that focuses entirely on a Native community, on a Native family, on Native individuals. And you get to know these characters, they are real. What makes it unique is they are developed without reference to white people or white society. It is also a balanced novel in that it speaks both of pain and of joy—which is what life is. About pain—it takes a long time to understand and comprehend or heal after some of these things that go on in one's community. But I hope she writes more.

*HL:* She has another novel finished. It is in the computer, and this time it is about a little boy, same age. I think it is going to be a nice one. I am looking forward to reading it!

*EL:* I mean, the world awaits! I feel like that. Sometimes I feel like I am wasting my life when I could be writing, because my heart and my head are full of characters from my community! Goodness, if Margaret Laurence can write from a small Manitoba community, so can we! We were no more "isolated" or "remote" than Laurence's home-town. We were human beings with our own craziness and our own love of life.

*HL:* Sure, human beings!

*EL:* Our "Dancing with the Wolves"! Or Wisakehcha!

*HL:* So if you want to add the final word, go ahead. Or if you want to draw the curriculum for Native Literature in Canada, go ahead!

*EL:* There are a thousand things that I would like to do. After you told me you were doing this book, I said, "Jesus, why didn't I think of that?"

*HL:* So, are you a bit annoyed that I am doing it?

*EL:* I am not annoyed at you. I am glad that somebody is doing it. Maybe I am annoyed with myself. That I haven't done it of all the things I have done, and thousands more things that need to be done.

*HL:* Yes, but you can't do everything! I wasn't going to do it either. I was going to sit down and write my own book.

*EL:* What I would like to do—I think it would be fun for all the writers to be on film. If we could sit together and have it filmed and we just chatted with each other—discussed each others works, ideas, or experiences—and we let Canadian society watch this. To me I think that would be great. That would be one of the things we could do.

*HL:* And that is something Native writers themselves should initiate.

*EL:* Well, that is something that some film makers, including Native ones, also could help out with.

*HL:* CBC could instead of cutting their regional programs.

*EL:* Yes, CBC, NFB, or some enterprising private film maker. There are just a thousand angles from which to see Native people—our vastness, our diversity, our different personalities, never mind, just plainly, our humanity. White North American, not to mention white European peoples, haven't even begun to see us. They haven't begun to see us because of centuries of stereotypes. How many years will it take before the film of stereotyping can be scraped away so that we can be taken at face value? As I said in my preface, I have spent years having to educate the audience first before I can even dialogue with them. That is partly why I am not a novelist or a voluminous poet or writer, because I am forever having to educate first. And one gets very tired. Also one gets very tired talking to one's self—this is why we need that engagement. We need that engagement with Canadian writers, with other Native writers and artists. We need to engage with each other, apart from politics.

*HL:* You mean the Native writers and artists among themselves and also mainstream?

*EL:* Both, back and forth, together, side by side. (LAUGHS) Sometimes, I really feel like I am talking to myself. And what has happened to me the last few years has been actually frightening. I found that I stopped talking, by that I mean I got very discouraged so I have withdrawn. How can you talk to yourself over and over again? You need to get comprehending feedback. You need to engage. No great literature is going to come unless we do that.

I would like it, after I have spoken or written, to be understood. I mean in a sense of comprehension, not in a sense of emotional empathy, but *comprehension*. There is still such a distance, I suppose it comes from our diametrically opposed experience in this country, between Native and white there is such a distance in comprehension. And as I said before, there is also some distance between Native writers and Native audience because of colonial forces.

*HL:* I think there is also something historically that stands between, and that is, as I see it, from the white side the guilt and the bad feelings. I can only explain it as, when I meet people my age or older or younger from Israel, before we can communicate, if ever, there are six million dead between us! There is incredible shame and guilt feelings on my side. There is bitterness. There are all these things, and unless they are addressed and whatever, whether we cry together or remember, we can't communicate directly. I think some analogy can be made to the Canadian situation.

*EL:* Absolutely!

*HL:* It is the mourning that hasn't happened.

*EL:* Exactly! It is interesting you bring this up because I often use it as an example. I should say, when I refer to what happened in Germany white Canadians sit here aghast and say "are you making connections to the holocaust?"

*HL:* Please believe me, I am not saying this to minimize German guilt! That is another thing. If I say that or make that connection it is "aw, you want to distract from your own guilt." I don't!

*EL:* No, I know. The point I make is that before reconciliation can happen, you have to go through the normal stages of grieving because there is a tremendous amount of grief. And one of those is guilt. But in order to move past guilt, you have to be willing to feel other things such as pain. I always say that there is no possibility of reconciliation between white and Native people—it will never happen without pain, without grieving together. That is the connection I make to German-Jewish experience. There are other lessons too, sociological and psychological ones.

*HL:* Well, there are theories with regard to Germany, and I *don't* want to say exactly it is parallel.

*EL:* Oh, absolutely not, no.

*HL:* But one of the psychological contents that makes it difficult to communicate is the displacement of history, literally the pushing under, "Verdrängung," is what Freud used. And if you push something aside, it is not gone, it is still there, and it hampers your learning. If you look at the official government policy towards Natives in Canada, it shows that white Canadians have learned too little in the last 200 years.

*EL:* But you know, speaking of the German-Jewish experience, I do want to say this about the Canadian context: part of the reason why white Canadian people keep pushing under the Native/white experience is because they don't really believe white people invaded and destroyed thousands of Native people. Now, maybe six million Native people did not die.

*HL:* It is not a question of numbers.

*EL:* Exactly! In the end it is not a question of numbers, which by the way, are also being revised in history. There were way more Aboriginal people in North America than was first propagated.

*HL:* I know, I know.

*EL:* So even in numbers, we may compete. But we had an experience, an incredibly destructive experience—in a way more powerfully destructive because it has happened and is happening over a span of five hundred years. And because the invasion is largely institutional, it is all the more insidious. But the destruction is there, the invasion is there, the deaths by the thousands are there, the dispossession stares at us everyday—therefore, the bitterness, the tension, the pain, the guilt, the anger are all there from both sides. Not guilt from the Native side but the anger, the frustrations. You will notice, too, in this country there is concern for the liberation of South Africa, or Central America, or the Philippines, or some place over yonder. Now Europe last year. Always some other people's liberation, not our liberation. Yet, we have documented our displacement, we have shared our oppression, we have talked until we are blue, nobody is taking us seriously! Because whites cannot see themselves as colonizers, Natives as the colonized.

*HL:* The reason I am sitting here in a way is similar. I am listening to Native people. I am not in Germany recording interviews with Turkish people. This I can explain in a very sort of academic way: I am in North American Studies, which maybe is a cop-out.

*EL:* You can't do everything! (Laughs)

*HL:* No, but I am very painfully aware of that and like you said, you can't do everything everywhere at the same time. But that is much easier.

I have used it quite often in presentations in Germany, to talk about Natives in North America. When I talk about Native Americans, people come to listen. Then I draw the parallels to our history. But if I would talk about gypsies, nobody shows up. But if I talk about Natives, and I say "let's look at the parallels in our country," and I do that all the time, people, hopefully, begin to understand. We have had evidence in the school projects that school kids understood. And sometimes I have told Native friends when I was still doing this research, "you know, sometimes I use you as a hook to get people," and to get information across because in

Germany everybody wants to know about Indians.

**EL:** Oh yes, I understand. Well, it is obviously threatening here for white Canadians to come to their own backyard and say, "Oh, yeah, we are not innocent either!" But it will take some time, you know. The self-images of Canadians have to change. White Canadians see themselves as nice guys. Their knowledge base has to change.

**HL:** I thought that Oka would have been a chance but Canada hasn't taken it.

**EL:** No, but you know, there is some ambivalence within the Native community about Oka.

**HL:** I know, I know. I looked at it from the white side and since they didn't understand what was going on ...

**EL:** I had quite an experience a few months ago on an Air Canada flight. There were tons of soldiers in our sitting area and the steward, who was a French Canadian, started joking with the soldiers with "going to Oka, are you?" And then he and the soldiers, some of whom also spoke French, were making Indian and Mohawk jokes. And there were three of us Native women on the plane, sitting about. The two other Native women overtly received racist/sexist treatment from the male steward. He didn't have a chance to do anything with me but I felt unsafe, and, I said a few words to him and the soldiers. I also complained to Air Canada, and I got a letter of apology and they tell me the steward was "disciplined." I doubt it.

But no, Oka was an event to vent your racism. These are the true colours of Canada, I am afraid.

**HL:** What had been swept under all the time, all of a sudden, was taken up.

**EL:** Yes, it was very ugly. I felt afraid but I couldn't sit there and not say anything. I thought, "Oh God, here we go again!" I experience this kind of racism very often—racism in Canada is not exactly "pushed under" but public events do bring racism out even more brazenly.

About Oka itself, I had some problems with the warrior model. I come back to the issue of words—so many words about "Indians" come from racism, much of it via Hollywood! Words like "squaw," "warrior," "tribe," "chief," "papoose," or "brave" come from the white myth that "Indians" were sub-human, were savages, so words had to be created to indicate that.

**HL:** For "squaw," according to the *Oxford English Dictionary*, there are many definitions, but it is also a kneeling figure used for target practice.

**EL:** Oh yes. The US cavalry used to use what they called the "kneeling squaw" for target practice.

**HL:** And the other explanation for the term in the *OED*, one that I didn't quite understand at the time, was a certain position in which a barrel is held when it is tapped. So that is a term denoting sexual penetration and violence. This was years ago, and since I didn't know all the terms,

I didn't quite understand it, but I think that is it.

*EL:* World rapist imagery, where rape and murder merge! Both are equally the grossest acts of the objectification of human beings. These are the reasons why "squaw" is so unreclaimable.

*HL:* Yes, I understand that.

*EL:* I have great difficulty with "warrior" as well. Only because of the context, not that I would go to "soldier" for a model either. (LAUGHS) This male macho violence, warring, is just so tiresome! I certainly understand the struggle for liberation, but must we adopt Hollywood's models? Must we always act in reference to white creations of our past? Is it not possible to move on towards the future? We need new symbols that speak to our contemporary presence. It is a tall order, I know, for we have been embalmed with stereotypes, but the challenge is to create symbols that retain our identities yet avoid the stereotypes.

Finally, I want to end by saying this: I dream for our liberation in our land. Many times I have felt I was in exile in my own country. I dream for our people to stop dying, to stop feeling so alienated and so marginalized. I dream for our collective and individual well-being. We certainly need to rearrange the institutional structures that keep us down, that keep us resourceless. But I think the most important sort of liberation at this time is psychological in nature. What if we have a semblance of self-government but are still deeply colonized in our self-images and thinking? If ever we need good writers, we need them now. We must do two things: we must write with intellectual and emotional comprehension of the places of invasion in our histories and lives, and equally, we must speak to our own human condition. We need liberation not only from the colonial legacy of the proverbial white man, we need liberation from our own untruths. To quote Adrienne Rich, we need to look at our "lies, secrets, and silence" in ourselves, in our homes, in our communities, in our politics. Only then will we produce great literature. Wisakehcha is a classic character in Cree legend. The reason? Because he mirrored to Cree society the good, the bad, and the funny in human beings who were the Cree. Thank you for this interview.

*HL:* Thank you!

## NOTES

1. Emma LaRocque, "Preface, or: Here Are Our Voices—Who Will Hear?" *Writing the Circle*, eds. Jeanne Perrault and Sylvia Vance (Edmonton: NeWest Press, 1990), xv–xxx.
2. Emma LaRocque, "Tides, Towns, and Trains," *Living the Changes*, ed. Joan Turner (Winnipeg: Univ. of Manitoba Press, 1990), 73–90.
3. Elisabeth Hermann, " 'Academic Squaws': Some Aspects of Culture Contact in the Literature and Criticism of Paula Gunn Allen and Wendy Rose." *Minority Literatures in North America*, eds. Wolfgang Karrer and Hartmut Lutz (Frankfurt/M.: Peter Lang, 1990), 175–191.

# RUBY SLIPPERJACK

▼

*Ruby Slipperjack (Ojibway) grew up in northern Ontario (White Water Lake) on her father's trapline. In her childhood she and her brothers and sisters listened to stories told to them by their parents and elders. In Ruby's case, this led to a strong interest in storytelling, and she began writing stories even as a child. She attended schools in Sault St. Marie and Thunder Bay, and later enrolled at Lakehead University, graduating with B.A. and B.Ed. degrees in 1989.*

*Ruby Slipperjack is a painter and writer. Her novel* Honour the Sun *came out in 1987, her only published poem, "A Spirit of Wings," in 1989. Honour the Sun subtly follows the psychological development of a young girl from age 10 to about 16, and in the process the novel records in realistic detail the gradual disintegration of a single-parent family in an isolated community where there is nobody to stop the abuse of women and children.*

*Ruby Slipperjack is married and has three daughters. She is presently enrolled as a graduate student at Lakehead University, Thunder Bay, working towards her Master's in Education. The conversation was recorded at Ruby Slipperjack's home in Thunder Bay, Ontario, on 16 December 1990 (copyright: Ruby Slipperjack/Hartmut Lutz).*

---

**HL:** What I would like to ask you is how you got started writing?

**RS:** I think we talked about this, one time.

**HL:** That's true.

**RS:** I remember the trapper's shack where we were all born and raised. There was storytelling in the evening as there was nothing else to do. So someone would start telling a story. Sometimes it was legends or whatever. If it was my brother or my father coming home, it would be a hunting story. If you are walking along, someone would tell a story. I guess I missed that.

The more I think about it, perhaps the writing had something to do with me going away to residential school. I was 11 or 12 years old.

I had no one to share my stories with any more. There was no one to tell me stories, so I started writing.

This had started back at the day school at home before I left. All we had was *Fun, Fun, Dick and Jane*, and some other readers that we had in school. But I really got off on the pictures! The cute little animals had little jackets and such. I was just flipping pages looking at the pictures. We could not identify with the stories we read at school.

I was on my way home one day, and there was a minister's house halfway home. Anyway, I ran into the minister's outhouse. We always had a box of rags at our outhouse. This place had nothing, and the only thing that was there was a paperback book. Of course, I didn't know what it was. Anyway I picked it up, and I started looking through the pages and said, "Hey, there is a story here." I started reading like crazy. Of course, I had to peek out once in a while to make sure the minister wasn't coming. I was reading as fast as I could. Towards the end there, I turned the page and the whole back section had been ripped off.

I could have gone in there and choked that old minister! I never knew the ending to that book and that plagued me.

**HL:** How old were you then?

**RS:** Gee, I don't know, 10 or 11, somewhere along there. Anyway, so that is when I started scrounging around. I had to resolve in my mind an ending to this book, because I wasn't about to go in and ask the minister how this book ended, then he would know that I was in there. I got a pencil from school. We were not supposed to take paper or pencils out of the school. Of course, there were no such things at home. And I remember peeling off the inner layer of a sugar bag. I wrote the ending to that book myself on that sugar bag. That was the very first time I came across the idea that you can actually write a story in book form.

**HL:** You kept it up after that?

**RS:** Off and on, when I felt like writing. Just the need to tell stories. I used to drive my mother crazy. She never knew if I was telling the truth or whether I was making up a story. I think that is where it started. Then, I just wrote here and there, on anything that I could get my hands on. All of what I wrote went in the fire. I couldn't chance someone finding and reading it.

So when I left home and went to residential school and then on to boarding homes after that, it was just my form of entertainment, I guess.

**HL:** You always insist that *Honour the Sun* is not autobiographical and I guess there are a lot of questions going into that.

**RS:** I can't say that it is all true, because it is not. Some of the things that are in there were taken out of sequence, things I had seen and heard in different places and times, filled in with fiction to complete the story and make it *seem* real. You know, when you are writing, things pop into your head. It is a part of me. I think when you look at it, it is a part of everybody else because there is one thing that we all have in common. We were all children at one point, so we all feel at certain points in our childhood, "Yes, I remember doing that, or I remember feeling like that!"

*HL:* That is also exactly my own reaction to the book, and I got the same reaction from a lot of students too, regardless of what their background was. This one student said, "This is so wonderful! It makes me remember things that I thought I'd forgotten." So it is a lot of basic experiences that children have, the way they play, the way they see the minute little details that we are very often too busy to actually pay attention to.

*RS:* You know what I liken it to? Children, little children, have invisible playmates. To them, they are not invisible. They can describe this thing that they are playing with. They can describe this little person or animal that they are playing with. They will tell you what colour of clothes little Old Man Jimmy here is wearing today, you know. But, as we grow older, we learn that this is not acceptable. That we can't do this any more. (LAUGHS) But who are these people that are telling us? It is the adults who are now blind that the child sees clearly.

You know what I am getting at?

*HL:* Yes.

*RS:* And it is the same, the things that we lose in our childhood because we have been blinded as we get older. Our vision goes, our internal vision.

*HL:* Well, we are brainwashed into perceiving reality as whatever we can touch, uh?

*RS:* Yes. When you read something, you remember. It jogs your memory, and that is when you say, "Yes, now I remember!" You know, all these little details come back. But you need that person there, you need the ... if I could speak Indian, I could tell you exactly what I am trying to say.

What I am getting at is, when one person starts talking and then when your mind is set, when you are in the same frame of mind as the other person, then you start "clicking." You start to understand, and your mind opens up and you know, you will understand what you are reading. Because the words themselves are just words written down. When you start reading and understanding between the lines, that is when you know that you are on the same wave length, or in the same communication link. I think that's all it is.

*HL:* You just said that if you could speak in, I guess, Ojibway, it would be much easier to explain? Well, that is your first language, so English is a second language for you too. But you write in English and you write so well! Do you feel that if you speak English, you have a harder time writing?

205

*RS:* When I am speaking English, I am fine on a conversational level, but when I am trying to explain something that is more personal, something more intense, then I would rather I do it in a Native language. Because, one or two words will explain what I am trying to explain in English until I am blue in the face! I can't get that right, or I can't get that right feeling across.

That drove me crazy because that character, the Owl, is a Native girl set in a Native environment, Native home, so the conversation is all in a Native language. There are some things in there, like expressions, like a shrug of the shoulder, that can mean so much. How do you put that into writing, and in another language too? So there were times I was just totally frustrated. I cannot get the right meaning of what I am trying to say, so what I do most times is, I parallel it. I use English words, I devise situations where the English language would fit, still keeping the Native content intact, hopefully, so that you would get the flavour of what I am trying to say in the Native language by using this English system in there. So the feeling comes across.

*HL:* If you put in something like a passage where you think, well, this I can only say adequately in Ojibway or Anishnabe, if you left it in that and then put in a translation or a footnote, would that help?

*RS:* No.

*HL:* Because some people switch codes.

*RS:* No, because I would break the thought, or the flow.

*HL:* But it would teach the non-Native audience, "Hey, this story, although it is so readable and I as a non-Native person feel I can relate to it, is all from a Native person! It should really be told in the Native language!"

It is so smooth in English that non-Native readers would not realize that. Why not give them a little jolt every once in a while, and put in some Native words, and say, "Hey, you haven't learned this language!" Some people do that! I know some Chicanos who deliberately put in some Spanish and say, "This is the language!" How would you feel about that?

*RS:* One of the main reasons is that I didn't want to intrude on this girl's story. If I had done that, then all of a sudden I as the writer of this thing would keep popping up in the middle of the page, when I am trying to be totally out of there altogether. You understand what I mean?

*HL:* Yes, I understand that.

*RS:* You know what I noticed, though, when we were just talking earlier about regions? There are sometimes words that mean something specific to that region. So, when you are writing something, the Native person from this region that you are from will read this passage and they will understand exactly what you are trying to say because they have understood the implied meaning, and all of a sudden, they are just cracking up laughing, because you would have to be from that region before you could understand what the big joke is! (LAUGHS)

*HL:* I think in the book, as an outsider you realize how closely it is connected to one specific place, and how there is this one walk by the water, where the kids are playing.

*RS:* Oh yes.

*HL:* Or, when Owl comes back and sits on her rock, you get this feeling how closely she is tied to this one specific region! That comes across very strongly.

*RS:* That is another thing. Everything is tied with nature. They may be just rocks to you, but that is Old Sammy there, you know. You have given it a name. So that was the character's way of personalizing the rock, this thing of "my rock," because then that was Suzie's rock over there, and that was Tommy's over there, because these are things that we know the land by. That was the island where Jimmy was born. This is where Suzy learned to walk. The land, rocks, trees are part of our history, a part of us. They live longer than we do. If you stay in one place, a tree will watch you crawl, run, walk, shuffle, and eventually see your children also complete the cycle behind you.

*HL:* So you are thinking of one specific surrounding that you have actually seen, and that you know? You said that rock is still there, so in your writing you were not creating a fictional landscape but you were referring to part of a landscape that you knew exactly.

*RS:* I know many, many rocks. I get to know the rocks and the trees everywhere I go. Now, when I say that the rock is still there, that rock may be in my mind. The one I am talking about right now may be in White Water Lake. I have a rock there, and I also have a rock at many other places I have been to! I have "my" rocks, (LAUGHS) and the same thing with the trees. There is always one tree, in fact, every time you walk by you say, "Hi, how are you? It is nice to see you again!" Of course, this is all communication in your head. Someone would probably think I was crazy if I did this out loud. (LAUGHS) You don't think about it. You don't think what you are actually doing when you are walking along when you have been gone for quite a long time, and you come back, and for some reason, you go down and touch the ground, or you touch the trees, the young trees, as you go by, "My! How you've grown!" Why do you do it? Did anybody ask you, "Why did you do that?" You never think about it because you just do it. It is second nature.

*HL:* It is saying "Hello," to connect again. Here I am back, you must feel me, I feel the earth or whatever it is. Yes. Especially if you have been away a while. Coming to critics. How do you cope with people from outside, maybe Native, maybe non-Native, reading the book, reviewing it? People like me coming and asking questions. How do you feel about that?

**RS:** I don't mind, because it tells me where your interest is. What type of questions are you asking me? These are the type of things that I had no way of knowing when I was writing it. You know, what is interesting? What is interesting to you? What kind of things don't you understand? Why don't you understand? Or what type of interpretations can you get, because I know what I was trying to do. I know what I was writing. You tell me what you got from this thing and I will see how close you are, how totally far off you are. But who am I to tell you your interpretation is not correct? I can't tell you that.

**HL:** So you think the text is out there, and it is open, and somebody from this direction might come and see this end of it, and somebody else may find something else? *You* know what you put in there but whatever people see in there may be a reflection of themselves, or it may not be. That is what it is?

**RS:** Yes, you hit the nail on the head! I cannot tell you what it is because, there we go, we are back to the child again. You only see what you can see. How well do you look at yourself? Well, that in itself will tell you what you will get out of that book. How many things can you remember of yourself? Is the child you were still in you?

**HL:** I think the visual detail and the way Owl perceives things are for me, and I think for a lot of other readers, too, the most striking things I remembered after the first reading. The way of looking at the world, at plants and animals, at the natural surroundings reminded me of playing as a child, and we always played outside. We played with grass and rocks and sand. Or we would watch a tiny insect, and say, "Where is this ant going?" And we'd try to follow it, and then there was another one, and you get carried away into a dream world. But then, all of a sudden somebody calls you, "Come in!" or, "Dinner!" or whatever, and you forget, because you were so far away in a different world!

Now I have read the book again and we were discussing it in class, I hadn't connected it that way. Now I see another dimension of it. You once said that you don't go for stridently political books that come with an open message, or preach, or whatever. Now I am reading it again, and in a way it is a very political book. It is a very strong statement about violence against women and children!

It makes connections between various forms of violence and abuse. There's not only this bully who kicks in the door, but also the teacher who takes the Owl and puts her on his lap, and all of a sudden, although she does not understand the situation, she realizes that there is something wrong. So it is all in there. And the attentive reader can get it out if he or she—"she" probably has less of a problem identifying the more subtle forms of abuse, whereas for me it really took a second reading to realize how all that is connected.

208

So, in that way, I think it is a very, very strong book that has some very pertinent social criticism. How do you react to that?

*RS:* Well, it says, "this is how I feel," "this is what I am feeling," "this is what is happening around me," and "this is how I am reacting," "this is how I am dealing with this situation." That is where it stops. I cannot tell you why this and this and that happens, you figure that out yourself.

Who am I to come and tell you something? It is there for you to see. The only thing I can do is to remind you of the person you once were, to wake you up and make you remember what it felt like to be that small. These are the many, many things that we forget as we get older, because we think we know more. These are the things that we don't see any more when we think we have seen so much.

There is the child again! The child is so honest, so open. The child has memory of creation, because the child has not yet lost that connection. That is one thing that we all have in common, and I think that is one way that we can all communicate. That is one thing that we can all understand. We all have that one thread that connects us all to creation.

*HL:* You said earlier that, as you were writing you didn't intend to ever have that published, you were not even dreaming of it. Now it is published and in a way you are now telling people that you put it out there and people have to figure it out themselves. When you were writing, and you didn't even dream of publishing, who were you writing for?

*RS:* For me. There was one manuscript I had written that I think about, and I burned it, like I burned them all, heaven knows how many dozens of other stories.

*HL:* Does that hurt you now, when you think about that?

*RS:* No, no. But of all the stories that I have written and burned, there is one that I would like to do over again. To see if I can remember.

But the thing is that you can never duplicate something you have done, because you have grown. It is like trying to redo a painting, it will never be the same. I think it would change, too, if I sat down and wrote for the sake of writing, or writing so it would be published and be read, because that personal thing would be gone.

I have a manuscript in there (the computer). I sat down and just started writing, the same thing I did with the first, and I am in no big rush. Maybe it will never be sent to a publisher but right now I don't care. That is not my main priority, I will get around to it when I get around to it, and if I don't, then that's fine.

*HL:* I think your readers will regret it much more than you would.

*RS:* The thing is if I start writing for the readers, I will be very conscious of what I put in there. So, I have to make sure that that is not there. That I as the writer do not pop up in the middle of a page somewhere, that the character is authentic and true to the story and everything that goes on in there. If I can't do that, then I will have failed.

*HL:* How is it different? You have this on the computer, and you have had a novel published, so you must be much more aware of readership now than when you wrote that book, the first one. Does that answer the questions?

*RS:* No.

*HL:* Does that sort of enter your mind as you write?

*RS:* No.

*HL:* Only afterwards? When you showed me those pages earlier this afternoon, wasn't that because you think eventually it might get published?

*RS:* No, I showed you those papers to make sure that I as the writer didn't pop up in there.

*HL:* Okay.

*RS:* Was I true to the character? And I showed it to you, I think, because I have never had a dialogue that long. Did it stand out too much? Should I just chuck it all out, you know?

*HL:* I think there, again, your yardstick would be, if you have developed this old man and he is like that, that is what he is like, right?

I read a poem by you that was published here in Thunder Bay last fall about the bird.[1]

*RS:* Yes.

*HL:* Do you write poetry, too?

*RS:* That was the one and only time I did that. I mean for the public.

*HL:* So you don't write poems otherwise?

*RS:* I shouldn't say, "No, I don't." Yes, I do, but those, again, I would never ever want someone else to see, because those are personal things. It's me coming out. It's me looking at this, and it's me chucking it out, you know. When I come back to it again, there it is, "Yes, I remember that!" As long as I can *see* the feeling, then I can still understand it, because it is not just words. If the feeling is not there, then it is worthless. In the stories I have to have that feeling between the sentences. If it is not there, then I have lost something. So I backtrack, and that is why I was saying that sometimes it takes a long time, because you can't just sit down and continue where you have stopped. You have to go back, sometimes right to the beginning, to capture the spirit of the character. The spirit has to be there, otherwise the character will be a chunky person that is broken up and the feeling will not be whole.

I find that really difficult sometimes! Other times, I just give up. I can't do it. You have to be in that frame of mind, to capture the spirit of the character before you can continue.

*HL:* What makes you write? Is that too personal a question? It sounds as if you also struggle and fight. Apparently sometimes it is very joyful, but sometimes it is also very hard, and yet you go back, and you do write. Does it help you?

*RS:* When I meet people, I don't see the face. I see the person inside. And there are so many souls out there that ... some are just totally ... they have no idea of who they are. That is very, very painful to see.

When I am writing I am searching for the person inside the character, so I can get to know the character. "What is the matter with you? What is this thing that makes you tick? Why are you the way you are? Let me see! Let me get to know you!"

So when I create a character, I throw in all kinds of things like, "Okay, Danny, what are you going to do now? I'll make this happen. How are you going to deal with this?" And it is amazing how Danny has to figure out how to deal with life's situations. Because you let the character grow, and it becomes real. It helps you to understand why people are the way they are. It is making you walk in this character's shoes so that you will understand why this character acts the way he or she does. Maybe it is a way for me to try and understand people.

*HL:* You know, that reminds me. I did some research on what people said, what storytellers said, what Native authors said, as to why stories are told, and why there are the stories. And what it seems to come down to is: the stories were always told so that people know where they are from, where they come from, who they are, and who the others are. The "others" meaning the whole surrounding, and if they know where they come from, they also know where they are going. I don't know whether you agree with that, but from what you just said it seems to me that in the writing process you go through for yourself, you are doing exactly that. You find this character, find out where he comes from or she comes from, and why he or she is like he or she is, and to establish identity, or let people know what they are about, and what other people are about, and how they should carry on.

*RS:* I don't always provide an answer though.

*HL:* No.

*RS:* When that character reacts one way or another to the situation, there is never a "because of this and this and that!" That is another thing that will drive you crazy if you are looking for answers as to why am I writing, why am I doing this, or, "What kind of message were you trying to put across to the reader?"

*HL:* No, you are very careful about that. I think that makes the book very intriguing, and that is why people will read it again and again. Because in the beginning, it may look like a "simple" story, you know, just this child. And then with each reading, there is more, and more, and more. And that is how good books should be.

You know Thomas King, or have you heard about him?

*RS:* Yes, I have spoken with him several times.

*HL:* He said, "She is so good, I think sometimes she doesn't even know how good she is!" I hope you *do* keep on writing, and that you will have the time to keep on writing.

*RS:* Well, I write for myself. I will always insist that it is a hobby. I am not a writer. I am not a good writer. I am not a good storyteller. But I do feel inside. If I can communicate this feeling inside with human beings I see every day, then maybe I have left something for other people. Because if they can see themselves in something that I have written, then I think I have touched that thread that runs through all of us.

*HL:* Anything else that you want to add? You know, when I started asking people for interviews, all I had in mind was to capture on tape the voice of a person, because if I am over in Germany and we read books by Native authors, it would make it not just a book by author "So-and-so," but this is a living person.

*RS:* Well, if I could just meet them! If I could talk to them! I need to see them before I can say something.

*HL:* Is that also why you didn't like the tape?[2]

*RS:* Yes.

*HL:* Yes, I can understand that. It is kind of awkward. There are some people, however, who are so "professionally unprofessional" that the tape actually gets them going.

*RS:* I am a non-verbal communication person.

*HL:* I don't know whether people do that here, but certainly down there people use body language and little signs a lot, pointing with their lips or eyes, you know. They are so very attentive, attuned to non-verbal communication.

*RS:* (LAUGHS) That is a big joke here! Because that is what Native people do here. (LAUGHS) It is really bad manners to point with your finger!

*HL:* Things like that can be very puzzling for an outsider. Sometimes, if you are a non-Native person in a group of Native people, all of a sudden, they get up and go some place. Because they have communicated, and since it was non-verbal, or you are so out of it culturally, you are the stupid one sitting there. And you are the only one who doesn't know what is going on.

It's happened to me!

*RS:* Words are very, very rare. That is another thing when you are writing, you have to put everything in words, right? And sometimes, like I say, it's frustrating, you come to a dead end. How are you going to put all this non-verbal communication that is going on back and forth into words, and English on top of that! (LAUGHS) It is a different language, and that is a very frustrating process, because we were raised in a non-verbal culture. You only used words when they were necessary or in direct conversations.

212

Most of the time, nobody said anything at all, because you didn't need to. I understand what you are thinking and what you are going to do next, or I just caught your comment right there.

I used to get a kick out of these people from the city, the white people from the city coming down to the Native communities. They walk into the local store, and everybody is quiet and doesn't say very much. And the ladies over there start giggling, and they burst out laughing, you know. And the person is just totally out of it! Like you were saying, he doesn't know what is going on. In the meantime, comments are flying back and forth. Somebody just said something over there and, unless you can interpret the messages, unless you can feel too, you know. The intuitive part of you has to be able to interpret the messages and catch what is happening. It is like when you walk into a tense room. You feel it! That is the kind of thing, the kind of communication.

*HL:* As non-Natives, we are far out! It must be hard for you, like you said, to try to get some of that into language, another language, and in written form.

*RS:* Yes. And as I mentioned, if there is a reader from that area, when I describe something in the book, you know, the child just did this, caught somebody's eye over there, and another person maybe shrugs their shoulders. They will know, they will get the message by just mentioning those things. They just burst out laughing because they have caught the unwritten communication in there.

*HL:* So, when you say that you write for yourself, and now that the book has been published for a couple of years and people are reading it, do you think then that you have written it more for Native people than for non-Native people? Because they will be more able to relate to it and understand those little messages?

*RS:* Oh yes! I hope they do get something out of it, like I said, and understand. That will make me happy. Especially the unwritten communication between the lines! If they can read between the lines and catch the jokes in there, yes, that is good to know.

*HL:* Do you get a lot of feedback from Native readers?

*RS:* No. You don't do that. (LAUGHS) It is like questioning someone! You don't question people. You don't make comments. That is why the lecture theatres are such a foreign environment in universities, the debates, and the discussions, the panels—those are totally foreign. It is just like pointing a finger at somebody. (LAUGHS)

*HL:* It is a fix in a way. You have written a book, and it is published, and it is out there. It is out there on its own, in a world that is dominated by forms of behaviour, by a literary culture, an academic culture that you have no control over and that is very alien to where you come from. So whether you like it or not, you are subjected to it.

*RS:* Yes, and I know there are people out there who will read from beginning to end, just reading the words. Where is the plug? Where is this typical European format? Right? I am sorry, but you are not going to find it there because it's of a different culture. I am not going to try to pound a circle into a square.

I stuck to my four seasons. I wanted that connection there, with the land.

*HL:* But the way it is set up now, you have the seasons coming back. And almost half of the book is set in the first year, or a little more than half, if you count the chapters. And so, as time goes on it moves much more rapidly towards the end, because of the bounds and leaps.

*RS:* Yes. Life is a circle. So I wrote how I was feeling and made it come across to the character. Days fly by as you get older. The older you get, weeks turn into days, etc. In the beginning the character's feelings were sort of lazy, spaced out, a very carefree childhood, so it dealt with quite a bit there. And the teenage years, they were just sort of skippy, full of anticipation and impatience, almost irritating in that section of the book, because that is exactly what that child is feeling at that time! And you as the reader were probably feeling the same way. And at the end, everything is happening so fast that, to the kid, it is suddenly, "Here I am!"

On page 210 it says, "I feel like I have just completed a circle." The book starts in the summer and ends in the summer.

*HL:* In your book there is so much humour, and warmth, and loving, and some of the situations are incredibly funny. But you can also read it as a sad book, because in the beginning there is this closeness and everybody is together, and in the end everybody has left, and the Owl is by herself. Fortunately, there is the Medicine Man she can talk to. But otherwise she is out in the open, and all the childhood, and security, and warmth is gone forever. So in that way it is also sad.

*RS:* Yes, but the old man says that life and hope are in us, as long as we know the sun is up there.

*HL:* And you have the feeling that she is strong enough to remember that.

*RS:* Oh yes!

*HL:* So, I understand that the book you are working on, which is almost finished, is about a boy.

*RS:* Yes.

*HL:* You want to talk about that?

*RS:* (LAUGHS) Danny? No!

*HL:* You know, reading Native literature and talking to Native authors, the more authors and more literature I get to know, the more I realize that criteria that I have learned about literature are inadequate. If I were to characterize *Honour the Sun*, also based on what you say now, I'd say it "shows a strong interest in psychological development." But you said

214

something about "plot." "Don't look for plot!" When writing do you think in categories like "poetry," or "this is novel, this is something from the oral tradition, and this is drama?"

*RS:* No, I chuck out any preconceived ideas. I chuck out anything that will interfere with my reading and my writing. When I read, I read to know that character, and from there I get to know the author very, very well. I know when that author has hit the dumps, you know. Because it comes out. It is in there, if the spirit is there. Mind you, I have read books that are absolutely nothing. They are just a string of words put together, which doesn't do anything for me. I don't bother to finish it.

*HL:* If you had to teach Native Literature here, are there some texts that you would really like to use, or that you would recommend?

*RS:* No, I haven't thought about it at all. In fact, I haven't really studied "Native Literature."

I would like to take the course, though, just to find out what it is they are teaching. What is their point of view? What is their interpretation? Because I know most are not Native people, how close are their interpretations, or how far out are they to my own understanding?

I wonder if Native people would get the same interpretation if they were teaching. There again, they would get different perspectives, because everybody comes from different backgrounds, and our experiences are different. So, we would get different meanings from what we are reading. Maybe this passage means something to me, has touched me, had something to do with my background, or has reminded me of something, whereas another person may say, "No." So it depends on the people. We are all different, and everyone will get different things out of it.

*HL:* That is the beautiful thing of it, also. It is good in the classroom, if you can share that with the students.

If there is something else that you would like to say, say so.

*RS:* Well, I hope that if I ever get around to finishing this second manuscript, and if it gets published, that it will generate as much discussion as this one has.

---

## NOTES

1. Ruby Slipperjack, "A Spirit of Wings," *Flight Pattern Uninterrupted*. Catalogue for exhibition of art by Alice Crawley, An Whitlock, and Michael Belmore, ed. Lynne Sharman (Thunder Bay: Definitely Superior, 11 November 1989), s/pp.

2. Ruby Slipperjack and I first met for an interview on 3 October 1989, at Renate Eigenbrod's home in Thunder Bay. Ruby was not comfortable with the tape recorder going, so we switched it off.

# JOY ASHAM FEDORICK

▼

*As the daughter of a Cree career serviceman overseas and an English mother, Joy Asham Fedorick grew up in various places throughout Canada and Europe. She decided to become a writer at an early age, but having to bring up two children on her own as a young divorced mother forced her to work in mainstream institutions for many years. The Indian Movement of the early 1970s in Canada led her to become active and reclaim her Native heritage — a process reflected in her writing and cultural work. Her poetry and critical essays have appeared in* Canadian Woman Studies/les cahiers de la femme, ArtViews, *and* Artscraft. *An active supporter of Native self-determination, Joy Asham Fedorick initiated and directed the Earthtones Project, an attempt to involve Ojibway and Cree communities in the production of books in their Native languages via computer communications in order to halt the erosion of Aboriginal linguistic identity.*

*Joy Asham Fedorick lives in Thunder Bay, Ontario, where the interview was recorded on 17 December 1990 in the kitchen of our mutual friend Renate Eigenbrod* (copyright Joy Asham Fedorick/Hartmut Lutz).

---

**HL:** How and when did you start to write?

**JAF:** I guess, when it comes to writing, I always have written. It is not something that I consciously learned to do. I know that by the time I was 10 years old I clearly knew that I wanted to be a writer. I got married at a young age, though, 18, and by the end of the marriage, three years later, I had two children. Meanwhile I was writing poetry, and I consider myself (at least in the early part of my career) primarily a poet. After my marriage ended I went to Winnipeg with my children, and there a few things got published. I guess it was because there my poetry changed: it became protest poetry, which at the time was a popular thing to do.

**HL:** Was that in the 1970s?

**JAF:** Yes, that was in the early 1970s. I ended up being published in a number of different places. Things were moving along for me quite well

217

in that area. I supported myself strictly through community development work, and through working with the Department of Education in Manitoba and doing a number of other jobs.

*HL:* Did you work with Indian or Métis people, or both?

*JAF:* Indian and Métis. That is where I think I got my education, because I virtually don't have an education of the sort that one normally considers to be such. But I think that doesn't mean that I don't know anything.

*HL:* No.

*JAF:* By the time I was 29 years old I had done many presentations of my work at libraries, universities, etc., and had numerous short stories and poems published. When I was 29, I was asked to do a national tv show. I wasn't the star or anything, but a poem of mine was featured and they wanted me to do the reading and an interview. But the night before the filming, something very violent happened to me. Somehow, because of the fact that I had a traumatic life, a strange connection happened in my head that said to me that it was because of my ability to communicate that this terrible thing had happened to me.

*HL:* You were also a communications officer for a government agency?

*JAF:* Yes, I was called "Information Officer."

*HL:* So that involved writing information, and other writing too?

*JAF:* Yes, that job and the violent incident happened about the same time. The violence resulted in a creative shut-down, and for three years I didn't write at all, other than what was necessary for the jobs that I had. I made a decision about six months after this thing happened. I decided that I had to get out of Winnipeg. I had to go to the people, and I had to find a better sense of myself, I guess, get a historical perspective to me.

I was offered a job in northern Manitoba. I went and it was disastrous! The community that I went to was very racist, and I was a divorced Native woman in a position of responsibility. The non-Native population had never seen such a thing before. I was only there about six months and I uprooted my little family one more time and my children and I went on what I call a traditional pilgrimage to a number of different places, such as the Indian Ecumenical Conference in Morley, Alberta. Eventually, we settled back in southern Ontario, where my mother is from. London.

While I was in Winnipeg, in that early part of my life, not only had I written protest pieces, but I had been very actively and prominently involved in the movement. In London I put that aside and started getting serious about how I was going to raise these children of mine, what kind of future could I offer them, and I came face to face within myself with a number of very complex issues such as "this is who I am," "this is who I am defined to be," and "yet I don't fit anywhere." I don't speak my language.

218

**HL:** Were you raised in an urban surrounding?

**JAF:** Many. My mother is English, so Cree was not spoken in the home. My father was in the services, and there was a lot of moving around—I was in Europe for two years, for example. So there had been a total separation from my roots. The repatriation period had started in Winnipeg. I think that is one of the reasons why I became very fervent about issues, because, all of a sudden, I was starting to see for the first time in my life the reality of what life can be like in Canada if you're a member of a non-favoured group. For some reason, my feelings about that had always been, "Well, I can live through that." I was very arrogant in a sense, because I also went on to think, "But these people around me and my children can't." That is why I think my work career became heavily involved in community development, looking at the social aspect and what can be done to bring us out of a state of powerlessness. I had become very involved in many activities and developed a new personal way of looking at things. But in those Winnipeg years I still don't think I was out of the egg yet, you know, still in the egg.

I had, as I mentioned before, a very traumatic life. One disastrous thing after another, and this followed me to London. Because I didn't have that education, I worked harder and harder all the time to prove myself, to deal with the self-esteem stuff that had never been allowed to grow. Through work I began to get "better and better" (I used this term tongue-in-cheek) jobs, and, at last, was transferred to northern Ontario, back near Manitoba.

I became quite successful indeed, on the outside. But inside I was dying.

I know this is a long story, to tell about how I got back to writing, but I think these things are important to why I looked at writing the way I looked at it. How these things changed.

When I was 37 years old I was confronted with a cancer scare, and I was put in the hospital and had major surgery. At the same time I was in a very bad relationship. I came out of the hospital and in a very short period I lost 90 pounds. My whole world just started to crumble around me, and right around this time I developed further along in progressive alcoholism. This never reflected in the work I was doing, other than spurring me on to work even harder and harder. So, when the Ontario Women's Directorate, where I then managed the northern office, called me back to work early I just put on the harness and went.

All these other things were going on, my relationship ended dramatically—it was just awful and I worked harder and harder and then, plop! I collapsed a year later. So, at 38 years old I confronted my own mortality again. This time, though, I said: "Hey, what's going on here?" and I began to make some fairly drastic decisions that were based on episodes of what I call vision quest, others have called epiphany. (LAUGHS) These are best described by Abraham Maslow as "peak experiences." It seems I was being told that I had been given a gift and that it was given to me for a purpose. There was something special I had to do. I felt the gift came with the responsibility of using it, and using it in an ethical, positive, even spiritual way.

And then, the way to use it presented itself, and, while I was on sick leave after the collapse, I was offered a job at the Ojibway/Cree Cultural Centre in Timmins. Those "coincidences" happen to me a lot, and, since I started exploring such things in writings and readings, I have found that they happen to a lot of people.

*HL:* I can tell you weird stories, and coincidences clustered, so that you don't believe they are coincidences any more. You said you were involved in leftist politics, and I come from a Marxist background myself. So, for me for a long time anything that was not tangible just did not exist. Those things happen so much that it really shook me in some of my beliefs. I had a hard time accepting that at first and now I am just grateful that they happened.

*JAF:* Yes, grateful! I think a lot of the changes and coincidences are reflected in my work. My earlier stuff is very different from the things that I write now. The change is reflected in my work very strongly.

*HL:* I think the idea of what I read in this one article, about how you went out with computers into the communities to produce books was very practical.[1] It was also a very practical political reason to help those languages survive. There is also a coming together. You started writing when you were 10, and the political activism made you write in a different way.

You said you were in a fix because you don't speak the language, and I see that dilemma too.

*JAF:* In fact, I looked at the creation of the 500 Aboriginal books required to provide refuge for Cree and Ojibway as a math problem.

There is a very logical, practical side of me. I said, "Hey, if we have 10 Native writers in Canada, they are going to have to put in 50 books each to come up with the 250 each needed to save the Cree and Ojibway languages. This is providing they write in their own language. This is mathematically impossible to achieve, given the 10 years left till our elders are gone (the oral keepers of our languages, predicted to die of old age by the year 2000). So, I am looking at this problem from the wrong end of the funnel. I have to turn this around and get back to the kind of belief I had when I was doing community work, which was it had to be the *people*! I don't own all of Native culture. Even our finest elders don't own it either. None of us own it. We are all an important piece of a massive jigsaw puzzle. Let's go about finding the pieces, and let's assemble."

So, that was the logical side. The other side said it was exactly the right thing to do, for people to read this stuff they have to know it is theirs. Community-based literature-of-the-people.

**HL:** Maybe you can explain just a little of how you went about that.

**JAF:** How I went about the project itself?

**HL:** Did you get the computers out to the communities?

**JAF:** Yes. There were a lot of problems with the things that happened. I had launched the project as an individual, since the Ojibway/Cree Cultural Centre that I had worked for was part of the larger bureaucracy. We, the oppressed, often think ourselves that we can't do anything unless we're well-papered, and the Cultural Centre was of this belief.

**HL:** I work at a college that was implemented through the bureaucracy from the top down. I know exactly what you are talking about. So, there was a lot of "politics"?

**JAF:** That is right, from the top down — descending power. But, I'm of the dammit-let's-do-it school and have a fundamental belief in the ability of people, not organizations, to do things. Unfortunately, though, funding agencies do not believe this, and the funding was drastically cut.

There was a lot of "politics," and when I left there, long before the project was started, I said to myself that my feelings haven't changed about what needs to be done. I — and here I get arrogant again! — as an individual have a gift, and where there is a gift there is a responsibility. I looked at it from the spiritual perspective and I said, "Something put me at the right place, at the right time, to do the right thing, and now I am obligated out of love and gratitude to do what I have been chosen to do."

That may be arrogant, but that is exactly how I felt, and how I feel. Unfortunately there is, at the same time, the state of powerlessness of this person. I am still a divorced Native woman, and I am not a status Indian. We were part of the whole enfranchisement scheme of the federal government, and my father finally got reinstated into status about a year ago, but he died in September before all the things were unravelled that would allow me, at some point in time, legally to say "I am Indian." There is a political game that you have to add to that, the fact that I have light eyes, and I end up in a lot of trouble.

But I said to myself, "I am going to do it anyway." Then, unfortunately, I became involved with another organization that systematically went about taking apart that dream. Just let me do it, I know what I am doing. I have the technical expertise and the social work expertise, I have the teaching ability, I have the experiential popular education. The organization did not understand any of these things but wanted to count a Native project to their advantage. It was terrible.

So, I finally realized that, yes, I had to do it alone. I applied as an individual artist to get funding back. Because of the cutbacks in the funding received, I had to go to communities that were accessible by road.

Not the communities where the languages are still strong, because they are remote fly-in. Pardon me, I get ethnocentric as hell, but the other problem with road access is the presence of many non-Aboriginal persons. Damn it, when it is advertised as a Native writing workshop, why do other people show up? When I went to communities, the non-Native people controlled those workshops, as much as I could sit there and say, "no, sorry, we don't like it." It is a very sensitive thing to attempt to deal with non-Native people within those situations. There can be seven Native people in the room, and the non-Native person will hog the conversations, hog the attention, and one has to go through a whole educational process to get that one person to the point where he can understand the basic symbolisms, and we are talking English. We are not talking another language.

*HL:* It is like the classic situation of one or two men in a women's workshop.

*JAF:* It was pretty disastrous on a field level. Because of the fact that I still don't know my own language, with the cutbacks came the inability to get the kind of support I needed to do the work, i.e., people who were familiar with the languages, familiar with the syllabics, and could install these into the computer system that I have. So, we got a book done at Wabigoon #27, a northern Ontario Ojibway reserve, but it is still in my computer.

*HL:* In syllabics?

*JAF:* No, in English; not only in roman orthography, but in the English language. So what I was capable of doing with the restrictions of the project is to show that a community can make their own book. There is no question about it. They can. But there is no support for this kind of thing in Canada. I was only able to get funding as an individual artist in media arts, not in literature, not in writing, not in anything remotely related.

*HL:* So much for multiculturalism.

*JAF:* So much for multiculturalism. I don't know whether you've come across it, but in the Fencepost article, I talked about Robert Bringhurst, in fact, said that he was a knight in shining armour.[2]

*HL:* That is a good term, because it is very ambivalent, right?

*JAF:* Well, the thing is that I quite appreciated his input, even though it could be construed in a sense as being paternalistic. There are times when we need to reach out our hands and have help.

*HL:* It is a dilemma that I was talking to Renate about also. We are in the dilemma, too, because we are "white liberals," well-meaning or so, and if we put together something which is useful, hopefully, for Native people, at the same time it upholds the structure, right?

*JAF:* Sure, but I don't know ...

*HL:* Or it reaffirms the sort of power relationship?

222

*JAF:* Yes, but I don't know how one gets around that. I had a situation a few years ago with somebody who had been a friend for a really long time, he and his wife, actually. He had been my boss, and after he was no longer my boss the friendship with the family remained. He had become quite ill, and he had to have eye surgery shortly before Christmas, but he hadn't gotten around to buying his wife's gift yet. So I said "why don't I take you around, I can do the driving, and I can guide you from store to store, and give you some input?," because I liked them both very much. I thought it would be a helpful thing to do. They agreed, and I arranged to pick him up the next day at an afternoon Christmas house party.

The woman who was the hostess was from South Africa. She was disgusted that I had come to the door. Just terrible. She was just awful. And these "good" people let her do it. I attempted to explain that I was there for a good purpose, but I was a non-entity to her. I was not recognizable to her as a human being, and how can I therefore influence that person? Even though it does reinforce the structure, those people should have said, "but I am your peer and it is not acceptable to me."

*HL:* Well, in that case, I think it would not have upheld the structure but destroyed it because they would turn around against that woman and say "you are so brainwashed, you can't even recognize human beings! To hell with it, this is a borderline!" That is what they should have done.

*JAF:* That is right.

*HL:* So they upheld the structure by not doing anything.

*JAF:* That is how it gets maintained—inability to see the need to act. Belief and words mean little without action. And, that is where I believe it must come.

*HL:* In that case, it is self-help because we need reeducation much more than the "victims." We are victimizing our own children. We have victimized ourselves into arrogance based on ignorance.

*JAF:* You are right! I believe that, yes, in some ways we need to change. Maybe some of that change has to do with the acquisition of certain kinds of transferable skills. I think, however, it is less easy to transfer a set of ethics, a spiritual way, than it is to learn how to operate a computer. Those are the easy things.

What I am talking about is what fundamentally forms good character, and that is the hardest thing to change. Personality reorganization is one of the hardest things to do because so very often we see no need for it if our basic needs are met. To step beyond and change on an ethical basis for the benefit of others—actually for yourself!—is seldom recognized, and less often successfully achieved. But it is from this bolt of red cloth that we see—usually long after they are gone—the true heroes, the ones history so often ignores. They are the ones who have allowed us to even progress as far as we have today, because great odds confront them.

223

There are ways in which we have to change—racism, sexism, and "classism" are all from the same root. Until that is systemically dealt with, we can take up arms, do all kinds of different things, but we can't change the thinking process within another human being. I don't know how that changes—epiphany perhaps?—maybe through peer pressure. Revolution, too, is the conclusion that I continuously reach. It can't go on the way it is. And that is not just for me and that is not just for my children, but it is because the circles of victimization are getting wider and wider. One of these days people are going to realize that 97% of the people are suffering for 3%. And, those social programs that I have struggled to protect in a sense defeat my long-term purpose, because those social programs ...

**HL:** Exactly. All social programs just put a little plaster on something, but they do not heal the root causes.

**JAF:** That is right.

**HL:** You were talking about this earlier. You said that you did an assessment, "where did this come from?" You said first, "it started October 12, 1492," but then you go back and say "to Plato." Okay, that sorts out the ideological side of it, but then, if you think of these evils like sexism, racism, and classism, they are triplets. They always come together and they help each other in many "wonderful" ways. I find it impossible to pinpoint when it really started, and where. It went on and on, but, certainly if you take the time of Columbus, right from Europe.

**JAF:** In the larger picture, I tend to think that there is a spiritual relationship between people and the land and that once a "dominion over" attitude is established, it goes wrong. All the major religions of the world have that. The only place—and I am not saying this because I am Aboriginal, but because I looked at it—the only place I don't see that is within Aboriginal culture and life-style. "Dominion over" is the process that comes through the establishment of hierarchy. When I talk circle, what I am saying is, part of that circle is not only "I am as valuable as you," and vice-versa, because that tree out there is part of the circle, and so is the sky, and the water. All these things need to be equally honoured and respected. That is another reason why I work with languages, because it may be that we are some of the last voices with that conception, the wisdom within the languages and culture, that have the ability to say "you do have to think unto the seventh generation," that say "I am not going to divert that stream, unless I can guarantee to my children's children's children's children's children's children that it will not negatively affect them.

That kind of thinking has been lost with the turning away from the belief in a continuum, a continuous state, a cycle. Instead it's like, "Hey, my life expectancy is 72 years and in 72 years I have to cram in everything, and to hell with everybody else, and everything else, because it doesn't continue beyond 72!" And, thus, these thinkers consume omnivorously and care not what they leave behind, if anything.

*HL:* No, it is the linear thinking which enables hierarchies. The thinking I am pretty sure about, but what interests me is, where did it start? What caused it? I mean, if hierarchies are established, who establishes hierarchy for what idea?—to preserve private property? Or is it earlier than that? So I think it is a much longer process, and it is not possible to pinpoint.

*JAF:* I think it does go back. I have a certain affinity for Neanderthal. And the reason I do is some of the findings of Shanidar Cave. They found people there with evidence of healed amputations, who continued to be protected, etc., by the rest of the people around them. They found pollen that showed that flowers had been gathered from miles and miles around to show honour and respect in ceremony. That says to me that somewhere along the line I wish we were descended from Neanderthal. I think, you know, that Homo Sapiens Sapiens, Thinking Thinking Man, is very stupid. We have overspecialized, which is one of the first indicators of a soon-to-be-extinct species. This is a very silly thing for me to say but, you know, my IQ is very high, about 185, so what? Intelligence and wisdom are not synonymous terms!

*HL:* No, of course not.

*JAF:* I know a man, listed in the *Guinness World Book of Records, 1984–88* as one of the world's five smartest people. IQ 197. I have known him well for four or five years. My IQ is such that I qualify for several egghead societies "above" MENSA, and these people are scary. They are not just scary because they are weird. I can understand what they are talking about, I am "up" there with them, but don't pontificate to me about thinking when that thinking doesn't end up with anything ethically usable. Where is the feeling part?

That is another thing I look at when I look at the early philosophers, or see the negation of the intuitive and spiritual aspects. I see that even in things such as the banning by Plato of the use of minor keys in music, which open up the right brain. We have to look and see how the manipulation of our minds has been going on for so damn long, the suppression of our feelings, our intuition, and ability to establish the spiritual links, unless they are within the rigid criteria of the institutional religion that I set down for you!

Right now, what is happening in the Aboriginal community is the institutionalization of the original directions. The original teachings, whether that be the use of tobacco, which way you walk around the circle—the trappings of this WAY, this spiritual way, the trappings are becoming rigid and institutionalized and oppressive of the spirit. To me, though, the Way is not whether I wear braids or not, it is how I am. I am not a ritualist. How I am, my relationship with everything, that, to me, is very much guided and part of my relationship with the Creator, the Great Spirit, and other beings around me, and that, to me, is the Way and what I have to work on. These things, you know, of which I speak, at times I can't see, touch, taste, hear, feel, or smell them. But they are real. They are just as real as everything else, and when the dust settles, more real!

This Way is why, within the articles I write, I try to come from a perspective that says, "There is another way of thinking and looking at things! Maybe that is what you need to be in touch with, instead of the Beginning, Middle, and End hierarchy." The circle, the continuum, is always looping back and reaffirming this Way. "There is no beginning, there is an always was, and with no end there is an always will be." [3] ... But, in articles I write I have only 2500 words to say all this stuff, now how can I incorporate all of that? I try, and sometimes have been told I succeed. I often use a storytelling approach to do this, as it helps to get into the right brain where non-linear things can happen.

*HL:* Well, you are certainly aware of the fact that quite a few minority writers, minority women of mixed descent in particular, really develop new ways. Maybe they are not new ways, but ways not vocalized previously, of looking at the world and teaching either side because they have this unique position "between." And, it is not "between." Take Gloria Anzaldúa, who talks about borderlines. She is Chicana, and not only in terms of geography and ethnicity but in terms of gender, in terms of culture, in terms of language. She says, "I am not the margin any more, I'm the centre." She doesn't say there are margins, but comes from the perspective that a critic in Europe is calling "liminality." "Limes" is the border. That liminality opens up such a complex way of relating to various parts and bringing together things that we, being "here" or "there," have no notion of. And I think it is this kind of perspective that brings together different world views, and maybe integrates in a person a totally new approach that is certainly needed, and that is helping. There are people out there in Europe who are very grateful for this, and who address that, and I want you to know that.

*JAF:* You see, like I believe, I call it "the straddle." The straddle between asphalt and boreal forest.

*HL:* She uses the same. "I have straddled the border all my life," exactly that!

*JAF:* And I have, at times, a foot planted firmly in midair! I'll just go back to this article that will be appearing in *Artscraft* magazine because what it is called is "Getting Out from Under: How to Avoid Professional Pathology." [4] I sort of treat professionalism as a disease, and examine the patho-type. (Laughs) I do it in a very strange way. I believe there is this sickness of spirit, or whatever one would want to call it. The thing that makes us struggle, strive like crazy to get to the top, like the children's book that talks about caterpillars climbing all over each other to get to the top of the post, and when they get up there they wonder what the heck is up there anyway!

Most people spend all their life keeping up with the Joneses, whom they don't like anyway. What is the sense of any of this stuff, I don't know. So what I try to do is take a very basic truth that few seem to see, and maybe address it in a different way and say, "Hey, this is what has been wrong!" I don't care what happens, without addressing the original problem bandaid solutions just won't work.

**HL:** Exactly, that is what we have been content with for centuries. That's what I said is the problem with social work, layers of layers, a little plaster here, a little drop there, and the underlying issue is not addressed so it just helps to keep the underlying structures intact.

**JAF:** And out of every "solution" arise more problems, and it just keeps going on like that and growing to where we have the "Imminent Doom" syndrome I see today.

**HL:** It is like redirecting the rivers, right?

**JAF:** Yes. They talk today about "sustainable development." My answer is "Just get the hell out of the way, just leave it alone!" (LAUGHS) Mother Earth is a power in herself, a greater power than those who "dominate over," but even Mother Earth cannot take too much more "help."

In writing I work in two or three different strategies, and those strategies include myself as a writer, for myself and my community. Myself as a writer for the larger global community. Myself as a catalyst for the use of emerging writers, avoiding like hell the pathology I see. These are the words that matter, the words from new lips.

What I do creatively is very different than what I do for *Artscraft* magazine. Those are the things I would like to share with you. I sit down at the computer, somebody else writes for a while, and then I get up and leave. And there is something there that is in simple language. Just because I can talk technically, use technical nomenclature, doesn't mean that this is how I write. Who does technical terminology really talk to? But, although I deal in simple language, some of the concepts are quite complex.

**HL:** You write poetry, too?

**JAF:** I write poetry as well. I don't write as much poetry as I used to, although I am kind of wondering why, and I think part of it is, where do you sell poetry? (LAUGHS)

**HL:** That is a good question.

**JAF:** And another part is, sometimes the medium really does dictate the message, and it is just like everything else! It is really hard to waltz to a polka! As a writer I must have several tools available to me and pick the right one for the job. Sometimes poetry restricts us. However, in my forthcoming tour of cross-cultural performances with a Ukrainian tsymbaly player, Ted Harasymchuk, I have once more picked up poetry as a tool. Actually, it picked me. I use several styles: free verse, parataxis, closed and rhyming, and even, for heaven's sakes, a limerick. In the prose I do and use for performing, I believe the poet is not very well hidden, lurking just below the surface. Sometimes, verbs, adverbs, and adjectives just begin to roll and nouns recede in the distance. Once again, the connection with the right brain as opposed to the material.

There are times when I use poetry to take a good poke at myself, because I tend to take myself much too seriously. I spend a lot of time in what I call "terminal introspection." I was inside poking around, lifting scabs, trapped there one day, and realized the ridiculousness of the whole thing. So I went to the computer and wrote a poem about that, and, I guess, about optimism. It's called "Midpoint Ponderings" and it goes like this:

> Periodically I reflect
> Upon the ruby
> In my navel
>
> Great things I see there
> Profound, philosophical
> And rosy
>
> Then I look again
> And see no ruby
> Just a wrinkled up
> Belly-button
>
> Rosy hue has fled
> But, at least,
> It's an innie!!

**HL:** Thank you!

---

## NOTES

1. Joy Asham Fedorick, "Recording the Truth and Truthful Records," by Fred Gaysek, *ArtViews* (July, August, September 1989): 28–30.
2. Joy Asham Fedorick, "Fencepost Sitting, and How I Fell Off to One Side," *Artscraft* 2.3 (Fall 1990): 9–14.
3. Joy Asham Fedorick, "Fencepost Sitting."
4. *Artscraft* 2.4 (Winter 1991), 11–15.

# BASIL JOHNSTON

▼

*Basil Johnston (Ojibway) was born on Parry Island Indian Reserve. He attended Cape Croker Indian Reserve Public School and later Spanish Indian Residential School, from where he received his high school diploma in 1950. He graduated from Loyola College, Montreal, and later attended the Ontario College of Education for a Secondary School Teaching Certificate. He has worked in various capacities, including hunting, trapping, fishing, and farming as well as administrative and educational work. For years he has been employed by the Royal Ontario Museum in Toronto as an educator and specialist in Ojibway culture and language.*

*Basil Johnston is known internationally for his many publications on Ojibway people, including* Ojibway Heritage *(1976),* Ojibway Ceremonies *(1983),* Moose Meat and Wild Rice *(1978), and* Indian School Days *(1989). In 1976 he received the Samuel S. Fells Literary Award for "Zhowmin and Mandamin." Besides, he has published several books of tales from the oral tradition, as well as numerous articles on Native languages, education, culture, and history. He is a prominent speaker who has given presentations throughout North America. In 1967 he received the Centennial Medal in recognition of his work on behalf of the Native community and was a recipient of the Order of Ontario in 1989.*

*The interview was conducted in Basil Johnston's office at the Royal Ontario Museum in Toronto on 18 December 1990 (copyright Basil Johnston/Hartmut Lutz).*

---

**HL:** I don't speak any of the Native languages myself. We were looking into something at the Saskatchewan Indian Federated College, which I strongly advocate—to make it compulsory for any person employed there to learn one of the Native languages, regardless of whether you are Native or non-Native. I only skim the surface. What is written in English is what I have access to.

**BJ:** Well, the requirement, I think, should apply also to ethnologists and anthropologists. Anyone who tends to work with any of the Aboriginal peoples should be required to take language and literature. And then their work will have substance. Right now, they are just dealing with the physical aspects of life. They can't get into the heart, and soul, and intellect of the people.

*HL:* No, I think this is certainly true of traditional ethnology. I am glad that in the articles you sent me you say it is not just the languages, it is the literature too!

*BJ:* Oh absolutely, you cannot separate the two things. You can't separate them, and if you do, all you have left is grammar, and that doesn't teach you language. That is one of my "apostolic missions." Whether anyone listens or not is something else!

*HL:* No, but you put it down in writing, and it is published, and it is there.

*BJ:* But it is difficult to make the universities listen to this stuff! It is difficult for a non-accredited person to have his ideas accepted by those who have accreditation. You are not supposed to know as much as they do, and it is difficult.

*HL:* If you look in terms of English Departments in Canada, some of them have a hard time even teaching mainstream Canadian literature, let alone Native literature. I was surprised on previous visits. I also do research in mainstream Canadian literature and I read some papers at Lethbridge and other places, and some academics said, "It is nice when you tell us something about our literature," because they are still hooked on England very often. I think if somebody comes from the outside and says, "Okay, over in Europe, in Italy and Germany, we do research into Native literature as scholars of North American literature," maybe it reflects positively on the situation of Native literature here too.

*BJ:* Really it hasn't been done yet. A lot of it has been passed off as "kid's stuff."

Another problem, of course, is trying to convince publishers. Publishers are not really resistant to publishing Native stuff, but it has got to be marketed. I've been very lucky with *Ojibway Heritage* and *Ojibway Ceremonies* and *Moose Meat and Wild Rice*. Those things have been on the market continuously since 1976, not spectacular but they are there, and they are the kinds of thing that are needed. I presume to think that these books are necessary for writers to have something to start with when they start writing plays—Tomson Highway is an example. But more needs to be done. We need poetry, operas, novels, novellas, all of these things need to be used. Prayers and chants, songs, all these things! There is a lot of material right now for Native people to come along and start writing about from their own perspective.

*HL:* I think this is coming along. In the US it has been on the agenda longer, but in Canada it is coming along if you think of the novels that have come out in the last two or three years. Not very many, but some.

You mention drama, and Canada has used Native literature, Native painting, Native carving to represent Canada culturally, abroad. George Kenny's *October Stranger* represented Canada in 1978 in Monaco. Then, at the Edinburgh Festival, it was Tomson Highway, and there is Evan Adams from B.C. who had his play in Sydney, Australia. So, on the one hand, mainstream culture says, "Okay it is here," and they advertise it, but Canadian English Departments, or the Literature Departments, are not generally addressing the issue. It is time to take the Canadian public to task and say, "If you do this, you should give acknowledgement to these writers here!"

*BJ:* You see it in the libraries—they separate "Indians" and "Canadians." You have to have a "reserve," a special place for Indian books and Indian authors in a library. They don't belong in Canadian literature. They don't belong with Leacock. They don't belong with Pierre Berton. You know, you have to put them aside, "Indians." (LAUGHS)

So we have been set aside and all these things are "Indian stuff." What has prevented the development of a greater readership for Native written books is that anthropologists have inadvertently massively massacred Indian life by depicting only physical aspects of it, medias, social organization, hunting, fishing, food preparation, dwellings, clothing, transportation. So, a lot of people look at that and say, "Oh god, not that stuff again!" This is the kind of thing you run up against. I don't blame readers for being discouraged.

*HL:* In one of your papers, you drew attention to the Five Nations' Great Law of Peace, and I have done that in a different context too. If you take that alone, if you think of the founding of the US, if you think of Marxism, if you think of contemporary feminism, they all look at that document and say, "Oh this is so wonderful!" They use it as a model, but there is a displacement at the same time of the Six Nations people as the people who have an ongoing tradition and who are still there!

I was very happy that you used that example. And there are many cases where Europe, Europeans, the world, have taken Native concepts and used them, not only at the material level but I think also at the philosophical level, without even knowing that these were Native in origin. And I think that research has to unearth that, too, and give it acknowledgement.

*BJ:* I think it has to be given practical application, not merely philosophical recognition. You take, for example, this phrase, "close to nature." It is just a phrase, and it doesn't mean a thing, when they have a tremendous respect for and a reverence for the land! When we speak about land, Natives generally include the other inhabitants, animals and birds, insects, fish. When they talk about the land, they also talk about the lakes, and the rivers, and the streams, and the mountains, all the land!

231

And they also include the weather, the seasons, the storms, the moons. Then what does the land do? It nourishes humankind. What nourishes you deserves respect.

It goes beyond that. The Earth is also a teacher. Everything that goes on in human life goes on and is reflected in human nature, by the other inhabitants. You see fights, generosity, parenthood, kindness, selfishness. The seagull is the great symbol of selfishness. They fight and they squawk. So you see a lot of these things, life-death, a law, a kind of harmony. A man is no greater than these creatures! He is a co-inhabitant. He has his place. Those other creatures have their place.

It is also an aesthetic source. I don't know if that is the right word or not, but if you appreciate the beauty of a valley, sunrise, moon setting, formation of clouds, it is tremendously fulfilling, and satisfying, and gratifying to be able to grasp this thing. Then to hear the sounds, and also the songs of birds—they really are not called "songs," birds don't really sing! Some of them whistle.

When you get all of that, this is when some of them become very philosophical. And they see some event, and then they try to connect that particular event with some other event—cause and effect. They start getting philosophical about this whole business: what is the connection between that and the weather? What is the connection between that weather and human conduct? It is all there! Trying to correlate human conduct, and the anger and the benevolence of the gods and their attitudes. There has been a tremendous contribution that the Five or Six Nations made, if you think of the adoption of their system of government by the US, and by other political social systems. But there is also this business of conservation. I don't know when it is going to get through to western Europeans that eventually our well-being is tied in with the well-being of the land. We have to look after it! Now there is too much of "who cares!," and also I suspect, there is a conviction that science will look after it. All they have to do is to throw some pellets into the water to purify it.

*HL:* But I think that certainty is gone! It is gone much more with the younger people than with the older people. We are on the road towards death unless we really turn and take other things into consideration. Why are there more and more people not using their cars any more, but going by bike in Europe? And I see it in Canada too—these are some beginnings.

*BJ:* Too many cars anyway!

*HL:* That is true!

*BJ:* If you look at the streets around here, how many times that is multiplying throughout the world! It is madness! This is some of the substance that must be dealt with, must be set down and explained. This is what I am doing now.

*HL:* What made you write?

232

***BJ:*** I was asked to start an Indian program in a museum which I carried out by teaching in the galleries and going out to the communities. I realized that neither students nor teachers were prepared to study, or to listen to a presentation, because the books available to them were poor in quality and in content.

I was asked to be a guest simply to look at this display that was mounted by a group of grade five/six students, Churchill Avenue Public School in North York in 1972, which they mounted after studying an Indian unit in depth for six weeks. It was a marvellous display. Over in one corner was this huge tepee and in front of this tepee was this young guy. A young chief wearing a paper headdress, with arms folded in the "traditional" manner of a Blackfoot chief, and he had on his lapel a cardboard label with the word "Blackfoot." So I went over to this little guy because he was all by himself. I greeted him with "How!," and he looked at me, and I said "How!" again, explaining that was the traditional Blackfoot greeting. So he said, "How!" Then I observed that he looked morose. "How come you look so sad, chief?" And he looked around to see that there were no teachers within the vicinity, and he explained, "Sir, I am bored!" "How so, chief?" "Before we started this program on Indians, I always thought Indians were neat, always wanted to be an Indian. But, sir, after six weeks of studying tepees that my team and I selected from these six aspects," he said, "is that all there is, sir?"

That is when I started to write! I wasn't even thinking about categories, I simply thought, there is a need for *Ojibway Heritage*. After that was finished, there was a need for *Ojibway Ceremonies*, and that became fiction simply because there was a fictional character in the thing that is based on ceremonies and rituals. Then it was *Moose Meat and Wild Rice* because Native people like humour, not subtle humour like Canadians want.

Then I did some basic books in my own language, and now there is a need for a text on literature, the reconstitution and rewriting of some of the stories in yet another language, at a higher plane, to convey the depth of the stories! The depth of understanding that has not yet been captured in the stories that have been written, recorded, and transliterated. So that is what I am working on.

***HL:*** Is that the Ojibway stories? Traditional stories?

***BJ:*** "Nishnabe." I use the term "Nishnabe."

***HL:*** Your book is about stories from the oral tradition of the Anishinabe people? Not contemporary fiction, or would that be included too, poetry, drama?

***BJ:*** Well, let's put it this way. There are stories that are universal, and I think almost eternal. Whether they were told 2–, 10–, 40,000 years ago, they still have application. However, some of these stories have to be redone in modern terms. These stories have lessons. Even though the circumstances change, the lessons still remain the same. And in one case, I am going to tell the story as it was told a long time ago, and then I am going to modernize it and also generalize it. The belief is that stories are supposed to be static. My approach is that they are not static. You change them and bring them up to date.

**HL:** So the book will give descriptions of those stories, and at the same time the implications, the vitality of those stories, because you are creating new ones?

**BJ:** Yes.

**HL:** That is an interesting book. You see, now I am trying to put *this* book together. Originally I planned to write a book *on* Native literature in Canada, just a survey. And then this book by Penny Petrone came out, and it covers at least some of the stuff that I would have covered. If you write something on the same topic someone else has written on already you inevitably end up saying you disagree with your predecessor at this point or that. I don't really want to get into that. Now, mainstream English Departments, at least some of them, start taking individual Native texts and analyze them exactly the way they analyze other literature too, very often. I think the analysis may be very intelligent, but may not be very meaningful in terms of Native literature. There is not much written by Native people *on* their own literature! It would be hard to get people to sit down and *write* about their literature—a lot of people do not have the time, or the resources to do that. So I thought of putting together a book with about 20 interviews, of writers from various perspectives, talking about their literature. That would be an opportunity to share what Native people say about the literature they are producing. That is the objective of this. So, when you say you are writing about storytelling, about the stories ...

**BJ:** I am retelling, writing these things hoping to give them their proper force. Many of them have been stripped of everything. You take a lot of those books that I have covered there, the skeletons of stories. So what I am doing is not explaining but simply retelling the story. If you tell a story properly, you don't have to explain what it means afterwards. This is why I am putting this together. I hope the story tells itself, is self-explanatory. If you have to explain then there is something wrong with that story, or with the storytelling. A lot of them are not immediately understandable. Some people can see it right away, some people take years.

I'll just give you one example. I was in Fort Francis, 10 or 12 years ago, at the request of professional tutors to address teachers on their professional development day. I told them that I would simply tell them stories and allow them to draw their own inferences about the meaning. And I said that some of them wouldn't understand the stories right away, and for some it would take a year, and for some 10 years.

After the presentation I was having coffee in a coffee room with these teachers, and the ones who felt they might not understand the story for 10 years were impatient. They wanted to understand now, and they asked me, "Would you tell me?" I said, "No, I want you to think about the story." Nevertheless they insisted, and persisted. Finally, there was an Indian lady, who may have had grade eight, and who had taken a couple of courses to be a teacher's aide. She was able to understand that story because she grew up with stories, and she went directly to the meaning of the story. It was a good thing! She had never taken any literature courses where they study structure, character, images, devices, all this nonsense! The people who had most insight in it were not academics.

This is the approach that I take in my writing. I am not going to explain structure, I am not going to explain conflict. I may do 15, 20 stories, but I am not going to write by the pound either. Two hundred and fifty pages perhaps, as long as it gives some other writer a start. That is all you need to do. You don't have to overwhelm him! (LAUGHS) So anyway, that is what I am doing. Also, you were suggesting that this is kind of an academic work? No! I think one of the reasons why Native writers, at the present time, don't write texts on literature from an academic point of view is that they are still proceeding on the basis of "Hey, do it!" Never mind talking about it, *do it*! In other words, "Never mind talking about writing! Write! Don't talk about telling stories, all this nonsense! Tell it! Write them!" This is what I am doing.

*HL:* That is very much in line with what I heard from a lot of other writers. You have been doing this kind of work for years and years.

*BJ:* Since 1976.

*HL:* And others have just started. There will be more and more!

*BJ:* Talking about literature—there has been no book on philosophy written. No book on psychology. In order to write truly about the Native insights, you have to know the language. We are only talking about English language writing.

There is even something prior to that and even more fundamental. One of the things that we can't get across here in Canada is to have books in *our* language. That is what is needed.

*HL:* I like a point you were making somewhere. You say those books will have to be published by museums or other government-sponsored organizations, because they are not the kind of books that will have a large reading public. They wouldn't be very profitable. But they must be preserved, because otherwise it is such a terrible loss.

*BJ:* I don't think you have to go outside for funding. Ask the Arabs, ask the Russians, they have been doing this for years. Maybe it is a deliberate withholding of funds! Maybe this country wants to be unilingual, suppress others.

**HL:** Once you said, "Those no longer speaking the language of the forebears cannot know themselves." This may be a very hard judgement on Native people who do not speak the language any more. Personally, as a non-Canadian, I agree with you. When people come up to me in Canada and say, "Oh, you are German?, I am German too!," I answer, "Ja? Woher kommst du denn?" Then, if they don't understand, and can't tell me where they are from, to me they are not German, they are German-Canadians, perhaps. So this may be okay in the case of Europeans, but what about Native people in Canada who perhaps grew up in an urban environment? It is thrown into their face all the time that they are Native, if they are looking for a place to stay, or whatever—because of the racism. There is no way of denying that they are Native, but they don't speak the language any more. Where are they? Caught in midair?

**BJ:** Yes.

**HL:** So you wouldn't say that they are Native? Or, maybe, you would say that they are not Nishnabe if they don't speak Nishnabe?

**BJ:** Well, they have lost that sense, that feeling. They cannot articulate any more those insights that are there. I sent you an article with some terms. If you can't articulate those things, you can't live by those principles, unless you know what they are. You will simply have to adopt western European life-styles, principles, everything! But you don't have to lose it! You can regain it! Now, what is to prevent that person from regaining that language?

The words work on several levels, anyway. There is the surface, where everybody understands. Then there are two or three other meanings, take for example, "manitou." It has many meanings, depending on the context of the conversation. The context will tell you the precise sense in which that is to be applied. "Medicine—strength," "Earth—strength." Then you think about that. How is its application? There is the person who is weak, debilitated by disease. To be restored to strength, he has got to get the strength of the Earth passed to him through this medicine. That is what medicine is, restoring of strength. That is why it is called that. But you have to know the language in order to be able to understand that. There is a lot of work that needs to be done. The spelling, the orthography, has to follow the prefixes. A lot of spelling systems are going at it "horse behind the cart." Linguists coming up with all kinds of orthographies. The logical development is: literature first and then orthography. It is the writer who is going to do the spelling first. Orthographers will come along and they find it, and I have got a list of the prefixes.

**HL:** Yes, the writing comes first.

**BJ:** Yes! Of course! That is what has to happen with people! Linguists who do not speak the language have to fiddle around, write texts to further their accreditation. I have books with lists of words, that is all! But the way my language works, if I am going to write about the ideas I have got to know how the language works.

*HL:* If you come to something like in *Indian School Days*, is language important there too? Because that is all in English?

*BJ:* Well of course it is! Nishnabe language, no! But, some of the ideas, the attitudes of Natives, are Native and it is tricky to try and get them across in English.

Earlier you mentioned *Moose Meat and Wild Rice*. Now was that fiction? No! When people say you must have made that up, they do flatter; tremendous imagination! Every single one of those stories is based upon some actual happening.

*HL:* And I guess the same is true with *Indian School Days*, right?

*BJ:* Yes. And that was the last one.

*HL:* Yes, I have the others at home, I didn't lug them all around, but this one I liked best, or to me it was more familiar, because I read other autobiographies. I also spent a year once in the United States and talked to a lot of Native people, especially about the residential school or boarding school. You hear a lot of horror stories, but you also hear a lot of humour, and this one stays almost on the humour level. There is all the hardship, and some of the meanness is in there, too, but it is not the main thing, the main accusation that is flung in your face.

*BJ:* See, I don't like doing what has already been done. It is simply a repetition. I want to do something a little different. Something that hasn't been done before. This is the main reason why I took that direction. Also, the former inmates of Spanish were the ones who suggested which stories were to be included.

*HL:* What you are writing actually happened, right?

*BJ:* Well yes! Of course!

*HL:* So it was partly a joint effort? I mean, you did the writing, but you had input from other inmates as well?

*BJ:* In the sense that since leaving in 1950, I see them all the time. When we get together we talk about it, and certain stories keep recurring. Those are the ones I have written.

*HL:* I see.

*BJ:* I took the approach from our point of view, the first graduating class who had gone together from 1940 on through to 1950. The perspective was narrow, and I didn't want to go into all these documents either, because that has already been done. And it would have been boring, you know. Read it, and there is this footnote, and another footnote. I wanted to write something different.

*HL:* Is there something that you would like to add, or anything that you think should be in this book?

*BJ:* I don't know. There is so much to say, and I am in the process of saying something right in this manuscript here. I wouldn't go any further than that, except to say that I hope I can get it done by spring. I would say the Yankees are far more generous people than our Canadians! I have had better reception for my books in the States than in Canada. I was on a cross-country tour two years ago, and I ended up in Regina on an open-line talk show. After an introduction by the master of ceremonies, the host of the radio show invited calls. The first caller said, "Why in hell don't you people forget the damn past!" (LAUGHS)

**HL:** The mainstream would like to forget the past, yes.

**BJ:** There was this question and the host asked, "Would you like to reply?" Imagine, you are out selling a book, you are a salesman, you have got to be gracious, and so I tried to reply to this comment as graciously as I could. I had a few other choice things to say but I didn't. They wouldn't be conducive for the sales of the book or even my reception. Then I asked the guy the question, "Did you read it?" "No!"

Let me say this, though, the people who are well disposed to minorities, to Natives, to a lot of issues, outnumber the rednecks. Now, the rednecks and people who are akin to them are far more aggressive than our own, and far more vocal. A lot of them use the government, and this is why governments suppress. Governments are instruments of these guys, so that the good guys are very often outshouted by these people. But they are there! There are a lot of good people out there, far more than these other guys, but the guys I described are far more vocal! I wouldn't go into any names but ... (LAUGHS)

**HL:** No, if you think of the discussion that is going on in Canada about the residential school system—would be an example where the residential school system hasn't destroyed people. But a lot of others were maimed for life. I live in Regina now, and some of the people have incredible problems actually staying together as a family. And if you think of people who for two and sometimes three generations were forced into residential schools, being separated from their kin, what do you expect than to see a lot of social problems, a lot of uprooting, and destruction of personalities? I think the residential schools have had much more impact than I ever thought before I came here. Would you disagree with that?

**BJ:** There are different ways of looking at it. I would agree in those cases, where a youngster was taken too soon from the parents, say age four, five, six, seven. Yes, but not always. Youngsters above that age, for example, 10, have been with their parents long enough to have firmed up their character to resist this kind of thing. And there are questions, not so much connected with the school. I think all of us there, including orphans and products of separated families, questioned, "Why did they give me away? Did they not like me?" Cast aside! And, of course, when you get beaten by the authorities, this feeling is intensified. There were many people who became alienated from their communities, their families, from a lot of people. But there were other people, and I think a lot of us, maybe all of us, were much more resistant afterwards to western Europeanization. Maybe we should be grateful for the residential schools for that. The other thing: you can't credit schools for everything, nor can you blame schools for everything. Somebody asked me one time and this is a difficult one to answer, "What did you learn? What did they instill in you?" I think the Jesuits instilled in us a desire to learn more. You don't need many lessons in life or from school. If you learn one, a good one, and if you learn it well enough, they have done something. What did I learn? I think from the beginning, you *played*, you play your heart out! And then there was this other one, "Be fair." Of course, it is hard. Be fair with the facts! But be fair with yourself, and you will be okay.

When you asked me to say something further, I think maybe those are some observations. After you go, I'll be saying, "Oh, god almighty, this is what I should have told him!"

**HL:** Would you say something about appropriation?

**BJ:** Appropriation what? That is too restrictive! Every idea that we express has already been expressed, and thought of, and all we have to do is give these new expressions new applications. That is what happens! If somebody hasn't done it before, does that prevent me from doing it, simply because it happens to belong to a German? Supposing that German idea can be expressed in an Indian way, with an emphasis.

**HL:** I would have no bad feelings about that at all. Anybody can write about Germans. But I think maybe it is a different matter here, though, if you think of the history of Native/non-Native relations, and colonialism, and the continued appropriation of Native materials.

**BJ:** That doesn't worry me at all. It is up to us. Let's get off our damn butts. Let's just write better books than those other guys! That is my attitude!

**HL:** You know, it is almost literally the same thing that I heard from a woman writer. I interviewed some women authors in Canada, and one of them, Aritha Van Herk, said, "the best revenge"—I mean on the men, she is a convinced feminist—"is to write better books!" I don't know if she said "revenge," but the best thing is to write better.

**BJ:** Yes, to write better. If these anthropologists had written so well in appropriating all these books there would have been nothing for me to do. But they have done it so poorly that I have so much work to do! (LAUGHS)

# RITA JOE

▼

*Rita Joe (Micmac) grew up in Micmac territory on Cape Breton Island, speaking Micmac as her first language. She began writing poetry, both in English and in Micmac, as a mother concerned about the experiences her children and other Native people had within mainstream society. In her poems she addresses both contemporary issues and Native traditions, and through all of her writing runs a deep undercurrent of love for creation. She has published two books of poetry,* Poems of Rita Joe *(1978) and* Song of Eskasoni *(1988), and for years she wrote her own column, "Here and There" in the* Micmac News. *Her works have also appeared in anthologies and journals. In 1989 Rita Joe was nominated for the Order of Canada, and in April 1990 she accepted the award "on behalf of all the Native people across the world."*

*The conversation was recorded in Rita Joe's home on the Micmac reserve, Eskasoni, Cape Breton Island, on 19 December 1991 (copyright Rita Joe/Hartmut Lutz).*

---

*To begin with, we were talking about how Rita Joe became motivated to write poetry, and she told the story of her daughter's experiences in high school in Sydney, Nova Scotia.*

**RJ:**  She came home one day and she said, "I want to quit school!" She was in grade 11. We were all so proud that she was in a high grade! And she came home and explained about the teacher asking her, "Since you are a Micmac, will you please explain why your people did this and that?" And one of the explanations that was in the book was about cannibalism, and she did not know that existed! And she said, "I just wanted to disappear! Or sink through the floor, or whatever!" And a young fellow behind her explained. And she was uncomfortable all the time. She and the four other Native girls were the only Native girls out of thousands of students, and the girls always went around together. They made friends, but they were still uncomfortable.

So, she wanted to quit. And I remember writing this:

A thousand ages we see
In a space of a moment,
And burdens follow
Out of old chronicles.

Submission I say, to obtain harmony,
But let the words die, that were written

So my children may see
The glories of their forefathers,
And share the pride of history

That they may learn
The way of their ancestors,
And nourish a quiet way.

Our children read and hate
The books offered—
A written record of events
By the white men.

Compromise I say, and meet
    our requirement,
Place the learning seed of happiness
    between us.[1]

That was one of my earlier poems. And then I wrote others on other occasions. And this went on and on and on like that.

But this earlier book, *Poems of Rita Joe*, was mostly crying, frustration—angry but hoping. Hoping, always hoping that it will turn to good. And that's when I began to write—that's about in 1969—for different Nova Scotia magazines that I picked up. I never tried newspapers until the *Micmac News* came out. I used *Micmac News* a lot. I imagine *Micmac News* went to China, Australia, and far different countries. And I began to receive mail. The people would write to me and comment.

One time I did not even know the English word for that herb, "flagroot." I never knew the English name of what I was talking about. I heard the Indian people always talking about "KiKweSu'sk." I kept hearing that and I pumped the old and elderly about "KiKweSu'sk." So by that time I began to question a lot.

Sometimes the elderly would tell me, "Why don't you know? You are Indian! Why don't you know?" And then I would say, "Well, I was an orphan, and I was never taught!" Usually, a grandparent or a parent tells their children. Well, I was not in that stage. I always sat out of sight, or out of the way, or outside, not picking up like the other normal children that have parents and a grandma and grandparents. So then I didn't pick it up, but now, when I wrote, I began to pick it up. And I asked a lot of questions.

When they were telling me a story I would say, "What did you say, Auntie? Say that again!"

So, I listen to people. And hearing something on the news, or reading something in the paper, or hearing something that just makes you so angry that you want to do something about it, I began to write! And after a while, around 1974, I'd seen a little newspaper article by the Writers' Federation telling writers, "You can send in a book, or a poem, or a short story, and you could win a prize." So I went to Roy Gould, the editor of *Micmac News*. I said, "I wonder if my poems are all right. Do you think they are okay?" I asked his permission. He said, "Oh, they are okay with me, and I guess by the majority of people everywhere."

And I remember he gave me advice a long time ago: "When you write something, don't step on toes!" And then he would explain to me which toes: the band council, the chief, Department of Indian Affairs officials, and secretary of state, or whatever, or prime minister, you know. "Don't say unkind things!" And I never did, I followed his advice. That was back in 1969.

But sometimes you feel you have to say something! In such a way to direct your thoughts to whoever picks up or opens some kind of page. You are talking to somebody but not necessarily a non-Indian—Indian people as well. They say I must live a white man's way—the day and age still being what they say, you've still got to do what they say.

I imagine that's me from the residential school. I ended up in residential school when I was 12. When my dad died I was 10. Then I was with him a whole year, and that's the happiest part of my life. And my dad is in most of my writing—what he said to me, or what direction he gave, because he is the one that I remember more clearly than Mom. Mom I remember as a loving person, but it's just like a smoky screen. Because I was five. So, Mom is like a "wishing figure."

So I go to the elderly. I hug them. I pay a lot of respect to them, because I want to have them as my mother or grandmother. So, it was like that most of my life. Unexpectedly, a woman at the bingo hall next door ran up to me and gave me a hug, a right tight squeeze, and I stood there and said, "What's the matter, what happened?" She said, "I love you!" No relation or whatever! And that meant more to me, she made my day! (LAUGHS)

So, I've been gathering information like that through the years. I wrote stories. I was working on legends, and one person would say it one way, and another one would tell it a different way. So I had a hard time. I'm still working on those legends, and I plan to come out some day with the legends.

*HL:* Would you write them down in English then?

*RJ:* Yes, I write them down in English. I wrote a story for *Tawow Magazine*, back in 1970 some time. They had asked me to write a story, two or three stories or legends or poems or what. So I wrote a story about "Ki'Kwaju." I kept hearing about this character Ki'Kwaju, and I never knew who it was. So I asked this elderly person, "What's the English name of Ki'Kwaju?" "I don't know," she said, "I know a lot of stories about Ki'Kwaju." I found out about a year later, it is "badger."

So I wrote the story. And I didn't have a tape recorder, it was all handwritten. And I kept asking them more questions. So, I finally had a rough sketch of Ki'Kwaju. For whatever person came in, I would ask that person, "What's Ki'Kwaju's English name?" They didn't know. Finally, Lee Cremo, a fiddling champ, came in and I asked him. And I thought, "He's been travelling all over Canada as a fiddling champ." So I asked him, "What's Ki'Kwaju's English name?" That's when he told me: "If you do not know the English name of something, write the Indian name! If people want to know, they will know." So, that's when I began to use that term.

*HL:* You also use Micmac in your poetry sometimes.

*RJ:* Yes, I do. Even my husband did, when he did his work for the university. I consider the original language very important. I use it in French, maybe, or if I heard the expression, or if I knew a German word I would use it, or Latin. I want the whole world to know how important it is to *me*, the Native! So, the perspective is mine. But I want the whole world to know what it is. I want him to know the Indian part. That's the most important part to me.

Speaking to students across the country, I try to encourage them to learn about different cultures. I speak to university students and I tell them, "Never forget who you are! The most important part is who you are. You are part of your culture! That you want to explain!" That's the most important part of it. And there are many people who come up to me after, and they'll say, "Oh, I appreciated you saying that! I felt good about myself."

When I'm talking to students or even the little wee ones, it's always in my mind. If you're a Native, you are the most important person. You are beautiful, you are ambitious, you are intelligent, you know how to do that. And sometimes I hold myself up as an example.

I slept in a wigwam. When I talk at school, teachers say, "But that's only 50 years ago!" And I say, "Yes, 50 years ago." Now it's 51, I was seven years old. But to me, sleeping in a wigwam was beautiful. That was my home! Well at one time I was ashamed. When I was going to school I would never talk about that part—my god, no! But now I am glad to proclaim to the whole world, "I slept in a wigwam!" I am not ashamed. And I have always taught my kids not to be ashamed of any part of their culture! I brainwashed my children from the time they were small: "If you hear something in the classroom that's not up to your expectations, put up your hand! Don't be afraid to put up your hand and explain it your Indian way!"

And when my daughter quit school that time, she went back later. She married, had a couple of children, and one day she came and said, "I want to go back to school!"

One time I was standing in front of them, grade seven. I took off my glasses and said, "I'm blind in one eye and nearsighted in the other. I have imperfect hearing." And I looked down at my feet and said, "And I don't even have socks that match." But I have to put in their heads that you don't have to be perfect.

**HL:** Were you born with a blind eye?

**RJ:** Well my sister used to tell me the doctor used to come and put medicine on my eye when I was a little baby. It was awful. My sister used to tell me, "We thought you were going to be completely blind." But as I grew up, Indian medicine, I think ... This one is blind—I can see, just barely see. I think if this one went, if I had to rely on that, I would see light and dark, or shapes. But this one is very nearsighted. That's why, when I read sometimes, it's blurry. So I usually take off my glasses. That's how nearsighted I am.

I try to urge so many of them to write.

My husband was my worst critic. I told you I would get up sometimes, at odd times, or when we were reading, or sometimes it struck me in the car when we were driving. And I'd take out a little notebook, and I would write down that thought. It would flit in my brain and I had to put it down. A story will come out of that one thought, or a poem. I had him climbing walls sometimes. But when I wrote something, I would read it to him, "What does it sound like?" He was the one with the university degree, not me. So I'd ask him, "What does that sound like?" "No, I think you better put that in another context," he would say. So I would fool around with words a little more.

My husband loved this one here:

Tears fall on the empty page
My thoughts wounding the heart
The bended wish unheard in the night
For soul-searching in the darkness black
What will I write?

I have nothing to fall back on
No wrongs I care to cleanse.
The engraved yesterdays not anymore

245

Or modernism I care to represent.
My revolt in dying embers
Peaceful my mission, I awaken.[2]

He loved that! There were some of them that he wanted me to read again, because something moved him.

I know this one moved a lot of people, not necessarily Indians.

Though it was natural for me to create my leather dress
the beads and quill my ornamentation[3]

It moves people. They say it makes them feel good, too. Even the non-Indian.

When I submitted the first book to the Writers' Federation I called it *The Valiant Race*, 111 poems. And in the front I put "The Valiant Race," because I considered my people valiant people. I tried to put it in neat form. I think I typed it, I had an old typewriter I borrowed from somebody. I had a hard time putting it together. And my English was poor, and as they say, "not in structure," or whatever the terms they use. And it won!

I was surprised. And they called me up: "You are one of the winners!" Oh gosh, I felt good! "You have to come up here to accept your award. It will be held at the Holiday Inn." I remember asking the woman, the executive director at that time, "May I come in Native dress?" Because that crept into my mind, to go in Native dress. She said, "Of course, of course." She was all excited I imagine.

And I went there. I made a polyester dress with leather fringes and I borrowed somebody's moccasins. And we went there.

There was a good feeling there. "Rita Joe, a Micmac Indian from Cape Breton," that's the way they said it. There were a lot of people there, tables, you know, polite clapping, and when they said "Rita Joe, Micmac Indian from Cape Breton," there was a roar. And I picked that up as meaning it meant a lot to them, to Nova Scotian people, or whoever was there, "this Indian!," so they gave loud applause. And I floated back, feeling the good feeling, being just one of them, of the writers.

*HL:* Do you have contacts with other Native writers?

*RJ:* Yes.

*HL:* Because you mentioned some.

*RJ:* Yes, once in a while. I know other poets, mostly. You know, Maria Campbell, and certain writers. When I go to education conferences, British Columbia, or Alberta, somewhere, then I get in contact with them. And I read their work, all the time. They show it to me, so proud! They are so happy, and I look at it, "Boy, that's beautiful!" That's how I feel about what they write down.

I do not know that much about literature. I read, too! I've got piles and piles of books. Now I feel like I have to read. But high school students and university students have to do an awful lot of reading. But I don't know that part. I'm lost there. But I consider it very important to put my touch on paper. The Indian! The Indian part of me! I consider it very important. I read, for example, Margaret Atwood, I look at her work, and her thoughts, and what she feels, and that's me, too! And receiving the feedback from the crowds that I talk to, I see it.

A couple of weeks ago I was at Laurentian University in Sudbury, and there were thousands of people there. After the speaking part there was a group, and then I was a dinner guest-speaker. And when I was a dinner guest-speaker I got more and more people to listen. So, I was reading the poetry, and I was singing a song for them, and then I got a standing ovation later! That moved me! I didn't want them to hear me sob, so I went away from the microphone and I put my head down for a few seconds, and then I looked back up at them. I moved up to the microphone and I said, "Thank you!"

And a lady said, "She will be there selling her books." And I sat down and I autographed them. And sometimes they just brought out paper, they couldn't afford the book. But the good feeling was right there.

The good feeling was just like when I was receiving the Order of Canada. I said, "I did it for you!" And I received the Order on behalf of all my people, on behalf of all the Aboriginal people, no matter where they are. They can be over in Norway, or somewhere, but that's what I felt like. And hopefully, I'm trying to get that little book out. I'm working on another one, to get out this year.

This one, *Poems of Rita Joe*, I feel I was born there! I don't know how to explain it, but it feels I was born as a writer, there.

The most requested one is "Aye! no monuments." [4] I wrote that in English, in about half an hour, 20 minutes. When I wrote it I was frustrated with no monuments for Native people. And the publisher wanted that in Micmac. So I got hold of Bernie Francis, who is a linguist, a Micmac linguist. He came here, and we had no Indian word for "monument." So I said, "God, what are we going to use?" So I said, "Let's go and ask my mother-in-law, across the road, she's elderly." And then I asked her, "What's the word for that mound where people put a pile of rocks, and put a stick there, and pointing, or telling your friends, you are blazing the trail where you have gone." And I remember she said: "knu'kaqann." Knu'kaqann means "showing." So, she came up with the word knu'kaqann at first. That's how it came in there! I imagine it's the first time it has been written anywhere. And Bernie and I used it. And we laughed about it—oh we were so happy! When I was at the University of Gettysburg—I was in the theatre, on a stage in front of people, and television was there—they asked me to read that one in Micmac. I didn't have the book, so I recited it from my mind. I didn't have the book with me at the time because I was there telling stories. And when I finished they gave me loud applause. Then I asked them: "Since you do not know a word of Micmac, why did you ask me to?" So they said, "We like to hear the sound!"

What does it sound like to you?

*HL:* It sounds very soft and subtle, and it has nice vowels, like a's and e's, and what I like is that you've got the "ch" sound. We've got that too, a lot. It's very gentle!

*RJ:* Aha, yes.

So then I got turned on, and I asked, "What does it sound like to you? Is it a guttural sound, or soft?" Sometimes they would say, "Like a singsong."

*HL:* Yes! It's very melodious!

*RJ:* Yes, like a melody. And when I hear other people talk, let's say I am standing near French-speaking people, I always listen. Or German!

A lot of German people came in! I had a craft store next door this summer, I opened July 1, 1990. A lot of people from Switzerland, Norway, United States, and England—they came from all over the world. They found that place in a short time! And I would hear two Germans discussing, and they're going around, two men, big men! And they bought different things, and they asked me for a box. And I gave them little boxes, for as many people as they were buying presents for. And they would say: "This is for my little girl, the little doll! This little basket is for my wife, this one is for my mother!" You know, they were explaining, and we would pack them right there.

At one time one of the men saw a headdress there, and he said: "May I borrow this?" He told his friend, they were talking in German. And then he said, "Would you please stand alongside of me?" And I had a grandson there, nine years old. He's right brown! "Will you stand alongside of me?" So, Nate and I, we stood right in the middle while he was wearing the headdress! (LAUGHS)

*HL:* (LAUGHS) He was so proud, eh?

*RJ:* I said, what about it? You want to send the picture home? He said, "Yes, I always wanted to put that on. I always wanted to know how it would feel to put it on." So I said, "How do you feel?," and he said, "Like a king!"

*HL:* That's a very German dream fulfilled!

*RJ:* Yes it is. And they tell me how much they want to know about Native people. They are curious. And they come out of their way. And they take pictures, they want to know why is this and that.

And another thing! Students come to my home! Honest to goodness! A lot of them come to my home. There's the song, "Come to my home, come see me as I am." By gosh, a couple of weeks ago, they came: 60!

Ooh, it was full! And I had a lot of artifacts hanging around for them. And I would tell them about these things, and they would ask questions. And I'd point out to them: "microwave," "electric stove," and that thing (fridge)! So I'll say, "Just like grandma? Just like your mother, eh? Just like home!" And they go, "yeah." And I say, "We don't live in wigwams any more." But they ask about that, you know, it's something they've read, and they ask. That's because children are honest, and they ask all sorts of questions. I tell them different stories. I like communicating with children. Oh god, I love that.

I stopped writing in 1970, and the year after. You know why? A comical experience. Something happened to me. Something very unpleasant had happened to me that time. I don't know what year it was, probably 1978 or 1979. Very unpleasant! I heard these people talking at the band office in Membertou: "Rita Joe." "Who? Who's that?" "You know, Here-and-There!" She was trying to explain who I was! You know, the article, "Here and There." When I heard that story, I said, "I'm not going to write that article any more if people are calling me Here-and-There." [5]

Indian people—Micmac, I don't know about the other tribes—they stick labels on.

*HL:* Oh yes.

*RJ:* Are you like that too, in different parts?

*HL:* Especially in smaller communities! Over in Europe also.

*RJ:* My mother-in-law, I picked up a lot of stories from her. You know, I picked up a lot from her, hearing stories. Or from my husband. We did not speak the same. We are both Micmac, but sometimes the words are not the same.

*HL:* So there are regional dialects?

*RJ:* Yes, regional dialects. But my husband and I learned from each other. When we first met in Boston in 1953, he came and knocked on my door, really. Somebody had told him where I lived. You know, Indian people move around a lot, but I was one of the people who stayed at that one address all the time. I was there until I married him. And then we moved away. I was there such a long time, so when anybody came, if they had no job, they had no home, I would take them in, no matter who it was, old, young, female, male, no matter who it was. Everybody knew that. It was only an apartment. "Rita will set you up!" But I tried to get them onto their own feet like that, because you don't like anybody underfoot. And he came, he was looking for his brothers, his cousins, and everybody knew that I would know where they were. I met this man in Portland, Maine, and he was looking for a job at the Massachusetts General Hospital, and he did get it. And I met him that weekend. He was knocking at my door. This handsome, skinny man standing there! Tall, and so neat looking! He was so neat! He spoke English, he was looking for his cousins, and I told him where, and he left. And my window was open a little bit, and I was up one floor. And after about half-an-hour, I heard Indians talking outside my window and I looked out. There's his cousin, getting out of the taxi. Four people getting out of a taxi, and I said, "Leo, a young man came here. I sent him over to your brothers' place." And Leo hollered and jumped back in the taxi. He thought that was his younger brother! But when he saw him, it was his friend, his cousin-friend. Leo was big, a muscular, hard-working man, and he came in and he said, "Joshua!" He called Frank "Joshua" from when they were kids, and he went up to him and lifted him up like that! Oh gosh!

I never saw him for another week. Then another week he came and we started, got married one month later! Thirty-five years last year! We celebrated 35 years!

It was a good relationship. We had eight children. We adopted two more boys. And the two boys, when we got them, were six years old and eight years old, and could swear in three languages. They were off a reserve. They swore in Scottish and English and Indian. Oh, they were bad! (LAUGHS) They grew up. I just got a call from one of them. He is married with three children. I am "Mum" to him! "How's the other brother?" We brought them up good! They are good boys!

*     *     *

This one, *Poems of Rita Joe*, needed a lot of housecleaning.
**HL:** Did it?
**RJ:** When the manuscript won that time, the writers' association assigned Chipman Hall, who in 1974 was an award-winning author. And Chipman and I got together and discussed it. And Chipman would say, "Oh, Indians never did that!" (BOTH LAUGH)
**HL:** Was he Indian? No, eh?
**RJ:** No! And I said, "What makes you think we didn't do that?" "Well," he said, "I studied Indians for seven years." (BOTH LAUGH) That's when I told him, "Damn it, I lived through that!" (LAUGHTER) "Don't question me, Chipman," I would say, "that stays just the way it is!" And he would want me to say it in another way. "No, that stays! That stays in there!" My own thoughts, I wanted them in there, and I didn't care who wanted what.
**HL:** The second book, *Song of Eskasoni*, I realized, was edited by Lee Maracle?
**RJ:** Yes!
**HL:** How much editing was done there?
**RJ:** That's everything, just the way it is.
**HL:** So she just wrote the introduction?

**RJ:** Yes, yes. They left everything. I said, "Is there anything in the book that I should work over," and she said, "No, there was nothing!"

**HL:** Was that Lee Maracle?

**RJ:** No, the publisher! She's not the publisher any more, it's a different woman now. She was the one who showed the manuscript to Lee Maracle, when they were at a publishing place somewhere in Ontario. She had the manuscript with her—she was going to have a discussion about it, you know, a workshop. She was going to discuss this Indian woman's work. So she happened to meet Lee Maracle, an Indian, and right away she said, "There's something I want you to see," and the way the publisher put it, she said, "I think an Indian should edit another Indian's work!" That's the way she looked at it.

So, I was surprised. And I received a letter from Lee. And in that letter she says, "I loved your work, and some day I hope we meet and talk." And I thought that was so great! Another Indian from somewhere else liking my work. She is a journalist.

**HL:** Yes, I know her.

**RJ:** Yes. And so I thought that was good. Nothing had to be corrected, not my spelling, my English, nothing! They just wanted it the way it was! And I thought that was great.

The only correction we made was about my brother Roddy. Roddy had disappeared, so I wrote on the disappearance of Roddy.[6] But just as the publisher phoned me and told me the book was going into print, first draft, I said, "Hold on to that Roddy poem, because I think Roddy has been found." Right at that time she phoned me for something, and Roddy was found.

I had just come from P.E.I. My husband and I were in P.E.I. in early August 1988. I was speaking there, and we were staying on this farm of a very famous poet. He died. So we were staying at his sister's farm.

My side of the family has unusual experiences. They are all dead, but I had two sisters, one half-sister and one real sister, and four brothers. I asked my sister, "Where did this ability come from?" We seemed to have a sixth sense, not me as much as my children have! I have six daughters and two sons, two of my own sons, and out of the six daughters, two have the ability to see things that we do not see, sometimes. They are spontaneous, though, they say that. We have a lot of unusual experiences. So I made it a point to put them down, or scribble them in a diary.

And that night at that farm, I had a strange dream. I saw a skeleton in the dream. There was sand blowing away from the skeleton. I could see some, some blowing on, some blowing off. Somebody in the dream told me to step over and identify this skeleton. "Step over here, and identify!" And in the dream I did not want to step over the skeleton, but I went around. But I could see the skeleton.

In the morning I told my husband, "Oh my god, I had a weird dream! I saw a skeleton and some sand blowing over!" "Ah," he said, "it must be the farm. Maybe somebody is buried here." You know, just joking around. And we thought no more of it.

But that morning he took me over to the publisher, and we had to look through and have a discussion of some of the book. She was sitting alongside of me, so she opened the book right away, just like that, just any old page. And "The Roddy Song" was right there. So I just got goosebumps all over me. And I didn't want to say anything to her because she'd think I was weird. But I was all goosebumps, and I looked at the poem and I said, "Oh, you think that's okay, the Roddy song?" And she said, "Yes! You are obviously talking about a mentally disturbed person?" And I said, "Yes." So she said, "That's important to the book." And I had not known that Roddy was found yet.

He disappeared in 1980, and this was in 1988. And we were talking away about other things. She said, "This 'Indian Song' is going to stay exactly the way it is."

But, later, when we came home, Roddy was found!

*HL:* You said that was the day after?

*RJ:* Yes, the day after. I did not know he was found. Evelyn, here, came in and she said, "A body has been found on Skye Mountain, Mom. It might be Roddy."

*HL:* Where is Skye Mountain?

*RJ:* Skye Mountain is in Whycocomagh, where Roddy last disappeared.

And so I called the RCMP, and I asked the RCMP, "Is it possible that might be my brother?" And they said, "We don't know. There has to be further investigation." So I said, "Will you please tell the district police to make sure?" I was the only living relative who was left, so I had to give the identifying marks. Roddy had a plate on his head and a pin in the left hip. He had a small build, and he walked with a severe limp.

*HL:* Was that from the war?

*RJ:* Yes, most of that. And he got hit by a car at the time when he was in Boston. So that hip always gave him a problem, and the war injury. And one of his eyes was like mine, too, blind.

So I phoned up the publisher and I told her, "Hold on! Don't put that one in there!" It was different, it was about the loss that I felt. So I said, "We'll remove that, and I'll write another one." And I wrote that in about half-an-hour. I just told what I felt. And the police called me later, and I said, "I'm pretty sure that's Roddy." So I told the policeman about my dream. And (LAUGHS) he said, "You know, police don't rely on dreams, not in a police investigation. But," he said, "it is possible, because nobody has disappeared in the last 20 years in Cape Breton — no man, and it appears to be a man. So it's possible that is your brother."

But *how* did he get up there? He walked with a very severe limp. I told the police that part. And he had cashed a $900 cheque that day, and no money was found on him, only a few pennies inside his pocket. I asked the policeman, "Was any money found?" And he said, "No, no money was found."

But he might have hid it. Because he was having problems that day. Some men coming off work at five o'clock saw him going into the water up to here! One of them was our nephew. And he saw Roddy going into the water up to his armpits. "Roddy," he said in Micmac, "what are you doing in the water?" And he hollered back, "White men are chasing me! It's like a war!"

*HL:* Oh, so he was still in the war in his mind?

*RJ:* Yes. So they told him to come out. And one of our nephews took him home and told him to get into dry clothes, and that he should come to the house for supper, or something like that. He lived just across the road from the nephew. And my nephew said, "After that I saw him walking on the road, going towards the church." So he didn't think anything of it. He thought he was going to come back later for supper. He said, "I saw him walking down the road. He went into the church, and he brought out the bell."

And he had put Kleenex inside the bell, and he showed it to the woman. He told the woman next door, "I had to put this inside of the bell, because every time this bell rings someone dies in the community." That's what he told the woman. And the woman looked at him. She said in Micmac, "Roddy, are you crazy?" (LAUGHS) And he just laughed at her and lifted it. "Put that bell back in the church like that!" So she said she looked out, and he took the bell back inside the church.

And somebody in there met him. There were some workmen in the church. They saw him going in the first time, taking the bell with him. And they were curious, but they didn't say anything to him. Then they saw him bring the bell back in and place it where it was before. But when he left the church, he walked backwards, like that! All the way to the door.

And another brother saw him walking. He said, "I was reading the newspaper near my picture window, and I saw him walking by." And he hollered out, "Roddy, I'm in here!," like that. And Roddy didn't come in. So, my brother Charly looked out, looking around for Roddy. He never saw him. So Charly explained to me, "When Roddy disappeared, that possibly was not the real Roddy, but the spirit of Roddy that I saw."

So, we didn't know.

*HL:* Did he act like that before?

*RJ:* About a year before that he forgot his name, and he was taken to the Nova Scotia Hospital. But I spoke to him the next day. My husband and I went to see him. We heard that Roddy was sick, and we went to the hospital to see him. And he was all right, he was normal!

So my husband asked him, "What is your name?" And he said, "Roderick Patrick Bernard." "How old are you?" "Fifty-seven," he said. Looked at my husband, said, "Why? Why do you ask?" (LAUGHS) Then my husband told him, "You know, we just wondered what was wrong with you yesterday." He said, "I don't know. I just didn't ... I don't know." He didn't remember what happened yesterday.

I imagine that was the start of the problem.

But he was normal. He went to the hospital. I didn't like what I saw when we visited him. Three months later I saw one of the doctors shaking his finger at Roddy: "Do not drink any more! Do not touch liquor any more!" But the way he was doing it, I told my husband, "Roddy may have been hypnotized!" You know, the shaking finger, "don't do it again!" Roddy was looking at the doctor so scared! "No, I will not drink again." You know, the frightened look, the puppy-dog look. I pitied him that time, and I hugged him and I told him, "You'll be all right!"

So he came home about two weeks after that. And he was all right for a whole year, until that time!

And we still don't know today what happened. But he was found on top. When he disappeared the elderly people told the searchers, "Roddy will not go up, because he is lame. He will go straight or downhill, because of his severe limp. Do not look for him up there, look for him level or down below." They looked for him in the water. All over. There were lots of searchers there, but they never found him.

And he was accidentally found eight years later by silvicultural workers. This guy was sitting down eating. Peeling an orange, and he went like that—to throw the peelings. He saw this body in the grass, in the tall grass.

I had gone to a psychic a few months after he disappeared. Last resort! We went to a psychic, my husband and I. My husband was cynical about psychics. So, he gave us tea, and he told my husband, "Turn your cup around a couple of times," and to give it to him. And I know why that was. The minute my husband handed him the cup and saucer, he told him right away: "The man you are looking for will never be found! Will not be found alive." That's the way he said it. Those were his very first words. And I just looked at him. How did he know what we were there for?

He told my husband a lot of things. My husband just looked at him with big eyes. And when he finally turned to me, I didn't even say a thing. I handed him my cup, and I never spoke. I never spoke! Not one word! Because I was too critical of the man. I wanted to judge him, see if he was real.

So he looked at me, right away, and he said, "What are you doing in a 12 by 15 room, and there is no window there, and a broom." And he was naming the things in that room. "What are you doing? And it's a little dark. What are you doing in that room?"

It registered: I am 12 years old, and I am being punished. I'm in a broom closet. It was at residential school. I recognized what he was telling me. And I said to myself, "How in the world did this guy know that I had been punished when I was 12?" I never met him before! And a few other things he said, from back when I was small, or a kid—he said these things out of the blue. And he questioned me about them, and that's when I believed him. He knew I was critical. He felt it.

So, I began to feel a little better towards him. He looked at me, and he said, "When you are writing, don't think back on the past! Write what it is today." I had not told him I was a writer!

He said, "When you write, write about what is happening today, not yesterday. Don't cry about yesterday." he said.

That's what he told me. And he told us, "That man you are looking for, he got hurt right here! Right there!" That's what he told my husband. "And he fell down. And he got up again, he walked, and he fell down, he got up again, he walked. The second time he did not get up. He fell in a hollow, an indentation in the ground. That's where he is. But," he said, "he will not be found."

My husband and I were driving home that night, and I asked my husband, "Did you believe that guy?" He said, "I don't know. What do you think?" "Well," I said, "some of the things he told me, nobody knew, not even you!" He said, "With me, too. Some of the things he said to me, I have not brought them up with anybody." We were trying to think that maybe he did some research on us. How could he do research on us when he hadn't even met us before? We kind of believed him.

So I said, "Well, Roddy will not be found." And he was not found until eight years later!

That man died. I found out he died, I asked about it. And when he told me that time, that's when I decided, from now on my writing will be of today! This man has given me direction. He doesn't know who I am, but he's given me direction.

I made a promise to myself, "I will write about what is today. Don't worry about the past. Always write positive." And I started to use the Indian language.

**_HL:_** So that's why in _Song of Eskasoni_ there is nothing about the past?

**_JL:_** Oh maybe if it is a colourful story, or something that was good that happened to me.

There is a negative one in here that people like. I don't like it. It's "She spoke of paradise/And angels' guests." [7] I don't like that one. I talk about that. My husband liked that poem. The reason why I don't like it is because I am speaking the truth there, and it is discrimination. That's what I am talking about.

*HL:* Oh yes, I see that. But why do you feel it is a negative one? Because discrimination is negative?

*RJ:* Yes it is.

*HL:* It is true, though!

*RJ:* Yes, it is true. Yes. I was going to write about residential school.

*HL:* She is a teacher, right?

*RJ:* This happened in residential school, yes. CBC contacted me a couple weeks ago, and they were doing something on residential schools. Somebody had told this lady that I went to residential school.

Right away I told her, "If I do go on the air about residential schools, it will not be negative. It will be *positive!*"

And some of my people say, "How can it be positive? After all those experiences, bad experiences, that you have had?" I know! All my life I had a lot of bad experiences, but I always look at the good side of life.

One time one of my people made a critical assessment of my work, and he said, "She doesn't know what she is talking about!" What did he say, now? "She looks at life through rose-coloured glasses," and all that stuff! Oh boy, Dr. Marie Battiste, she is the curriculum director— you've never met her?

*HL:* No.

*RJ:* She is very good! Well, she was at the University of California, and she read this poem, and she read about me, and way back she had admired my work. So she blasted that guy! (Laughs)

Then a month later my husband and I happened to walk into the *Micmac News.* My husband is big, he's five foot eleven. And he meets this guy, this fellow was standing there ...

*HL:* The one who had written that?

*RJ:* Yes! He said, "Ah, you said something unpleasant about my wife." And he went on like that, and went on and on. And that guy happened to have a black eye. And Roy, the editor of the *Micmac News* jumped out and said, "Frank, Frank, Frank," talking Micmac. Frank, of course, was teasing, he did not mean it. So he asked the guy, "Where did you get the black eye?" And that fellow said, "Oh, I got into a fight in Newfoundland." He was at a conference up there somewhere. I guess he took somebody's girl, I don't know what the story was.

*HL:* Maybe he wrote another review?

*RJ:* (Laughs) I looked at it and I laughed, and I said, "I have friends up in Newfoundland, too!"

We had a big laugh out of that! And that man is a friend of mine today. I met him one time about a year later on the street, and I said, "I'm working on a book about residential schools." And he had written a manuscript about a year or two years before that. It was not accepted by any publisher! No publisher wanted to touch it. Well, you are speaking against nuns and priests. That was back in the 1960s. So, a couple of years later I told this same fellow, "I'm writing a book about residential schools." And he said, "I'll give you all of my pictures that I have." And I told him, "Conrad, the book I am writing is positive. It's nothing negative." When I told my sister-in-law about it, the positive part of the book, she said, "Boy, you are going to have a hard time!"

*HL:* Did he ever get his book published, that Conrad?

*RJ:* No. They still have it.

*HL:* Maybe there is a chance now, with all these investigations coming up.

*RJ:* I told him, hold on to it!

*HL:* Yes, I think it should be documented! Because if you see some of the effects ...

Well, in Regina, officially I think there are about 6 or 8% Indians, but really there are about 20%, 25%. There is so much racism going on. And there are so many people out on the street, and there is so much violence, and misery, and alcohol, and you wonder, "How come?"

Also in some Native families, people are really hurting each other. Abandoning their children, or buying booze, and the kids go hungry, and all these really bad things! Ten years ago I did a book with interviews, also, people talking about boarding school.[8] And if you think that for two, sometimes three generations, people, families were being broken up, and they don't even *learn*, some of the kids, that their parents love them! What do you expect them to do when they are parents?

So, I think some of the problems, or a lot of the problems that we see today, are really the result of the residential schools. And that must never happen again!

I don't know, but that's how I see it.

*RJ:* Yes, well, some of it! Some of it!

*HL:* Yes, some of it. And then others pulled through and stayed straight, like you.

*RJ:* But let me tell you about the positive part that I have tried to research.

The positive part of the residential school — and I will say that across the nation! — the positive part was: the people that came from it, the good ones, learned a lot from there. And so many people have gone on, and they have become chiefs, counsellors, and social workers, and they went on to learn!

My own husband went back to school because of the negative experiences he had when he was a little boy there. And he didn't want that to happen again, so that's why he went into social work. So the motivations and some of the experiences they had being in that Native environment were more positive for them. That's what I feel, you know?

I tried to speak to my husband about that part. The 35 years we were together he was always speaking about that place negatively. All through the years! And I did, too! But talking! I have found out that when you are frustrated, when you are trying to analyze what you are talking about in your writings, it makes you feel better. But again, I look at that 10 years later, what I have written, sit down, and rewrite it again and the positive part comes out!

I refuse to talk about that "hated structure," that building, it stood there for the people to see. Especially Shubenacadie in Nova Scotia. Every time they saw that building, they would feel the hate, they would feel the anger. And after a while there were some people who would drink there. They had this mattress, and they would drink there.

I know a woman who wrote a book, a historical account, about the Europeans finding us, and things, and she did a part about the residential schools.

We were so many children there, over a hundred girls, and over a hundred boys. We had a spiritual encounter. Unusual things happened in that school. We tried to tell the sisters. I'll give you an instance of one. I called it "Sticks in the Night." I wrote a story "Sticks in the Night."

In the summer months, I heard the girls talk about this sound they heard in the night. I even asked an elderly man here what it could possibly be. And he talked about some kind of a bug that made that sound. But I said, "This was not a bug. It was as if you took two sticks, and it had a nice sound, like they were drumming. But they were two sticks. It sounded like that."

Well, I heard the girls talking about it, and I'd never woken up then. When I'd sleep, I'd sleep right through. But one night I woke up about three or four in the morning, and I was lying there, and I did hear them! I could not describe them any other way, but as two sticks. Somebody playing with them. And it had a nice tune to it. And then they would go off, and they would fade. And then they'd come back. It was like marching! I was petrified! I put the blanket over my head, and I tried to shut out the sound, but I couldn't. And I kept hearing it.

Next day I told the girls, the older ones. We would talk about our experiences. "I heard those darned things you people were talking about!" And then I was trying to analyze them today. Was it the power of suggestion? But how can you hear this sound, power of suggestion?

I'll tell you about one experience I had many, many years ago, when I first wrote that book. It had just come out. I met a journalist in Antigonish. We had gone to the same funeral. There was this Indian friend that died. And this non-Indian guy was curious about what Indian people do. Well, we all went to church. I was standing outside, it was warm. My brother had spoken to this journalist and told him about me writing something. I remember the man coming to me, and he asked, "Now what do we do?" Coming from the church, we go to the burial and the observance of the traditional hymn that is sung when they lower the body into the ground. We were not doing that hymn for a while until it was revived by one of the priests, here. He came in and told us, "Do what you have always done! Bring out your customs!" So, I remember that hymn, I even have a portion of it, I sing it when I am telling the stories. Now, that journalist, I told him, "Well, see what we do! Just look and observe, and see what we do."

Then, after the burial, we go to the community hall or some place, and food is served. "Now, what do we do?" he said, sitting over there somewhere. And I said, "See, there is an auction going on?" Well, when they set up the tables outside, people bring things and put them on that table. Maybe I took a set of dishes, or a flower pot, or something. People were bringing all sorts of things. Then an auction was held. And it takes a long time, five or six hours. And he came over to me, and sat down beside me. He said, "I'm gonna leave. But I'm gonna do a story for the *Casket*. Do you mind if I write about my friend? And about this part of it?" He said, "Do you mind?" And I said, "Write about what you want. And if you need any information, call me up," and I gave him my phone number. He said, "I don't know how much money will come in." I said, "Well, phone somebody in the community tomorrow, they'll tell you." And he phoned me about a week later, that man, and he said "Eleven hundred was raised that day." And I said, "You did your story?" And he said, "Yes. That's the first time I've seen that happen in the community." And then I wrote it for the book. I wrote that part, because I've seen it done so often in the community here.

My husband used to be an auctioneer at the hall for a long time. So when he died, I was thinking to myself, "Now I will experience it first hand, what I have seen happening." So, other people auctioneered the time my husband was buried. Forty-two-hundred was raised that day. I paid off all our bills, I paid the funeral expenses, even our phone bill. I paid all that, and got a beautiful headstone.

So, that's the beautiful part of that custom that I am so proud of. And I look at people, the sorrow in people. I was broken-hearted when he died. But that part I feel good about.

Well, one time, it was done without money. When I was small, that's 1937, I remember going away to Grandma's. I was told to go to Grandma's. And I wondered why I had to go to Grandma's so early in the morning. But my mother was in childbirth. She was in bad pain, and I had to be taken to Grandma's. And from Grandma's, with my older sister I went

259

to school. I'd never been to school before, but I went to school that morning. I imagine Grandma did not want me underfoot, being worried about her daughter, my mother. So I was in school, and the bell began to ring, "one"—two seconds—"one"—two seconds—"one"—like that. Angelus! So, teacher let us out. And I remember going out with my sister. We were glad, it was like recess.

But I saw my father standing at the corner, at a post. He was holding onto the post. And I asked my sister, "Why is Dad hanging onto the post?" So we went over there. "What's the matter, Dad?," you know, in Micmac. He just looked at us, and he couldn't speak. He was crying. That's the first time I saw my dad cry. He couldn't tell us, so he said, "Go to your Grandma's!"

So everybody went home, and we went to Grandma. And I remember Grandma standing at the door. I was sitting against the wall on a bench, and I saw Grandma standing by the door, and a man came by on the road, and I heard her say, "What's going on, Gabriel?" Gabriel was the chief at the time. And Gabriel, the old man, told her, "Annie has died!" And she fell back on the floor. And I remember my older sister putting a face cloth on her, trying to wake her up, putting water on her. And she was all right after. And she stood up. I can't forget that finger! Her pointing the finger at me, "It is your fault!" You know, all through the years, I always had the feeling that it was my fault my mother died. But it wasn't, you know?

And when I grew up, got older, and married, and my own children slept with me sometimes, that's when I found out why it was my fault. Because a child moves around sometimes, and accidentally kicks you. So I think, I rationalized it like that, being a mother myself. But I know she died of childbirth, because I spoke to the woman that held her when she died. I asked her why my mother died, and she said, "Your mother died with the baby inside of her." She was cold. That's from the cold. She used to fish, smelts, you know. And she was on the cold ice too long. She had branches there, under her feet, but that is not enough. And I imagine that's why she died.

She asked my dad if he would allow them to save the child. They usually cut the woman open and save the child. And they saw movements. My dad came in. A doctor came in first, and he took my mother's pulse and everything. And he went towards the door again. The midwife said she jerked him back, "Hey, aren't you going to do something?" "She's beyond help," that's what he said. "She's beyond help!" So, she said, he walked out the door! The doctor! The person they depended on! So, she held my mother. It was her friend. And she said sweat, as thick as sap, was rolling down my mother's face, but she didn't cry, she didn't holler. She says she suffered silently until she died.

And she said, "She whispered in my ear, something. I have not told a living soul what she told me that time." And I said, "Can you tell me now? She's dead." She said, "No! I have kept that promise to your mother as long as I lived."

A little while later, that particular lady had gangrene in her leg. So they had a mass at her house. They used to do that, went to different people, each other's house. And when it was over, she looked around. She said, "Is Rita Joe here?" And they said, "No!" I hadn't heard they were going to have a mass, because I would have gone. And she looked at the priest, and she said, "Father, I had a strange dream about Rita Joe's mother last night." And she named two others. There were four on a sleigh, and she said my mother was in white robes, and she was on a sleigh. And she went behind the moon! She went behind the moon and did not come back!

The reason why she thought about that was, when they were young married women, 18 or 20, they used to coast down those hills. They used to coast for hours—bobsleigh, a whole lot of them. All women together. They had one young man, maybe two young men, push that thing up the hill again. And they said my dad used to be jealous. (LAUGHS) That's what I heard, later. Because he was much older than her. He was in his 60s when he married her, and she was 16. She had five children by him. I was the youngest one, and the next one died with her. I used to ask a lot of questions about Mother.

And another thing I asked my sister was: "Why do some of my children have a sixth sense?" I have it, but it's only in dreams, or intuition, or something. One of them sees things that are not of this world. And I asked my sister that. She said, "Our mother used to 'wasiget,' that's tell fortune, with cards." I said, "I didn't know that." I learned a lot from my older sister. She knew more because she was 12 when Mother died, I was only five. So that's how I learned. I asked her, and I asked grandmothers.

I didn't learn so much from my dad, because he was old. But I remember sitting on his lap, and I used to ask him, "How do you say 'Rita' in Micmac?" I used to ask him, why was I given that name, "Rita"? And he used to say "Lita." There's no "r" in Micmac pronunciation. So I wanted to know the Indian name for Rita. "Sosep" is "Joseph." I imagine it's pretty near in different dialects. "Mali" is "Mary," "Buxima" is "Simon," "Gabliel" is "Gabriel," "Bi-el" is "Peter," "Sanwel" is "John." A lot of Indians are named "John Noël," I don't know why, I guess the missionaries, some saint's name.

*HL:* Are all the Micmac Catholics?

*RJ:* Yes, the majority here, in the community, I can count on my hand how many of them are not practising.

*HL:* Is there any of the old Micmac religion around?

**RJ:** Traditionals? Yes, there are some traditionals, but they are more spiritual. But they don't go to church. Their church is in the woods, or whatever, Earth! Sometimes I think to myself, "That's a poor excuse for not going to church, being a traditional." I think that. I do not like to criticize my own culture, but I always think that.

Being more spiritual, I listen to their stories, too. And there is half-a-percent who are bad apples, but the majority of the people in this community are good spiritual people. They work their way, even the traditionals! Now, that one traditional guy, he doesn't go to church. And he practises sweat lodge and everything, but when there is an auction, he is an auctioneer, he works in there all day, for somebody who died. So that's the good part.

**HL:** Well, that's probably where the auction comes from. It's probably older than the church.

**RJ:** Yes, older than the church. Oh yes, yes.

And then there is a story!

I had a little quill box—did you see some of my quillwork?—I only have a few, but I had over 30, 40 pieces this summer. I sold a lot of it to a museum.

Now, I had this box that this woman made me. There was a white cross on the top, a wide white cross, like that, eh? And one day we were talking about this chief, warrior chief, who was sick. He was in a coma, and he was hurt bad, and they kept him alive. And we were talking about that, I was telling Mary Ruston this story. I said, this warrior chief was kept alive by the people for one moon, that's one month, and when he woke up he took a stick, and he drew on the ground, and he drew a cross, and a little cross over on each side standing on the cross bar. And the spirit told him, "You will be better if you wear this symbol on you! Then you will become progressively better! And your people as well." And there was an epidemic that time, something was wrong. And he told the people, "Wear this! Wear it on our clothes, let's put it on." So he gave them direction. I imagine they followed just like Membertou. So that's the symbol.

And LeClerque came along, and they already had this symbol. He asked, "Where did you get this symbol?" So they just told the story about the chief.

So, I was telling Mary this story. She's a friend of mine. She lives in Sydney. And we were laughing at it. And she said, "So, our people knew about this symbol before the Europeans?" I said, "Yes." And she didn't say anything. We talked about other things. We are cousins, so we talked about other gossip.

About two weeks later she called me up again. She said, "Rita, I have something special." Because I asked her all the time to make me

quillboxes for the gift shop. She said, "I have something special for you."
So I went. Audrey took me. And she brought out three little boxes. Oval,
and different shapes. "Oh, they are beautiful!" I bought them right there
on the spot. And she said, "There's another one." She was sort of hanging
back with it. "There's another one that I want you to see!" And she brought
out a little box, with the white cross on it. I said, "Oooh!" I said, "the
Kji-klujiaway! You did it!" And she said, "Yes." She said, "I made it for
you, because of the story."

So I had that. And I put a $1,000 price on it, because I didn't want
anybody to buy it. I had it in my craft shop, in the showcase. And that
was there, and people looked at it. "Oh, one thousand!" Even European
people, yes!

"Thousand?" they said. I said, "Yes!" "Why? Why that one?" Then
I would tell the story! Well I had that, and I took it to the University of
Gettysburg, and Maine, and California and told that story. And I said,
"I will not sell this box! This is not for sale. This is for me personally."

And something unusual happened in November. Two people came
from Shubenacadie. This priest, this Oblate father, came, and this woman,
Jino, Mrs. Knockwood. "Came to see you about quillwork, because you
are famous for quillwork!"

I brought out my little boxes. I said, "Here they are!" I didn't bring
out that little cross, because I had no intention of selling it. He said, "We
want a container for the Eucharist. And we want a traditional container.
The host would be held in there."

Right there: BING! I go to my room, and I said, "I have this ..."

He was looking at the other little boxes, he was going to buy. He
had them all. "This one maybe!" You know, they had a discussion there.
But when I brought out the little box, I said "Here, father! Here!"

He looked at the price, "Ah, gee no, you think we'll be able to afford
that?" He looked at her. She's the one with the pocket of money. And
I said, "I'm going to knock the price down, father!" He looked at me
hopefully. He is a big guy. He is six feet. "I'll knock the price down father!"

"Yeah, how much?"

I said, "A hug!"

Oh, I don't know how that guy got up off that seat. (LAUGHS) He
hugged me. I had a beautiful experience that time! I felt something right
there, right there. It was—oh, I cannot describe it. Some day I'll write
about it!

And there was another one he got, a $200 one. "This one is mine.
I'm going to give it as a gift to somebody." Now, he had me sign a document,
To Kutjinu—"kutjinu" means "father"—to Kutjinu Gilbert and that date.

And I know that little box will make history! Because it will be taken
good care of. And made by Mary Ruston.

**HL:** Did you tell her?

**RJ:** Yes, I told her. I went to her house, and her husband said, "You did that?" He couldn't believe it. "Mary, the Eucharist! You'll become famous!"

Mary is famous for her work already, because I sold a lot of her work to museums, and I made it a point. "This is a 57-year-old woman who made this, Mary Ruston!" Her work will be on display at the Museum of Nova Scotia.

So that's what I have been working on.

You know, I have received fame. I have my rewards, personal triumph, or personal achievement, or something. That's mine, all of it. I did get mine, I'm working on other things. But the most important part is showing what these people have done.

A woman here, Irene Julian—she is 58 years old—has been making baskets since she was seven years old. Nobody knew how beautiful her work was. This past summer I got her to make me a man and a woman, basket woven, and dressed. I sold them to the museum. Now they are going on a North American tour. And I told her, "This is what's going to happen to your work!" That woman cannot read or write, but her work is beautiful!

You know, I was going to turn this building into something, a museum or cultural centre. And I think I will do it next summer, because next year, 1991, is Year of the Aborigine.

It has to be shown, the things that we do. There's so much. Look how beautiful that painting is way over there! There's a woman here, she is in her 30s. She did not know she could paint something so beautiful. But when it was displayed downstairs, she couldn't believe it. She said, "I did that, I did that!"

"Yes, you did!"

---

## NOTES

1. Rita Joe, *Poems of Rita Joe* (Halifax, N.S.: Abanaki Press, 1978), 21.
2. "The Empty Page" (first two stanzas), *Song of Eskasoni*, (Charlottetown, P.E.I.: Ragweed Press, 1988), 62.
3. "My Shadow Celebrates," *Song of Eskasoni*, 88.
4. Joe, *Poems*, 10.
5. "Here and There in Eskasoni" was the title of Rita Joe's article in *Micmac News*.
6. "The Roddy Song," "My Brother Roddy Disappeared, Then Found," in: Rita Joe, *Song of Eskasoni*, 28–29, 30.
7. "She spoke of paradise/ And angels' guests./ She spoke of Niskam/ And the Holy Spirit./ She spoke religiously/ Of man's true brotherhood./ Yet once when she must sit beside me/ She stood." *Poems*, 20.
8. *"Achte Deines Bruders Traum!" Gespräche mit nordamerikanischen Indianern 1978– 1985.* (Münster: Wurf Verlag, 1987), [Translation of title: *"Respect Your Brother's Dream!" Conversations with North American Indians 1978–1985.*]

# BIBLIOGRAPHY

▼

## Canadian Native Literature

Adams, Howard. *Prison of Grass: Canada from a Native Point of View.* Toronto: General Publishing, 1975f. Rev. ed. Saskatoon: Fifth House Publishers, 1989.

——. "Öffentliche Grundschule und katholischer Konvent, Saskatchewan, ca. 1940." *Achte Deines Bruders Traum! Gespräche mit nordamerikanischen Indianern 1978–1985.* Eds. Hartmut Lutz and Indianerprojektgruppe Osnabrück. Münster: Wurf Verlag, 1987.

Ahenakew, Freda. *Wâskahikaniwiyiniw—âcimowina: Stories of the House.* Winnipeg: University of Manitoba, 1985.

——., ed. *Kiskinahamawâkan – âcimowinisa: Student Stories.* Winnipeg: University of Manitoba, Native Language Program, 1986.

——. *Nâpêsis êkwa âpakosis âcimowinis: How the Mouse Got Brown Teeth.* Saskatoon: Fifth House Publishers, 1988.

——. *Wîsahkêcâhkêkwa waskwayak âtayohkêwin: How the Birch Tree Got its Stripes.* Saskatoon: Fifth House Publishers, 1988.

Annharte [Marie Annharte Baker]. *Being on the Moon.* Winlaw, B.C.: Polestar Book Publishers, 1990.

Armstrong, Jeannette. *Enwhisteetkwa: Walk on Water.* Penticton, B.C.: Okanagan Tribal Council, 1982.

——. *Neekna and Chemai.* Illustrated by Kenneth Lee Edwards. Penticton B.C.: Theytus Books, 1984.

——. *Slash.* Penticton, B.C.: Theytus Books, 1985.

——. "Words." *Telling It: Women and Language Across Cultures.* Edited by S. Lee, L. Maracle, D. Marlatt, and B. Warland. Vancouver: Press Gang Publishers, 1990, 23–29.

Association of Métis and Non-Status Indians of Saskatchewan, eds. *Louis Riel: Justice Must Be Done.* Winnipeg, Manitoba Métis Federation Press, 1979.

Assu, Harry (with Joy Inglis). *Assu of Cape Mudge: Recollections of a Coastal Indian Chief.* Vancouver: University of British Columbia Press, 1989.

Bemister, Margaret. *Thirty Indian Legends of Canada.* Vancouver: Douglas & McIntyre, 1973.

Blondin, George. *When the World was New: Stories of the Sahtu Dene.* Yellowknife: Outcrop, 1989.

Bopp, Judie. *Unity in Diversity.* Lethbridge: Four Worlds Development Project, 1988.

265

Bouchard, Randy and Dorothy Kennedy, eds. *Shuswap Stories*. Collected 1971–1975. Vancouver: Comm Cept Publications Ltd., 1979.

Boulanger, Tom. *An Indian Remembers: My Life as a Trapper in Northern Manitoba*. Winnipeg: Peguis Publishers, 1971.

Brant, Beth, ed. *A Gathering of Spirit: Writing and Art by North American Indian Women*. Montpelier, V.T.: Sinister Wisdom Books, 1984. Toronto: Women's Press, 1988.

——. *Mohawk Trail*. Ithaca, N.Y.: Firebrand Books, 1984.

Brass, Eleanor. *Medicine Boy and Other Cree Tales*. Calgary: Glenbow Museum, 1978. Repr. 1982.

——. *I Walk in Two Worlds*. Calgary: Glenbow Museum, 1987.

Campbell, Maria. *Halfbreed*. Toronto: McClelland & Stewart, 1973. Repr.: Goodread Biographies, Halifax: Formac Publishing, 1983.

——. *People of the Buffalo: How the Plains Indians Lived*. Illustrated by Douglas Tait and Shannon Twofeathers. Vancouver: J.J. Douglas Ltd., 1976.

——. *Riel's People: How the Métis Lived*. Illustrated by David Maclagan. Vancouver/Toronto: Douglas & McIntyre, 1978.

——. "Introduction." *Achimoona*. Saskatoon: Fifth House Publishers, 1985.

Campbell, Maria, and Linda Griffiths. *The Book of Jessica: A Theatrical Transformation*. Toronto: The Coach House Press, 1989.

*Canadian Fiction Magazine*, no. 60 (1987). Guest editor Thomas King. (Special issue on Native Fiction)

*The Canadian Journal of Native Studies*, 1981ff. Edited by Dept. of Native Studies, Brandon University, Manitoba.

Capek, Peggy. *Mirna and the Marmots*. Penticton, B.C.: Theytus Books, 1982.

Cardinal, Harold. *The Unjust Society: The Tragedy of Canada's Indians*. Edmonton: Hurtig Publishers, 1969.

——. *The Rebirth of Canada's Indians*. Edmonton: Hurtig Publishers, 1977.

Carpenter, Jock. *Fifty Dollar Bride: Marie Rose Smith—A Chronicle of Métis Life in the 19th Century*. Hanna, Alta.: Gorman & Gorman, 1977, 1988.

Chester, Bruce. *Paper Radio*. Penticton B.C.: Theytus Books, 1986.

Chrystos. *Not Vanishing*. Vancouver: Press Gang Publishers, 1988.

Clutesi, George. *Son of Raven, Son of Deer*. Fables of the Tse-shaht. Sidney, B.C.: Gray's Publishing, 1967.

——. *Potlatch*. Sidney, B.C.: Gray's Publishing, 1969. Repr. 1973.

Cornplanter, J.J. *Legends of the Longhouse*. Oshweken: Iroqrafts Ltd., 1986.

Crate, Joan. *Pale as Real Ladies: Poems for Emily Pauline Johnson*. Coldstream: Brick Books, 1989.

——. *Breathing Water*. Edmonton: NeWest Publishers, 1989.

Culleton, Beatrice. *In Search of April Raintree*. Winnipeg: Pemmican Publications, 1983. 6th repr. 1987.

——. *April Raintree*. Winnipeg: Pemmican Publications, 1984. 3rd repr. 1987.

——. *Spirit of the White Bison*. Illustrated by Robert Kakaygeesick, Jr. Winnipeg: Pemmican Publications, 1985. Repr. 1987.

Cuthand, Beth. *Horse Dance to Emerald Mountain*. Vancouver: Lazara Publications, 1987.

——. *Voices in the Waterfall*. Vancouver: Lazara Press, 1989.

Daniels, Greg, and Eugene Stickland. *The Third House From the Corner*. Regina: Laughing Dog Productions, 1990.

Day, David, and Marilyn Bowering. *Many Voices: An Anthology of Contemporary Canadian Indian Poetry*. Vancouver: J.J. Douglas Ltd., 1977.

Dion, Joseph F. *My Tribe the Crees*. Edited and with an introduction by Hugh A. Dempsey. Calgary: Glenbow Museum, 1979.

Eber, Dorothy Harley. *When the Whalers Were Up North: Inuit Memories from the Eastern Arctic*. Kingston, Montreal, London: McGill's University Press, 1989.

Elston, Georgia, ed. *Giving: Ojibwa Stories and Legends from the Children of Curve Lake*. Lakefield, Ontario: Waapoone Publishing & Promotion, 1985.

Enosse, Susan (teller), Mary Lou (writer), Melvina Corbiere (translator). *Why the Beaver has a Broad Tail/Amik Gazhi Debinung We Zawonugom*. Cobalt, Ontario: Highway Book Shop, 1974. 9th repr. 1985.

Fedorick, Joy Asham. "Fencepost Sitting and How I Fell Off to One Side." *Artscraft* 2.3. (Fall 1990): 9–14.

——. "Getting Out from Under: How to Avoid Professional Pathology." *Artscraft* 2.4 (Winter 1991): 11–15.

Fiddler, Chief Thomas, and James R. Stevens, eds. *Legends From the Forest: Told by Chief Thomas Fiddler*. Translated by Edtrip Fiddler. Kapuskasing and Moonbeam: Penumbra Press, 1985.

Freeman, Minnie Aodla. *Life Among the Qallunaat*. Edmonton: Hurtig Publishers, 1978.

Gardner, Ethel B. "Ka-Imi's Gift: A Sto:lo Legend" (with commentary by author) in *Canadian Journal of Native Education* 15:3 (1988): 101–108.

*Gatherings: The En'owkin Journal of First North American Peoples*. Edited by En'owkin Centre/Theytus Books, Penticton, B.C. Premiere Issue, 1.1 (Fall 1990).

Geddes, Carol. "Growing Up Native." *Homemaker's Magazine*. (October 1990): 36–38, 40, 42, 44, 46, 48, 50–51.

George, Chief Dan. *My Heart Soars*. Sydney, B.C.: Hancock House, 1981.

——. *My Spirit Soars*. Sydney, B.C.: Hancock House, 1982.

Getty, Ian L., and Antoine S. Lussier, eds. *As Long as the Sun Shines and Water Flows: A Reader in Canadian Native Studies*. Vancouver: University of B.C. Press, 1983.

Geyshick, Ronald, and Judith Doyle. *Te Bwe Win* (Truth). Toronto: Summerhill Press, 1989.

Gooderham, Kent, ed. *I Am An Indian*. Toronto: J.M. Dent & Sons, 1969.

Goodwill, Jean, and Norma Sluman. *John Tootoosis*. Winnipeg: Pemmican Publications, 1984.

Goudie, Elizabeth. *Woman of Labrador*. Toronto: Peter Martin Associates, 1973.

Grant, Agnes, ed. *Our Bit of Truth: An Anthology of Canadian Native Literature*. Winnipeg: Pemmican Publications, 1990.

Greene, Alma (Gah-wonh-nos-do). *Forbidden Voice: Reflections of a Mohawk Indian*. Illustrated and cover design by Gordon McLean. London, N.Y., Sydney, Toronto: Hamlyn, 1971.

——. *Tales of the Mohawk*. Illustrated by R.G. Miller. Toronto: J.M. Dent and Sons (Canada) Ltd., 1975.

Gros-Louis, Max (in collaboration with Marcel Bellier). *First Among the Hurons*. Translated by Sheila Fischman from the French text. Montreal: Harvest House, 1974 (original: *Le "Premier" des Hurons*).

H., Arthur, with George McPeek. *The Grieving Indian: An Ojibwe Elder Shares his Discovery of Help and Hope*. Indian Life Books. Winnipeg: Intertribal Christian Communications (Canada) Inc., 1988.

Hardin, Herschel. *Esker Mike and his Wife, Agiluk*. Vancouver: Talon Books, 1973.

——. *The Great Wave of Civilization*. Vancouver: Talon Books, 1976.

Harris, Chief Kenneth B. *Visitors Who Never Left: The Origin of the People of Damelahamid*. Translated and arranged by Chief Kenneth B. Harris in collaboration with Frances M.P. Robinson. Vancouver: University of British Columbia Press, 1974.

Heath, Caroline, ed. *The Land Called Morning: Three Plays*. Saskatoon: Fifth House Publishers, 1986.

Highway, Tomson. *The Rez Sisters: A Play in Two Acts*. Saskatoon: Fifth House Publishers, 1988.

——. *Dry Lips Oughta Move to Kapuskasing*. Saskatoon: Fifth House Publishers, 1989.

Hodgson, Heather, ed. *Seventh Generation: Contemporary Native Writing*. Penticton, B.C.: Theytus Books, 1989.

Hungry Wolf, Beverly. *The Ways of My Grandmothers*. New York: Quill, 1982.

*Inuktitut* (Magazine). Edited by Dept. of Indian Affairs and Northern Development, Ottawa.

Joe, J.B. "Shale" (radio drama based on a Nitinaht legend). *Whetstone*. (Native Issue, Spring 1987): 71–85.

Joe, Rita. *Poems of Rita Joe*. Halifax, N.S.: Abanaki Press, 1978.

——. *Song of Eskasoni: More Poems of Rita Joe*. Charlottetown: Ragweed Press, 1988.

Johnson, Emily Pauline/Tekahionwake. *Canadian Born*. Toronto: George N. Morang & Co., 1903.

——. *Legends of Vancouver*. Vancouver: Vancouver Daily Province, 1911. Repr. Toronto: McClelland & Stewart, 1983.

——. *Flint and Feather: The Complete Poems of E. Pauline Johnson*. Toronto: Hodder & Stoughton, 1911. Repr. Markham, Ontario: Paper Jacks Ltd., 1972. 3rd repr. 1981.

——. *The Moccasin Maker*. Introduction, Annotation, and Bibliography by A. LaVonne Brown Rouff. Tucson: University of Arizona Press, 1987.

Johnston, Basil. *Moose Meat and Wild Rice*. Toronto: McClelland & Stewart, 1978.

——. *Tales the Elders Told: Ojibway Legends*. Illustrations by Shirley Cheechoo. Toronto: Royal Ontario Museum Publications, 1981.

——. *Und Manitou erschuf die Welt: Mythen und Visionen der Ojibwa*. 2. Aufl. Köln: Diederichs, 1981.

——. *Ojibway Ceremonies*. Illustrations by David Beyer. Toronto: McClelland & Stewart, 1982.

——. *By Canoe and Moccasin. Some Native Place Names of the Great Lakes*. Illustrations by David Beyer. Lakefield, Ontario: Waapoone Publishing & Promotion, 1986.

——. *Indian Schooldays*. Toronto: Key Porter Books, 1988.

Jones, Chief Charles, with Stephen Bosustow. *Queesto, Pacheenaht Chief by Birthright*. Penticton B.C.: Theytus Books, 1981.

Jonker, Peter. *Sitting Wind: The Life of Stoney Indian Chief Frank Kaquitts*. Biography of the 20th-century Albertan Indian chief. s.l.: LPP, 1988

Kelly/Kinew, Peter. "Pow Wow: Der große Tanz vereint die indianischen Nationen." *Geo-Special: Kanada* 6 (1988): 48–60.

Kennedy, Dan (Ochankugahe). *Recollections of an Assiniboine Chief*. Edited and with an introduction by James R. Stevens. Toronto & Montreal: McClelland & Stewart, 1972.

Kenny, George. *Indians Don't Cry*. s.l.: Chimo Publishing, 1977.

Kenny, George, in collaboration with Denis Lacroix. *October Stranger*. Toronto: Chimo Publishing, 1978.

Keon, Wayne. *Sweetgrass II*. Stratford, Ont.: The Mercury Press, 1990.

King, Thomas, guest ed. *Canadian Fiction Magazine*, no. 60 (1987). (Special issue on Native writing)

——. *Medicine River*. Markham, Ont.: Penguin Books-Canada, 1990.

——., ed. *All My Relations: An Anthology of Contemporary Canadian Native Fiction*. Toronto: McClelland & Stewart, 1990.

Kirk, Ruth. *Wisdom of the Elders: Native Traditions on the Northwest Coast*. Vancouver: Douglas & McIntyre, 1986.

Kusugak, Michael, and Robert Munsch. *A Promise is a Promise*. Willowdale: Annick Press, 1988.

LaRoque, Emma. *Defeathering the Indian*. Agincourt, Canada: The Book Society of Canada Ltd., 1975. [Editor's note: Since 1984 Emma LaRocque has used her family name of "LaRocque" rather than "LaRoque."]

Lee, Bobbi. [Lee Maracle] *Indian Rebel: Struggles of a Native Canadian Woman*. SLM Information Center, 1975. Repr. Toronto: Women's Press, 1990.

Leon, Ed. *The Story of Chehalis*. As told by Ed Leon. Stó:lóSitel Curriculum. Sardis, B.C., V0X 1Y0: Coqualeetca Education Training Center, Box 370, 1983.

*The Magazine to Re-Establish the Trickster: New Native Writing*. (Fall 1988): 1.1, (Spring 1989) 2:1.

Maracle, Brant Joseph. *The Fever and Frustration of the Indian Heart*. Oshawa, Ontario: Maracle Press, 1977. Repr. 1979.

——. *Questions We Indians Are Asked*. s.l.: Maracle Press, 1977.

Maracle, Lee. *I Am Woman*. Vancouver: Write-on Press Publishers Ltd., 1988.

——. "Moving Over." in *Trivia: A Journal of Ideas*, no. 14 (Spring 1989): 9–12.

——. *Bobbi Lee: Indian Rebel*. Toronto: Women's Press, 1990.

——. *Sojourner's Truth and Other Stories*. Vancouver: Press Gang Publishers, 1990.

Maracle, Lee, Daphne Marlatt, Betsy Warland, and Sky Lee. *Telling It: Women and Language Across Cultures.* Vancouver: Press Gang Publishers, 1990.

Markoosie. *Harpoon of the Hunter.* Illustrated by Germaine Arnaktauyok. Montreal and London: McGill-Queens University Press, 1970.

McClellan, Catharine. *The Girl Who Married the Bear.* Publication in Ethnology, no. 2. Ottawa and Manitoba: National Museum of Canada/Museum of Manitoba, 1970.

McEwan, J. Richard. *Memoirs of A Micmac Life.* Edited by W.D. Hamilton. Fredericton, N.B.: Micmac-Maliseet Institute/University of New Brunswick, 1988.

McGrath (Gedalof), Robin, ed. *Paper Stays Put: A Collection of Inuit Writing.* Illustrated by Alootook Ipellie. Edmonton: Hurtig Publishers, 1980.

McLellan, Joseph. *Nanabosho: The Birth of Nanabosho.* Winnipeg: Pemmican Publications, 1988.

Metayer, Maurice, ed. and transl. *Tales From the Igloo.* Illustrated by Agnes Nanogak. Edmonton: Hurtig Publishers, 1972.

Miller, Jay. "The Early Years of Watonuka (James Bouchard): Delaware and Jesuit," in *American Indian Quarterly* 13:2 (Spring 1989): 165–ff.

Moore, Patrick, and Angela Wheelock, eds. *Wolverine Myths and Visions: Dene Traditions from Northern Alberta.* Lincoln: University of Nebraska Press, 1990.

Moses, Daniel David. *Delicate Bodies.* Vancouver: blewointmentpress, 1980.

——. *The White Line.* Saskatoon: Fifth House Publishers, 1990.

——. *Coyote City: A Play in Two Acts.* Stratford, Ont.: Williams-Wallace Publications, 1990.

Mountain Horse, Mike. *My People the Bloods.* Edited and introduction by Hugh A. Dempsey. Calgary: Glenbow-Alberta Institute/Blood Tribal Council, 1979.

Mowat, William, and Christine Mowat, eds. *Natives in Canadian Literatures.* Toronto: Macmillan of Canada, 1975.

Nanogak, Agnes. *More Tales From the Igloo.* Introduction by Robin Gedalof McGrath. Edmonton: Hurtig Publishers, 1986.

New, W.H., ed. *Native Writers and Canadian Writing.* Vancouver: UBC Press, 1990. Repr. *Canadian Literature,* no. 124/5. (Native Issue)

North American Indian Travelling College, ed. *Legends of Our Nations.* Cornwall Island, Ont.: North American Indian Travelling College, s.a.

Nowlan, Michael O., ed. *Canadian Myths and Legends.* Toronto: Macmillan, 1977.

Nuligak. I. *Nuligak.* Edited and translated by Maurice Metayer, illustrated by Ekootak. Markham, Ontario: Simon & Schuster, 3rd paperback ed. 1975. Orig.: Peter Martin, 1966.

Nungak, Zebedee. *Inuit Stories.* Hull: Canadian Museum of Civilization, 1988.

Pagtatek. Edited by S. Inglis, J. Mannette, S. Sulewski. (Policy and Consciousness in Mi'kmaq Life.), vol. 1 (1991).

Pelletier, Wilfred, and Ted Poole. *No Foreign Land: The Biography of a North American Indian.* Toronto: McClelland & Stewart, 1973.

Perrault, Jeanne, and Sylvia Vance, eds. *Native Women of Western Canada: Writing the Circle: An Anthology.* Edmonton: NeWest Publishers, 1990.

Petrone, Penny, ed. *First People, First Voices*. Toronto, Buffalo, London: University of Toronto Press, 1983.

——. *Northern Voices: Inuit Writing in English*. Toronto: University of Toronto Press, 1988.

Pitseolak. *Pitseolak: Pictures Out of my Life*. Edited from recorded interviews by Dorothy Eber. Montreal: Design Collaborative Books/Toronto: Oxford University Press, 1971.

Pitseolak, Peter. *People from our side: A life story with photography* by Peter Pitseolak and oral biography by Dorothy Eber. Edmonton: Hurtig Publishers, 1975.

Poelzer, Dolores T., and Irene A. Poelzer. *In Our Own Words: Northern Saskatchewan Métis Women Speak Out*. Saskatoon: Lindenblatt & Hamonic, 1986.

Racette, Calvin. *Flags of the Métis*. Regina: Gabriel Dumont Institute, s.a.

Ray, Carl, and James R. Stevens. *Sacred Legends of the Sandy Lake Cree*. Illustrated by Carl Ray. Toronto: McClelland and Stewart, 1971. Repr. 1988.

Redbird, Duke. *We Are Métis: A Métis View of the Development of a Native Canadian*. Willowdale, Ont.: Ontario Métis and Non-Status Indian Association, 1980.

Redsky, James. *Great Leader of the Ojibway: Mis-quona-queb*. Edited by James R. Stevens. Toronto: McClelland and Stewart, 1972.

Reid, Bill, and Robert Bringhurst. *Raven Steals the Light*. Vancouver: Douglas & McIntyre, 1988.

Richardson, Boyce, ed. *Drum Beat: Anger and Renewal in Indian Country*. Introduction by George Erasmus. Toronto: Summerhill Press/Assembly of First Nations, 1989.

Riel, Louis. *The Collected Writings of Louis Riel/Les Ecrits complets de Louis Riel*. General editor George F.G. Stanley. Edmonton: University of Alberta Press, 1985. 5 vols.

Robinson, Gordon. *Tales of Kitamaat*. Kitimat, B.C.: Northern Sentinel Press, 1956.

Robinson, Harry (as told to Wendy Wickwire). *Write it on Your Heart: The Epic World of an Okanagan Storyteller*. Vancouver: Talon Books/Theytus Books, 1989.

Rustige, Rona, ed. *Tyendinaga Tales*. Montreal: McGill-Queen's University Press, 1988.

Sark, John Joe. *Micmac Legends of Prince Edward Island*. Charlottetown: Ragweed Press, 1988.

Schwarz, Herbert T. *Tales from the Smokehouse*. Illustrated by Daphne Odjig. Edmonton: Hurtig Publishers, 1974.

Sewid, James. *Guests Never Leave Hungry: The Autobiography of James Sewid, a Kwakiutl Indian*. Edited by James P. Spradley. Harvard: Yale University Press, 1969. Repr. Kingston and Montreal: McGill-Queen's University Press, 1972.

Shilling, Arthur. *The Ojibway Dream: Faces of my People*. s.l. Tundra Books, 1986.

Silman, Janet, ed. *Enough is Enough: Aboriginal Women Speak Out*. Toronto: The Women's Press, 1987.

Skogan, Joan. *The Princess and the Sea-Bear and Other Tsimishian Stories*. Illustrated by Claudia Stewart. Prince Rupert, B.C.: Metlakatla Band Council, 1983.

Slipperjack, Ruby. *Honour the Sun*. Winnipeg: Pemmican Publications, 1987.

——. "A Spirit of Wings." *Flight Pattern Uninterrupted* (catalogue for exhibition of art by Alice Crawley, An Whitlock, and Michael Belmore, with a written work by Ruby Slipperjack.) Edited by Lynne Sharman, curator. Thunder Bay, Ont.: Definitely Superior, 11 November 1989.

Smith, Barbara. *Renewal: The Prophecy of Manu; Book I*. Penticton, B.C.: Theytus Books, 1985.

——. *Renewal: Teoni's Giveway: Book Two*. Penticton, B.C.: Theytus Books, 1986.

Smith, E.A. *Myths of the Iroquois*. Oshweken: Iroqrafts Ltd., 1983.

Snow, Chief John. *These Mountains are our Sacred Places: The Story of the Stoney Indians*. Toronto & Sarasota: Samuel Stevens, 1977.

*Speaking Together: Canada's Native Women*. Edited by Jean Goodwill. Ottawa: Secretary of State, 1975.

*Spirits Rising. A Collection of Native Writings and Illustrations*. Toronto: Frontier College Press, 1987.

Stonechild, Blair. *Saskatchewan Indians and The Resistance of 1885: Two Case Studies*. Regina: Saskatchewan Education, 1986.

Stump, Sarain. *There is My People Sleeping*. Sidney, B.C.: Gray's Publishing Ltd., 1970.

Suluk, Donald. *Inummariit: An Inuit Way of Life*. Special Issue of: *Inuktitut* (Winter 1987). Ottawa: Indian and Northern Affairs. Canada, 1987.

Taylor, Drew Hayden. *"Toronto at Dreamer's Rock" and "Education is Our Right." Two One-Act Plays*. Saskatoon: Fifth House Publishers, 1990.

Tetso, John. *Trapping is my Life*. Toronto: Peter Martin, 1970.

Thrasher, Anthony Apakark. *[The Three Lives of] Thrasher, Skid Row Eskimo*. In collaboration with Gerard Deagle and Alan Mettrick. Toronto: Griffin Press, 1976.

Trindell, Ted. *Métis Witness to the North*. Edited by Jean Morisset and Rose-Marie Pelletier. Vancouver: Tillacum Library, 1986.

Tyman, James. *Inside Out: An Autobiography of a Native Canadian*. Saskatoon: Fifth House Publishers, 1989.

Ungalaaq, Martha Angugatiaq. *Inuit Life of Fifty Years Ago: Recollections of Martha Angugatiaq Ungalaaq*. Eskimo Point, N.W.T.: Inuit Cultural Institute, 1985.

Waubageshig, ed. *The Only Good Indian: Essays by Canadian Indians*. Toronto: New Press, 1972.

Wheeler, Bernelda. *A Friend Called Chum*. Winnipeg: Pemmican Publications, 1984.

——. *I Can't Have Bannock. But the Beaver has a Drum*. Winnipeg: Pemmican Publications, 1984.

Wheeler, Jordan. *Brothers in Arms: Three Novellas*. Winnipeg: Pemmican Publications, 1989.

*Whetstone*. Edited by Dept. of English, University of Lethbridge, Alberta (Special Native issues Spring 1985, Spring 1987, and Fall 1988).

White, Ellen. *Kwulasulwut: Stories From the Coast Salish*. Penticton, B.C.: Theytus Books, 1981.

Whitehead, Ruth Holmes. *Stories From the Six Worlds*. Halifax: Nimbus Publishing, 1988.

Williams, Stephen Guion. *In the Middle: The Inuit Today.* Toronto: Fitzhenry & Whiteside, 1983.

Willis, Jane. *Geniesh: An Indian Girlhood.* Toronto: New Press, 1973.

Wolfe, Alexander. *Earth Elder Stories: The Pinayzitt Path.* Saskatoon: Fifth House Publishers, 1988.

Zeilig, Ken, and Victoria Zeilig. *Ste. Madeleine: Community without a Town.* Winnipeg: Pemmican Publications, 1987.

## Secondary Sources on Canadian Native Literature

Armstrong, Jeannette C. "Writing from a Native Woman's Perspective." Proceedings from *in the feminine: women and words conference,* 1983. Edited by A. Dybikowski et. al. Edmonton: Longspoon Press, 1985: 55–57.

——. "Words." *Telling It: Women and Language Across Cultures.* Edited by S. Lee, L. Maracle, D. Marlatt, and B. Warland. Vancouver: Press Gang Publishers, 1990: 23–29.

——. "The Disempowerment of First North American Native Peoples And Empowerment Through Their Writing." Paper prepared for the Saskatchewan Writers Guild 1990 Annual Conference in *Gatherings: The En'owkin Journal of First North American Peoples,* Premiere Issue. 1:1 (Fall 1990): 141–146.

Atwood, Margaret. "A Double-Bladed Knife: Subversive Laughter in Two Stories by Thomas King." *Canadian Literature* nos. 124–125 (Spring-Summer 1990): 243–250.

Bataille, Gretchen M., and Kathleen Mullen Sands. *American Indian Women Telling Their Lives.* Lincoln: University of Nebraska Press, 1984.

Brant, Beth. "Coming Out As Indian Lesbian Writers." Proceedings from *in the feminine: women and words conference.* Edited by A. Dybikowski et. al. Edmonton: Longspoon Press, 1985: 58–59.

Bringhurst, Robert. "That Also Is You: Some Classics of Native Canadian Literature." *Canadian Literature* nos. 124–125 (Spring-Summer 1990): 32–47.

Brown, Alanna Kathleen. "Mourning Dove's Canadian Recovery Years, 1917–1919." *Canadian Literature* nos. 124–125 (Spring-Summer 1990): 113–122.

Charnley, Kerrie. "Concepts of Identity, Anger and Power and the Vision in the Writings of First Nations Women," in *Gatherings: The En'owkin Journal of First North American Peoples,* Premiere Issue 1.1 (Fall 1990): 10–22.

Cornell, George L. "The Imposition of Western Definitions of Literature On Indian Oral Traditions." *The Native in Literature: Canadian and Comparative Perspectives.* Edited by T. King, C. Calver, H. Hoy. Oakville, Ont.: ECW Press, 1987: 174–187.

Currie, Noel Elizabeth. "Jeannette Armstrong and the Colonial Legacy." *Canadian Literature* nos. 124–125 (Spring-Summer 1990): 138–152.

Cuthand, Beth. "Transmitting Our Identity as Indian Writers." Proceedings from *in the feminine: women and words conference,* 1983. Edited by A. Dybikowski et. al. Edmonton: Longspoon Press, 1985: 53–54.

Debenham, Diane. "Native People in Contemporary Canadian Drama." *Canadian Drama/L'Art dramatique canadienne.* 14:2 (1988): 137–158.

Fee, Margery. "Upsetting Fake Ideas: Jeannette Armstrong's Slash and Beatrice Culleton's April Raintree." *Canadian Literature* nos. 124–125 (Spring-Summer 1990): 168–180.

Freeman, Victoria. "The Baffin Writers' Project." *Canadian Literature* nos. 124–125 (Spring-Summer 1990): 266–271.

Godard, Barbara. "Talking About Ourselves: The Literary Productions of the Native Women in Canada." *The CRIAW Papers/Les Documents de l'ICREF,* no. 11. Ottawa: Canadian Research Institute for the Advancement of Women/Institut Canadien de Recherches sur les Femmes, 1985.

——. "Voicing difference: the literary production of native women." *A MAZING SPACE: Writing Canadian Women Writing*. Edited by. S. Neumann and S. Kamboureli. Edmonton: Longspoon Press/NeWest Press, 1986: 87–107.

——. "Listening for the Silence: Native Women's Traditional Narratives." *The Native In Literature: Canadian and Comparative Perspectives*. Edited by T. King, C. Calver, H. Hoy. Oakville, Ont.: ECW Press, 1987: 133–158.

——. "The Politics of Representation: Some Native Canadian Women Writers." *Canadian Literature* nos. 124–125 (Spring-Summer 1990): 183–225.

Grant, Agnes. "Contemporary Native Women's Voices in Literature." *Canadian Literature* nos. 124–125 (Spring-Summer 1990): 124–132.

Harry, Margaret. "Literature in English by Native Canadians (Indian and Inuit)." *Studies in Canadian Literature,* 10.2 (1985): 146–153.

Johnston, Basil H. "One Generation from Extinction." *Canadian Literature* nos. 124–125 (Spring-Summer 1990): 10–15.

Johnston, Denis W. "Lines and Circles: The 'Rez' Plays of Tomson Highway." *Canadian Literature* nos. 124–125 (Spring-Summer 1990): 254–264.

Karrer, Wolfgang, and Hartmut Lutz. "Minority Literatures in North America: From Cultural Nationalism to Liminality." *Minority Literatures in North America: Contemporary Perspectives*. Edited by W. Karrer and H. Lutz. Frankfurt: Peter Lang, 1990: 11–64.

Keller, Betty. *Pauline: Biography of Pauline Johnson*. Goodread Biographies. Halifax: Formac Publishing, 1981.

King, T., C. Calver, and H. Hoy, eds. *The Native in Literature: Canadian and Comparative Perspectives*. Oakville, Ont.: ECW Press, 1987.

King, Thomas. "Introduction." *The Native in Literature: Canadian and Comparative Perspectives*. Edited by T. King, C. Calver, H. Hoy. Oakville, Ont.: ECW Press, 1987: 7–14.

Klooss, Wolfgang. *Geschichte und Mythos in der Literatur Kanadas: Die englischsprachige Métis–und Riel-Rezeption*. Heidelberg: Carl Winter, 1989.

——. "Fictional and Non-Fictional Autobiographies by Métis Women." *Minority Literatures in North America*. Edited by W. Karrer and H. Lutz. Frankfurt: Peter Lang, 1990: 205–225.

Klooss, Wolfgang, and Hartmut Lutz. "Minority Studies and Intercultural Perceptiveness." *Anglistentag 1989 Würzburg*. Edited by Rüdiger Ahrens. Tübingen: Max Niemeyer, 1990: 92–107.

Kroeber, Karl. *Traditional American Indian Literature*. Lincoln: Univ. of Nebraska Press, 1981.

Krupat, Arnold. *The Voice in the Margin: Native American Literature and the Canon.* Berkeley: University of California Press, 1989.

LaRocque, Emma. "Preface, or Here Are Our Voices—Who Will Hear?" *Writing the Circle: Native Women Of Western Canada.* Edited by Jeanne Perreault and Sylvia Vance. Edmonton, Alta.: NeWest Publishers, 1990: xv–xxx.

——. "Tides, Towns, and Trains." *Living the Changes.* Edited by Joan Turner. Winnipeg: University of Manitoba Press, 1990: 76–90.

Lutz, Hartmut. "The Circle as a Philosophical and Structural Concept in Native American Fiction Today." *Native American Literatures.* Edited by Laura Coltelli. Pisa, Italy: Servizio Editoriale Universitario, 1989: 85–100.

——. "Native Literatures in Canada Today." *Zeitschrift der Gesellschaft für Kanada-Studien* 10.1 (1990): 27–47.

——. "Cultural Appropriation as a Process of Displacing Peoples and History." Publication pending in *Canadian Journal of Native Studies,* (1991).

Maracle, Lee. "Just Get in Front of a Typewriter and Bleed." *Telling It: Women and Language Across Cultures.* Edited by S. Lee, L. Maracle, D. Marlatt, B. Warland. Vancouver: Press Gang Publishers, 1990: 37–41.

——. "Ramparts Hanging in the Air." *Telling It: Women and Language Across Cultures.* Edited by S. Lee, L. Maracle, D. Marlatt, B. Warland. Vancouver: Press Gang Publishers, 1990: 161–175.

McGrath, Robin. *Canadian Inuit Literature: The Development of a Tradition.* Ottawa: National Museum of Canada, 1984.

——. "Oral Influences in Contemporary Inuit Literature." *The Native in Literature: Canadian and Comparative Perspectives.* Edited by T. King, C. Calver, H. Hoy. Oakville, Ont.: ECW Press, 1987: 159–173.

——. "Reassessing Traditional Inuit Poetry." *Canadian Literature* nos. 124–125, (Spring–Summer 1990): 19–28.

——. "The Development of Inuit Literature in English." *Minority Literatures in North America: Contemporary Perspectives.* Edited by W. Karrer and H. Lutz. Frankfurt: Peter Lang, 1990: 193–203.

Mingwôn, Mingwôn (Shirley Bear). "Equality Among Women." *Canadian Literature* nos. 124–125 (Spring-Summer 1990): 133–136.

New, W.H., ed. *Native Writers and Canadian Writing.* Special Issue of *Canadian Literature.* Vancouver: University of British Columbia Press, 1990.

Petrone, Penny. *Native Literature in Canada: From the Oral Tradition to the Present.* Toronto: Oxford University Press, 1990.

Ramsey, Jarold. "Ti-Jean and the Seven-Headed Dragon: Instances of Native American Assimilation of European Folklore." *The Native in Literature: Canadian and Contemporary Perspectives.* Edited by T. King, C. Calver, H. Hoy. Oakville, Ont.: ECW Press, 1987: 206–224.

Ridington, Robin. "Cultures in Conflict: The Problem of Discourse." *Canadian Literature* nos. 124–125 (Spring–Summer 1990): 273–289.

Swann, Brian, and Arnold Krupat, eds. *Recovering the Word: Essays on Native American Literature.* Berkeley et. al.: Univ. of California Press, 1987.

——., eds. *I Tell You Now: Autobiographical Essays by Native American Writers.* Lincoln: Univ. of Nebraska Press, 1987.

*Tiger Lily, The Voices That Dare,* Stratford, Ont.: Earthtone Women's Magazine Inc., 1990.

Vangen, Kate. "Making Faces: Defiance and Humour in Campbell's *Halfbreed* and Welch's *Winter in the Blood." The Native in Literature: Canadian and Comparative Perspectives.* Edited by T. King, C. Calver, H. Hoy. Oakville, Ont.: ECW Press, 1987: 188–205.

"Whose Voice Is It, Anyway? A Symposium on who should be speaking for whom." *Books in Canada* 20.1 (January/February 1991): 11–17.

Printed in Canada